Dynamics 365 Field Service

Implementing Business Solutions for the Enterprise

Sanjaya Yapa
Indika Abayarathne

Apress®

Dynamics 365 Field Service: Implementing Business Solutions for the Enterprise

Sanjaya Yapa
Mount Waverley, VIC, Australia

Indika Abayarathne
Victory, WA, Australia

ISBN-13 (pbk): 978-1-4842-6407-2
https://doi.org/10.1007/978-1-4842-6408-9

ISBN-13 (electronic): 978-1-4842-6408-9

Managing Director, Apress Media LLC: Welmoed Spahr
Acquisitions Editor: Smriti Srivastava
Development Editor: Laura Berendson
Coordinating Editor: Shrikant Vishwakarma

Cover designed by eStudioCalamar

Cover image designed by Pexels

Distributed to the book trade worldwide by Springer Science+Business Media LLC, 1 New York Plaza, Suite 4600, New York, NY 10004. Phone 1-800-SPRINGER, fax (201) 348-4505, e-mail orders-ny@springer-sbm.com, or visit www.springeronline.com. Apress Media, LLC is a California LLC and the sole member (owner) is Springer Science + Business Media Finance Inc (SSBM Finance Inc). SSBM Finance Inc is a **Delaware** corporation.

For information on translations, please e-mail booktranslations@springernature.com; for reprint, paperback, or audio rights, please e-mail bookpermissions@springernature.com.

Apress titles may be purchased in bulk for academic, corporate, or promotional use. eBook versions and licenses are also available for most titles. For more information, reference our Print and eBook Bulk Sales web page at www.apress.com/bulk-sales.

Any source code or other supplementary material referenced by the author in this book is available to readers on GitHub via the book's product page, located at www.apress.com/978-1-4842-6407-2. For more detailed information, please visit www.apress.com/source-code.

Printed on acid-free paper

Table of Contents

About the Authors

Sanjaya Yapa currently works as a Microsoft Dynamics CE/FS Solution Architect in Melbourne, Australia. He has more than 14 years of experience in the industry. He has been working with various Microsoft technologies since 2005 and possesses a wealth of experience in software development, team leadership, product management, and consultancy. He specializes in Dynamics 365 Customer Engagement, Field Service, and Application Lifecycle Management.

Indika Abayarathne is from Melbourne, Australia, and currently works as a Lead Consultant/Solution Architect. He started the Dynamics CRM journey in 2008 and has performed different roles in software development and consultancy. He blogs about technology and his development experience and expertise at `crmfortress.com`.

About the Technical Reviewer

 **Scott Durow** is a Microsoft Business Applications MVP specializing in Dynamics 365 and Power Platform. He is a passionate software architect, technologist, blogger, and speaker, as well as the author of multiple tools, including the Ribbon Workbench. His software career spans more than 20 years, during which he has moved from assembly language device driver programming to industrial control software to enterprise business applications. Find him on Twitter as @ScottDurow and read his blog at scottdurow.develop1.net.

Acknowledgments

About six months ago, we took over the mammoth task of writing this book. It would not have been possible without the kind support and help of many individuals. We would like to extend our heartfelt gratitude to all of them.

We are thankful to Scott Durow for providing valuable technical reviews.

We would also like to express our thanks and appreciation to our families for encouraging us to achieve this milestone. We are also indebted to all our mentors for their guidance, encouragement, and the opportunities they gave us throughout our careers. Special thanks go to Nadeeja Bomiriya and Ajith Premaratne.

Finally, we would like to express our gratitude to our friends for their encouragement and inspiring words to move us forward.

Introduction

Managing field operations is one of the tedious tasks faced by modern businesses that provide services to their clients at the doorstep. These organizations face many challenges when providing services to their clients, including allocating work, tracking live inventory movement, etc. Dynamics 365 Field Service overcomes most of these challenges—and can be extended to meet the specific needs of a business.

Since there is a huge demand for this product in the market, Dynamics 365 Customer Engagement developers should be able to learn the product swiftly. The objective of this book is to provide a complete guide with practical examples of how to configure and customize Field Service. This book is a step-by-step guide to provide a solution to a business problem.

The book begins with an introduction to Dynamics 365 Field Service and how to set it up with your Dynamics 365 subscription. We then explore how to configure the application. In the beginning, the book will guide the reader on allocating work, resource management, and inventory movement. We explain how to configure both Field Service and Field Service Mobile using the Woodford configuration tool. One of the main topics covered is how to apply security to both Field Service and Field Service Mobile.

The book provides suitable examples for the reader to better understand the concepts and apply them in practical scenarios. We also elaborate the best practices for configuring and customizing Field Service. This book is a stepping stone for Dynamics 365 Customer Engagement developers/consultants to become a professional in Dynamics 365 Field Service.

CHAPTER 1

Introduction to Field Services

During the past few years, we all have seen a major shift in technology—the use of mobile devices in our day-to-day lives. Gradually, organizations started to use mobile devices for their business processes to provide better and faster services to their customers. Some organizations provide services or sell goods at the customer's doorsteps. In such businesses, the mobile device is playing a key role. Apart from that, organizations must also manage their workforce in the field. This is where the concept of *field services* came into the market—that is, delivering services or selling products on-site and managing the field staff. For this type of business, the software that is used to carry out the business process is equally important.

Initially, the Field Service application was known as *FieldOne*. When you set up Dynamics 365 Customer Engagement, Field Service is one of the available applications that you can install. Installing Field Service enables businesses to serve their customers through the full customer life cycle. Also, Field Service is mobile-enabled, and it works in both online and offline situations. Primarily, it operates on Android, Apple, and Windows mobile devices. The application comes with a plethora of features, such as creating and scheduling work, inventory management, and field staff management. Apart from these, at the enterprise level, you can integrate Dynamics 365 Field Service with financial operations, a.k.a. FinOps.

Before digging into Field Service, it is important to understand Dataflex Pro (formerly known as Common Data Service [CDS]) and model-driven apps. Dataflex Pro is the data modelling capability that Power Platform offers for power users to build business applications. (For more information about CDS, visit `https://docs.microsoft.com/en-us/powerapps/maker/common-data-service/data-platform-intro`.) Model-driven apps provide a no-code or low-code component approach for business application development. Model-driven apps run in a responsive behavior on browsers and on

1

© Sanjaya Yapa and Indika Abayarathne 2021
S. Yapa and I. Abayarathne, *Dynamics 365 Field Service*, https://doi.org/10.1007/978-1-4842-6408-9_1

mobile devices, as the apps are built on the Unified Interface client. The Dynamics 365 Field Service app and the Field Service (Dynamics 365) Mobile app are two model-driven apps built on Dataflex Pro.

Capabilities of Dynamics 365 Field Service

As mentioned earlier, Dynamics 365 Field Service is designed and developed to facilitate field business operations. Out of the box, the application can be easily used to execute the following actions:

- Define work/jobs to perform in the field

- Schedule work

- Manage field staff

- Manage inventory, purchasing, and returns

- Provide billing and invoicing capabilities

- Provide time and location tracking

- Generate reports and dashboards

A small business that provides field services can easily adapt the Field Service application to their business without any modifications. The out-of-the-box features of the application are well defined and easy to use. But, as we all know, every business is unique in various ways, and the out-of-the-box features of Field Service might not be enough to fulfil the needs of such organizations. With the help of developers or consultants, you can easily extend the capabilities of the application. Since the application is installed together with Dynamics 365 Customer Engagement, the full customer life cycle is enabled to the business. For example, Figure 1-1 shows a customer sales and service cycle.

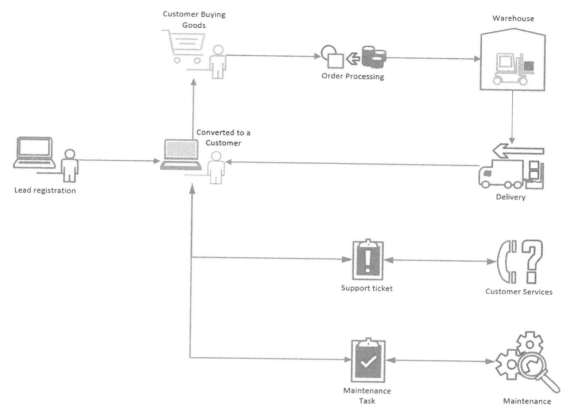

Figure 1-1. *Customer sales and services life cycle*

This is a generic flow of a customer sales and services life cycle. In this process, both Dynamics 365 Customer Engagement and Dynamics 365 Field Service can be used. Tasks such as lead registration, lead conversion, and customer order processing are typically Dynamics 365 Customer Engagement activities, whereas tasks such as dispatching and delivering are typically Dynamics 365 Field Service activities. All the support and maintenance work can span across both applications.

Installing Dynamics 365 Field Service

In this section, we will look at how to set up Field Service. We will be setting up a trial instance and installing Field Service on top of it. Go to the following link to set up a trial instance of Dynamics 365 Customer Engagement: `https://trials.dynamics.com/`. Click the **Sign Up Here** link to initiate the registration process (Figure 1-2).

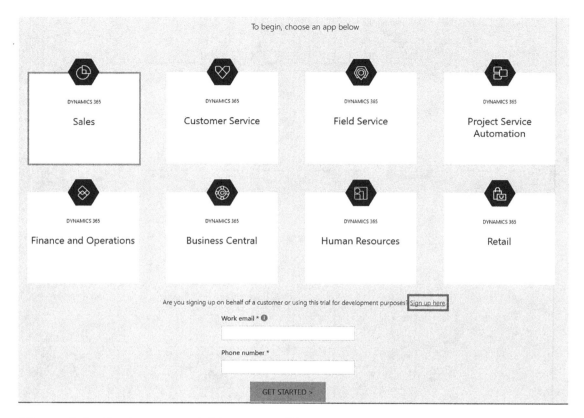

Figure 1-2. *Setting up a trial instance of Dynamics 365 Customer Engagement*

On the next screen, enter your company details, create login credentials, and enter a valid phone number for verification. Your phone will receive a 6-digit code. After entering the code, you will be directed to the trial details page (Figure 1-3). Make sure to save the details shown.

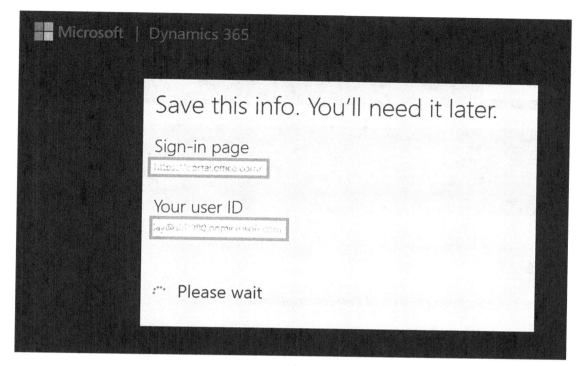

Figure 1-3. *Signing user account details page*

On the next screen, select the application that suits your business. For the purpose of this book, we will be using the Field Service application. Click **Complete Setup** (Figure 1-4). It will take several minutes to set up the application in your instance.

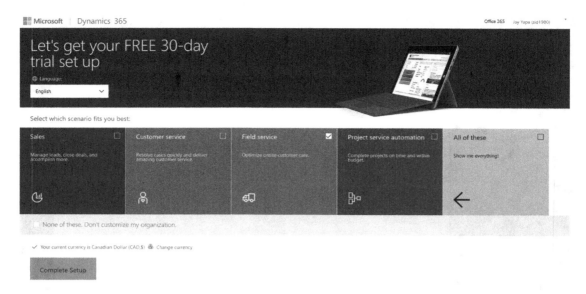

Figure 1-4. *Selecting the Field Service application*

Figure 1-5 shows that the Field Service application has been successfully installed.

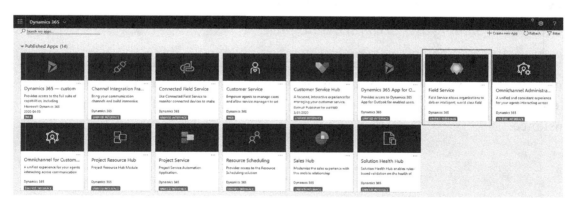

Figure 1-5. *Field Service installed on the instance*

Click the **More Options** button and then click the **Manage Roles** option (Figure 1-6).

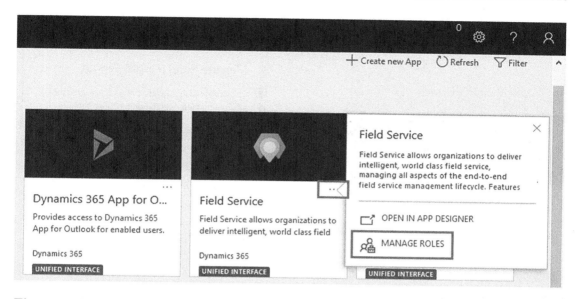

Figure 1-6. *Managing Field Service security roles*

This will show the default security roles applied to the app (Figure 1-7). In order for a user to use the application, they must be assigned a security role. Later, you can add any other security roles, as required. We will discuss the security roles related to Field Service in a later chapter.

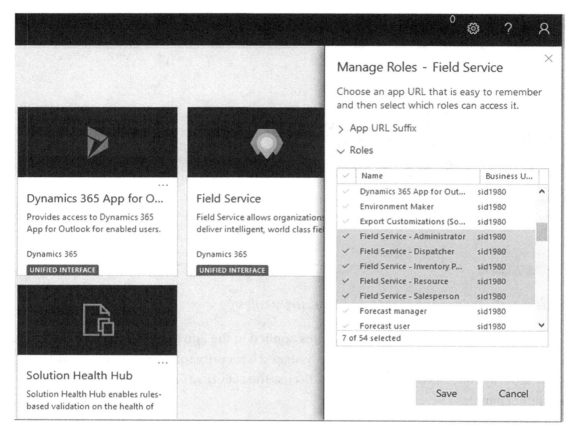

Figure 1-7. *Security roles assigned to Field Service*

Note   These same security roles will also be used to grant access to the Field Service Mobile application. When the mobile applications are created, mobile apps' configurator tool will prompt to the configuring user/admin to select the security roles so that the users with the security roles will have access to the app.

Click the **Field Service** app tile. You will be directed to the new installation (Figure 1-8).

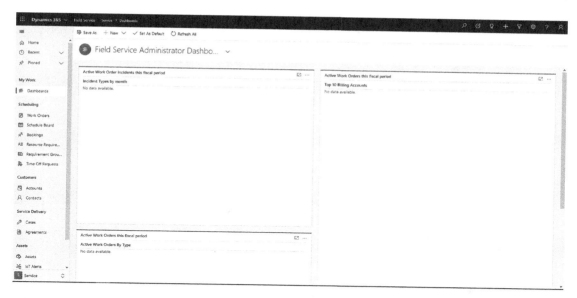

Figure 1-8. *The new installation of the Field Service app*

Setting Up the Field Service Mobile

When it comes to field services, mobile apps are essential. Field operatives must capture data related to the work they do in the field. With the massive development in mobile technology, all field operatives are equipped with mobile devices to easily access the information. So, Dynamics 365 Field Service also includes a mobile app that works on both Apple iOS and Android. In fact, there are two options: Field Service (Dynamics 365) and Field Service Mobile (Figure 1-9).

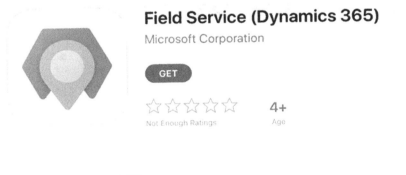

Field Service (Dynamics 365)

Microsoft Corporation

GET

☆ ☆ ☆ ☆ ☆   4+
Not Enough Ratings   Age

Field Service Mobile

Microsoft Corporation • Business > CRM

🔗 Share   ♡ Wish list

★ ★ ★ ☆ ☆ 2

Dynamics 365 for Field Service provides the cross-platform, multi-device Field Service Mobile application that is specifically crafted to the field service worker's needs. Robust offline capabilities allow

More

Figure 1-9. Dynamics 365 Field Service Mobile apps

Both of these apps are great options for mobile field services solutions. At the time of writing, the Field Service (Dynamics 365) app is new and evolving. Microsoft is continuously releasing updates to the app. Field Service Mobile has great offline capabilities and is a good option for complex solutions. According to Microsoft's documentation, the support for Field Service Mobile will end by June 2022. All new solution development on field services commencing by June 2021 must use the new Field Service (Dynamics 365) app. Therefore, this book is going to focus on the new Field Service (Dynamics 365) app.

The new Field Service (Dynamics 365) app is built on top of Microsoft's Power Platform. It is a model-driven app that can be customized using the same admin console. The app is available in both Apple App Store (Figure 1-10) and Google Play (Figure 1-11).

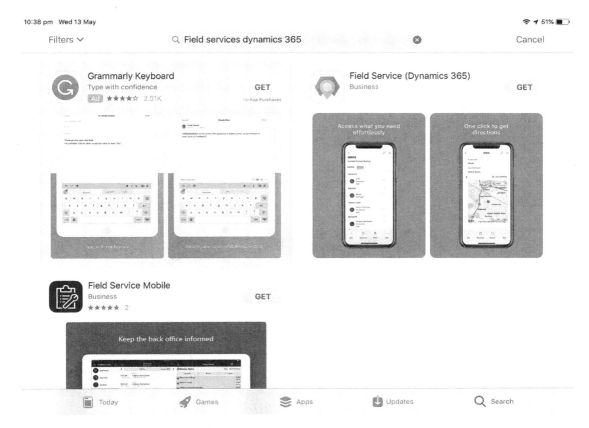

Figure 1-10. *Field Service (Dynamics 365) app on Apple App Store*

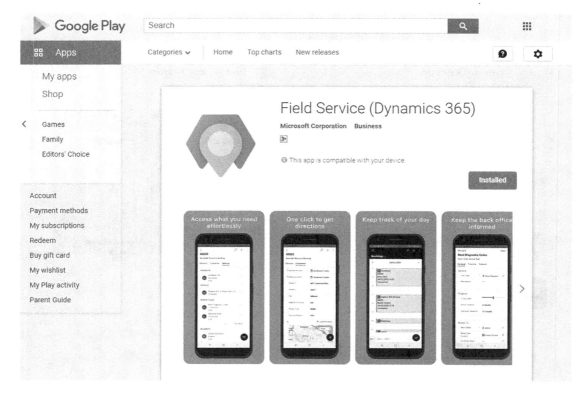

Figure 1-11. *Field Service (Dynamics 365) app on Google Play*

To install the app on your device, select the app on the screen and click **Get**. Figure 1-12 shows installing the app on an Apple iPad.

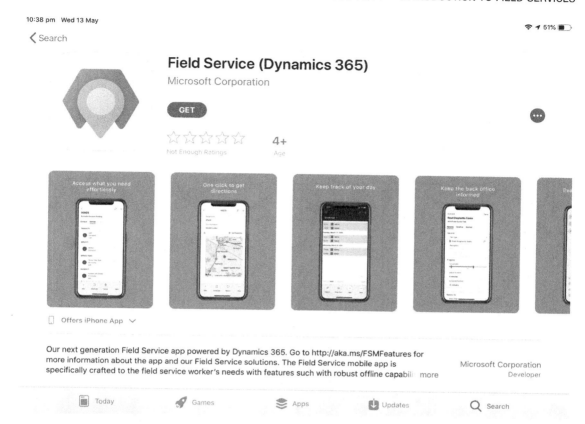

Figure 1-12. *Installing the app on an Apple IPad*

Once the installation completes, you will be directed to the screen shown in Figure 1-13 to enter your login credentials.

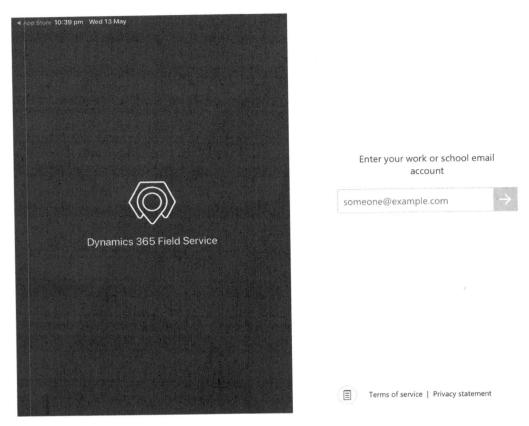

Figure 1-13. *Field Service (Dynamics 365) login screen*

After entering your Office 365 login credentials, you will be directed to the bookings assigned to you (Figure 1-14).

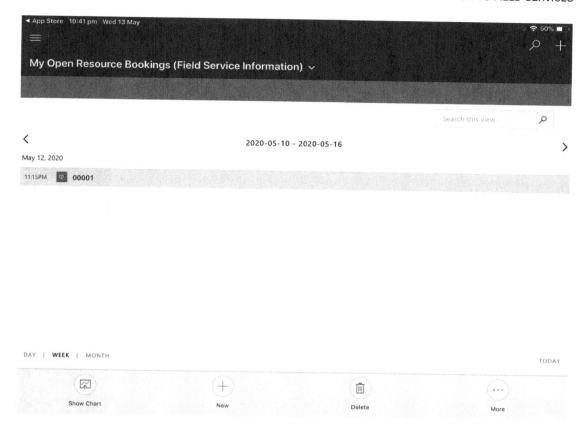

Figure 1-14. *Current user's bookings*

When you click the hamburger button on the top-left corner of the app, the left navigation pane opens (Figure 1-15).

Figure 1-15. *Left navigation of the app*

You can configure this navigation using Sitemap Designer within App Designer (Figure 1-16).

In order to reach Sitemap Designer, you need to go through the following steps.

The Field Service Mobile app is a model-driven app that has been added as a solution component to the base solution. The solution can be accessed through Power Apps (make.powerapps.com), and the correct environment needs to be selected. The components can be edited using the menu option shown in Figure 1-16.

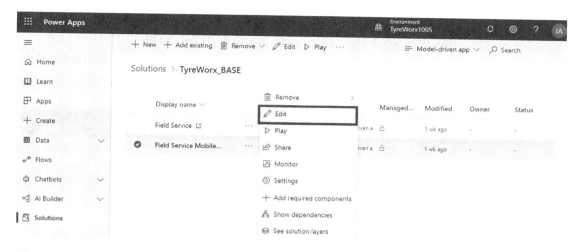

Figure 1-16. *Power Apps home*

Alternatively, you can open Field Service Mobile App Designer under the Dynamics 365 Home (`https://home.dynamics.com/`), as shown in Figure 1-17. Note that, you have to have a user account with Dynamics 365 Field Service App access in order to see this App.

Figure 1-17. *Dynamics 365 Home*

Sitemaps can be edited using App Designer (Figure 1-18). You can also use App Designer to select dashboards, business process flows, entities, views, etc. to be shown in Field Service Mobile. Figure 1-19 shows an image of a Sitemap Designer of the Field Service Mobile model driven app.

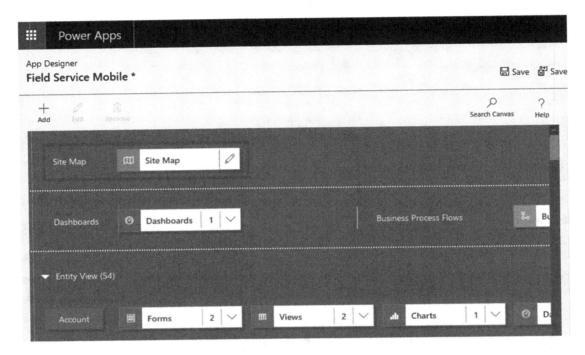

Figure 1-18. *App Designer*

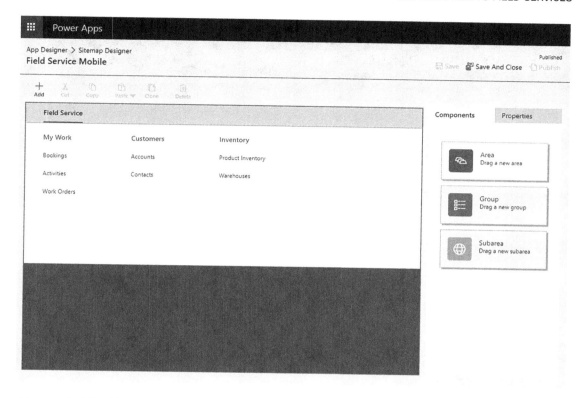

Figure 1-19. *Sitemap Designer of the Field Service (Dynamics 365) app*

The same views in the Field Service Dynamics 365 app can be exposed in the Field Service Mobile app. For instance, the Active Accounts view in Field Service can be exposed in the app (Figure 1-20).

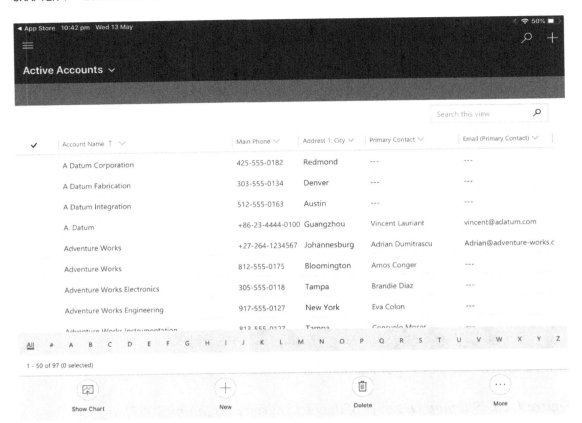

Figure 1-20. *Views in the Field Service Mobile*

When you open the records, the information is displayed on the form(s) configured in App Designer (Figure 1-21).

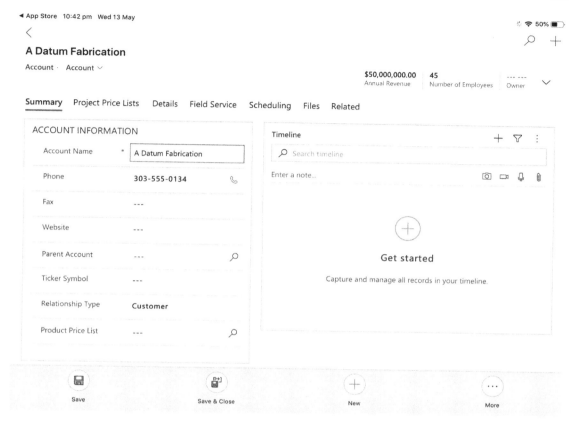

Figure 1-21. *Account record opened on the Field Service Mobile*

We will be looking deep into how to customize the form to fit into the Field Service Mobile interface. This is essential and depends on the real estate of the device used by the field technician. For instance, there are hundreds of fields in entities, such as Work Orders, Accounts, etc. You should carefully pick the fields that satisfy the field operations requirements. If the device used by a field technician has small real estate, then showing more tabs and fields may not work out. It will be cumbersome to the end user. Figure 1-22 illustrates the Work Order form in the mobile interface. The work order entity is the heart and soul of field services; it's where everything happens. Therefore, special consideration should be given when exposing fields and functionality for this form.

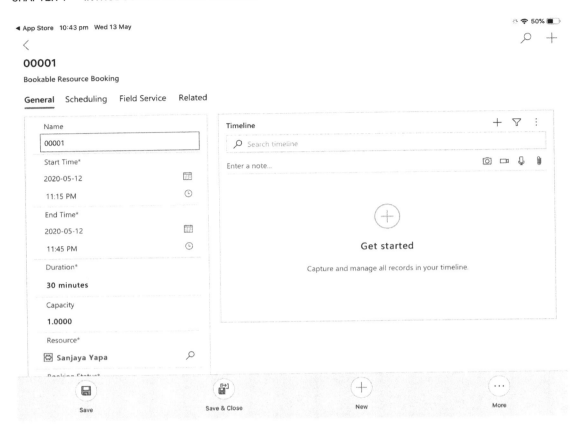

Figure 1-22.   *Work Order form on the Field Service Mobile app*

Figure 1-23 shows the booking related to this work order. The booking is the mechanism that assigns the work order to the resource.

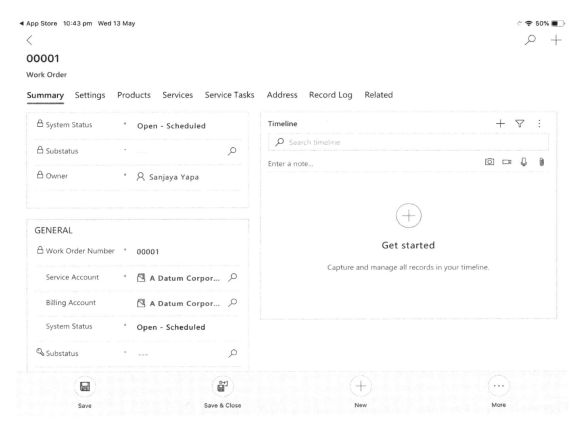

Figure 1-23. *The booking form on the Field Service Mobile app*

Note   The application is configured out of the box to support general field services operations. Sometimes, however, we cannot use the processes as they are and have to extend them by further customizing them. For instance, there are certain steps in these out-of-the-box processes that a field operative may not be doing but that are required by the process flow. In such scenarios, the steps can be automated through customizations. We will discuss these customizations in detail in the upcoming chapters.

Field Service Mobile

Field Service Mobile consists of two parts: the mobile app and the configuration tool. Before you can work with the mobile app, you must install the configuration tool on the Dynamics 365 Field Service instance. The following link provide a step-by-step guide to install the Woodford configuration tool: `https://docs.microsoft.com/en-us/dynamics365/field-service/install-field-service#step-3-install-the-field-service-mobile-configuration-tool`. Once the tool is installed on your instance, it will be located in Advance Configuration ➤ Settings area (Figure 1-24).

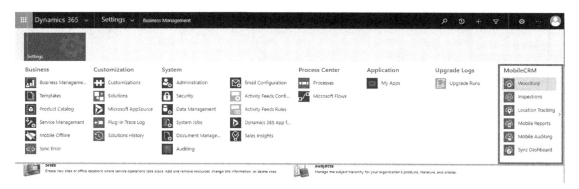

Figure 1-24. *Woodford Mobile CRM menu items under Dynamics 365*

As part of the setup process, you must import the Mobile project template. You can clone this template and configure it based on your business requirements (Figure 1-25).

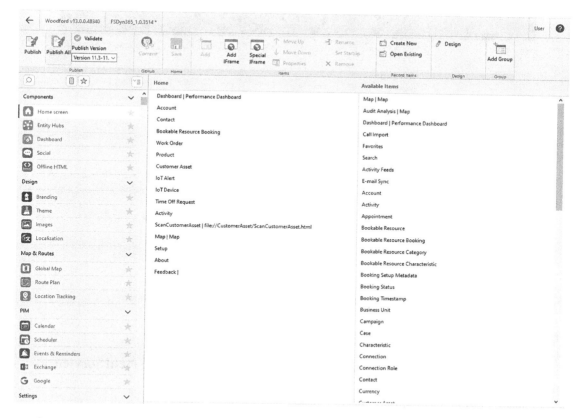

Figure 1-25. *Woodford configuration tool*

Then, you can install the mobile application. The app is available in Microsoft Store, Apple App Store, and Google Play. Visit the following link to install the app on Windows: `https://docs.microsoft.com/en-us/dynamics365/field-service/field-service-mobile-app-user-guide`.

Before logging in, you must create a bookable resource for the user(s) creating the app and enable them to use the Field Service Mobile. As shown in Figure 1-26, open the **Resources** section of the application and search for the resource.

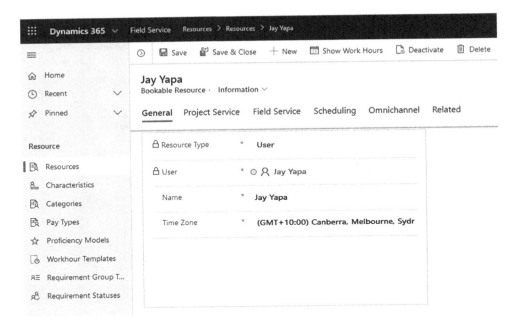

Figure 1-26. *Resource details*

Under the **Field Services** tab, set the value of the field **Enable for Field Service Mobile** to **Yes** (Figure 1-27).

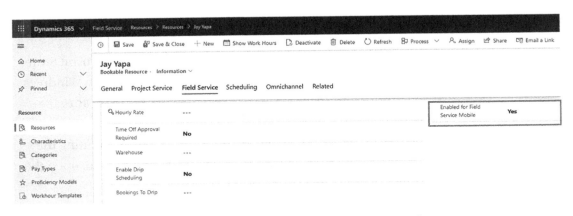

Figure 1-27. *Enabling resources to access Field Service Mobile*

Once your login is verified, you will be directed to the home page of Field Service Mobile (Figure 1-28).

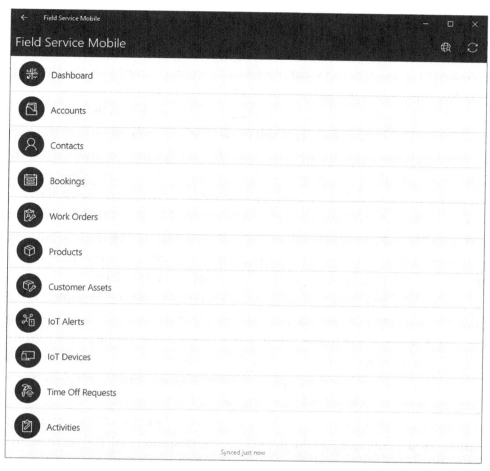

Figure 1-28. *Field Service Mobile home page (Windows version)*

As mentioned in the previous section, we will not be focusing on configuring and customizing this Field Service Mobile for this book.

The Example Scenario

This book will demonstrate the configuration and customizations of the Dynamics 365 Field Service and using a real-world implementation of Field Service Mobile as the mobile app. This section provides a brief introduction to the scenario and a high-level design overview.

The Business

TyreWorx is a Canadian company that sells and services tires throughout Canada. The business offers various services for commercial clients and for individuals. The company consists of two businesses: wholesale and retail.

The retail operations are handled through the call center. When the client runs into a problem, they call the call center. This will create the job for the vehicle in the area and send the service person to the incident location. The service person could either change the tire to a new one, which is a new sale, or they could repair the tire, which is a service.

Technicians in the retail business have allocations. For instance, one field technician may work from Monday to Wednesday from 6.00 a.m. to 4.00 p.m. Another technician may work from Thursday to Sunday from 7.00 a.m. to 9.00 p.m. The technicians drive vans full of tires and have access to tire storage facilities across the provinces. The company caters to both private-use vehicles and commercial vehicles.

The business also sells tires to wholesale customers. These are the small shops that buy tires from TyreWorx at wholesale prices. The sales reps have scheduled visits and the customers buy tires based on the requirements. The wholesale customers are given 30 days of credit as a payment method. That is, the customer must settle the invoice within 30 days from the purchase. Payment options also credit card, check, and cash. The wholesale business does not provide any services, only product sales.

An invoice is issued after every sale in both business domains. The company is going "eco-friendly" and wants to email the invoices to the customers. All the services are followed up by the company in a different periodical. Tires are stored in the warehouses and in vehicles for onsite use. Vehicles are stocked up with tires from the warehouses. Every province has main distribution centers. From the distribution center, they will make tire purchases from vendors quarterly.

Apart from the main distribution centers, the company also has store locations spread across each province. All the other company store locations are filled from these main distribution centers. The field technicians and sales reps can go to this seller warehouse and refill tires in their vehicles.

Retail Work

Following are some of the activities a retail technician would do during a day:

1. The service desk staff at the call center receives calls regarding service requests from customers.

2. The service desk staff captures the request and creates jobs in the system.

3. They search for the availability of resources in the area and assign the job.

4. The job is assigned to the nearest technician who is available at that time.

5. The technician checks their vehicle's stock when they start their shift and refills it with the required stock from the nearest company store location.

6. When a job is assigned, the technician can see the job on their device.

7. Then the technicians can drive to the customer location defined in the job.

8. The technician attends to the job and fills in the job based on the actions/tasks carried out and the products/services used in the job.

9. Onsite payment is captured. The customer can pay via credit card or cash. In case of a credit card payment, the last four digits of the credit card are captured against the payment.

10. Once the job completes, the technician captures the customer signature and the invoice will be emailed to the customer.

11. The business sends an email to the customer and reminds him to post job check-ups.

12. In a warranty replacement, the technicians will collect the old tires and send them back to the warehouse.

13. Services include fixing tire punctures and rotating tires.

Wholesale Work

Following are some of the activities a sales rep would do during a visit to a wholesale customer:

1. Medium- to small-scale tire shops are registered with TyreWorx as wholesale customers.

2. Sales representatives purchase tyres in bulk and sell the tyres to the customers.

3. Agreements are generated every year for each wholesale customer. These agreements define how often the company's sales reps visit the customer.

4. These agreements are the schedule for inventory updates of wholesale customers.

5. The sales rep is responsible for inventory management.

6. The sales rep checks the stock levels of different tires.

7. Based on the requests from the customer, the sales rep can restock tires for the customer.

8. When tires are restocked, the customer buys the tires at wholesale prices. They have 30 days of credit.

9. The customer's payments are captured and an invoice is generated and emailed to the customer.

10. Onsite payment is captured. The customer can pay via credit card or cash. In case of a credit card payment, the last four digits of the credit card is captured against the payment.

New System

The company wants to improve the services they provide to the customers and make more profits. The top management has decided to build a new system to replace the old system, which is spread across multiple technologies. Since their current system is spread across multiple systems, maintenance is challenging and reporting is more difficult, as the internal staff must do manual comparisons of the various reports extracted from different systems, which have duplicate data.

The main objective is to bring the scattered system into one single platform so that the company can cut off the burden of maintaining multiple systems. Above all, they want the new solution to be operational in a short period of time. They have chosen Microsoft Dynamics 365 Field Service as the ideal platform to meet these requirements. Following are some of the expectations of the new system:

- It should support both the wholesale and retail sides of the company.

- It should maintain a live inventory of the products sold by both business domains.

- The field operatives should be able to easily record the data—that is, the system should be user friendly.

- It should provide interactive reports to the decision-makers.

The High-Level Design

Figure 1-29 shows the entity-relationshiop (ER) diagram for the proposed new system. This is based on the entities in the Dynamics 365 Field Service. This will give you a high-level idea about how the information is going to be stored from the back end. There are several other entities between some of these relationships, which will be discussed in detail in Chapter 2.

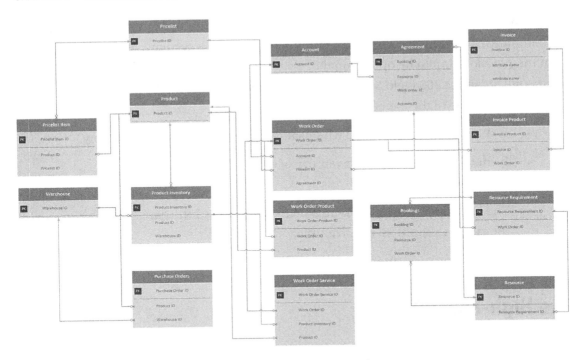

Figure 1-29. *High-level ER diagram of the proposed system*

High-Level Process Flows

As explained at the beginning of this section, the company consists of two main business streams: the retail business and the wholesale business. This subsection illustrates the high-level process flows for these businesses.

Figure 1-30 illustrates the retail process flow.

Retail Process

Figure 1-30. *Retail process flow*

Figure 1-31 illustrates the wholesale process flow.

Wholesale Process

Figure 1-31. *Wholesale process flow*

Summary

This chapter began by discussing what Dynamics 365 Field Service is, where it is used, and its benefits to field services businesses. The next section provided guidelines for installing and setting up Dynamics 365 Field Service. Finally, we took a brief look at an example scenario to explain the implementation of a Field Service solution.

CHAPTER 2

Core Entities and Configuring the Mobile App

Dynamics 365 Field Service is a prebuilt solution with functionality specific to field operations, resource management, and inventory management. This means the solution already has several core entities specific to the solution. Each entity has a specific purpose in the solution. Before we continue further, you should gain a basic understanding of the core entities. The objective of this chapter is to introduce you to the Field Service core entities and then move to extend the solution to implement specific requirements.

Understanding the core entities and their position in the solution is essentialbecause there are out of the box underlying processes explicit to Dynamics 365 Field Services. When extending the solution, you should be extra careful not to break the core processes. Even though you can customize the system, you should always respect the boundaries and follow the best practices. Microsoft is always updating the Dynamics 365 ecosystem, and the platform should absorb these new features without breaking customizations.

Services and Scheduling

This section describes the primary entities of Dynamics 365 Field Service and its reference entities. In conjunction, these entities drive the core operations conducted by the field operatives.

© Sanjaya Yapa and Indika Abayarathne 2021
S. Yapa and I. Abayarathne, *Dynamics 365 Field Service*, https://doi.org/10.1007/978-1-4842-6408-9_2

Work Orders

The *work order* is the primary entity in Dynamics 365 Field Service and has references to dozens of other entities to drive the work. It is located in the Service area of the Field Service app by default.

The primary purpose of the a work order is to store all the information about the job that needs to perform for the customer. The work order records can be considered as transactions records in the system. A work order also includes incident details, location information, products and services that need to perform the job, resource bookings, expenses, taxes, tasks, communications, billing, and more.

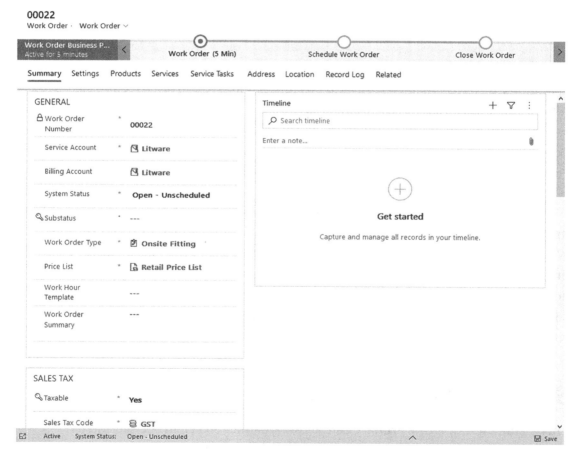

Figure 2-1. *Work Order record*

To provide a quick status at a glance, the Work Order record contains a default business process flow (Figure 2-1). The record also include System Status and Substatus fields that describe more of the job status. The Address tab contains the site location and the geolocation information, which will be helpful for technicians to find the job location on the map. Multiple products, services, resource bookings, and activities can be available under the relevant tabs, depending on the job to be performed in the work order.

Work orders can be created in one of the following five ways:

1. Case records can be converted to work orders.

2. Opportunity records can be converted to work orders.

3. Work order records can be created directly from the site map items of the Field Service app without converting cases or opportunities.

4. Agreements can generate work orders automatically in the system.

5. External systems can communicate with Dynamics 365 Field Service via an integration layer to create work orders.

Figure 2-2 shows the work order life cycle.

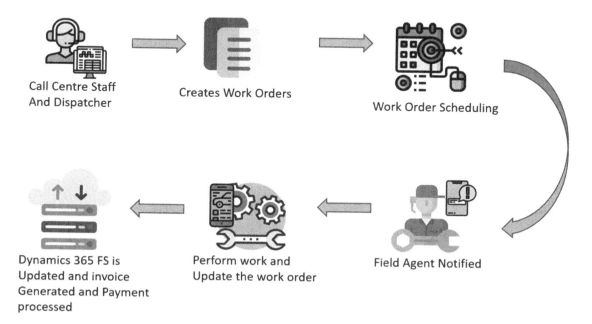

Figure 2-2. *Work order life cycle*

A work order can go through different statuses, as defined in System Status field of the Work Order record. Following are the out-of-the-box statuses:

- Open - Unscheduled

- Open - Scheduled

- Open - In Progress

- Open - Completed

- Closed - Posted

- Closed - Cancelled

These statuses are used to define the current point of the work order in the life cycle.

Important   These statuses are part of the Dynamics 365 Field Service that drive back-end processes and should not be edited at any cost. Note, also, that the booking status defined in the bookable resource booking is used to set the system status of the work order. This flow will be discussed later in this chapter.

The statuses can be given more meaning by using the Work Order record's Substatus field. The statuses can be defined based on each organization's requirements.

Work Order Types

Work order types are used to differentiate work orders. This differentiation is important in scenarios where the organization is providing various types of services. Few default work order types are available in Field Service, but you can create additional work order types from the Settings area of the Field Service app. Figure 2-3 shows the Work Order Type record.

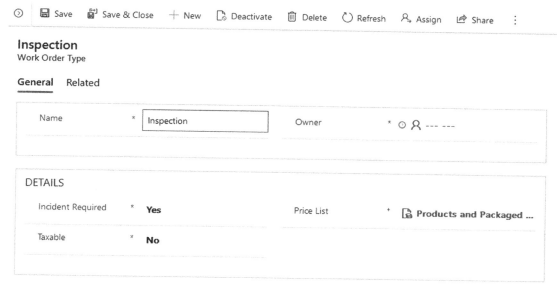

Figure 2-3. *Work Order Type record*

Work order types can be kept deactivated so that those records cannot be used to create work orders. The values in the Incident Required, Taxable, and Price List fields of the Work Order type record can change the behavior of the work order. For example, if the value of Incident Required field is Yes, then the associated work order must contain an incident type with it. The Work Order Type records are master records in the system.

Incident Types

Incident types define the various types of incidents/issues that a customer could raise. Fundamentally, work orders are based on these incident types. The primary incident type on a work order will be mandatory when the Incident Required field of the Work Order Type record is set to Yes.

⊙ | 🖫 Save 🖺 Save & Close + New ▭ Deactivate 🗑 Delete ↻ Refresh ⅋ Assign ⬑ Share ⋮

New Retail Tyre Sale
Incident Type

General   Details   Products   Services   Service Tasks   Characteristics   Notes   Related

Name	*	**New Retail Tyre Sale**
Owner	*	⊙ ⅋ **Indika AB**

Description

Description	**New retail tyre sale at onsite.**

Figure 2-4. *Incident Type record*

The Incident Type record contains the specific products, services, and service tasks to perform the job described by the incident type (Figure 2-4). An incident type can contain zero or more products (incident type products), services (incident type services), and service tasks (incident type service tasks), depending on the type of the work to be performed. Essentially, an incident type can be considered as a template to create work orders. This makes work order creation very easy and productive because, when the request received from the customer, the call center staff knows which type of job this is and can easily select the incident type, and Dynamics 365 Field Service will do the rest.

It is important to note that at the schema level, products, services, and service tasks are different types under the Incident Type and in the Work Order. When the work order is created, the system automatically creates and associates products (work order products), services (work order services) and service tasks (work order service tasks) according to the primary incident type selected on the Work Order record. Incident Type records are master records in the system.

Work Order Products

Work order products are sold to the customer as part of completing the job described in the work order. Work order products are based on products in the product catalog. The products categorized as inventory under the Product tab on the Work Order record will be listed here (Figure 2-5).

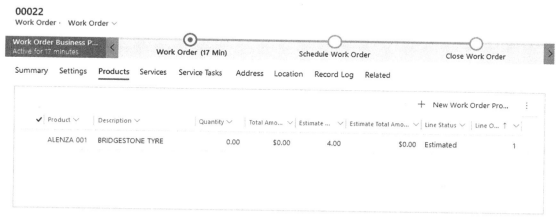

Figure 2-5. *Work Order Product sub-grid on the Products tab of the Work Order record*

If the selected incident type has a product defined, then Work Order Product records are automatically created when the work order is created. New Work Order Product records also can be created manually under the work order. If the incident type does not define any products, the field operative can add products to the work order as and when required. Also, the Work Order Product records can be deleted from the sub-grid on the Work Order record. As shown in Figure 2-6, when a product is added to the Work Order record, the Line Status field is set to Estimated. Only when this is set to Use will the product will be fully utilized.

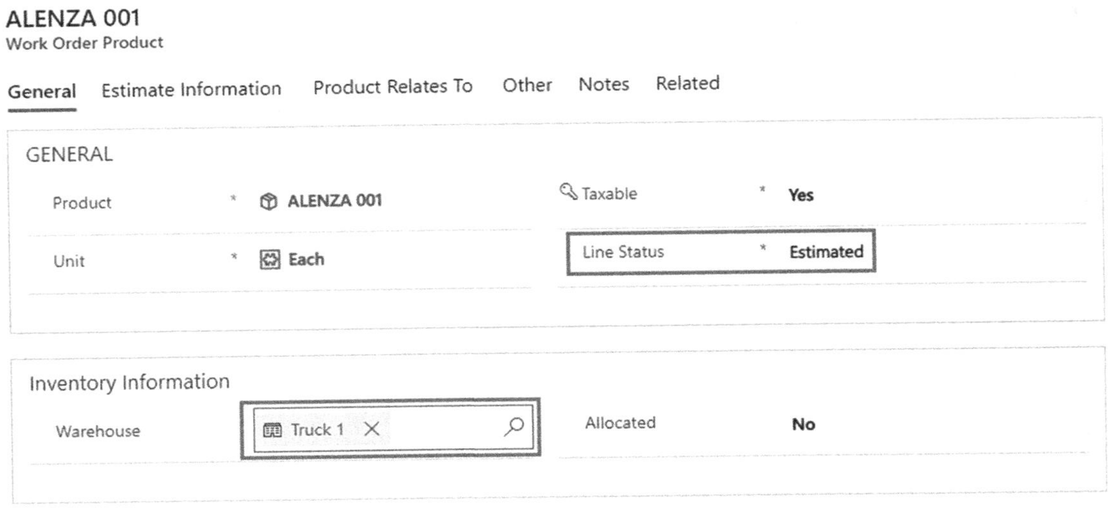
ALENZA 001
Work Order Product
General
Estimate Information
Product Relates To
Other
Notes
Related
GENERAL
Product
ALENZA 001
Taxable
Yes
Unit
Each
Line Status
Estimated
Inventory Information
Warehouse
Truck 1
Allocated
No

Figure 2-6. *Work Order Product's Line Status and the linked warehouse*

Similarly, the Warehouse field will determine where this product is taken from. Once the product is fully utilized, the product inventory of the selected warehouse will be depleted. Warehouse and Inventory related topics will be discussed in detail in the following chapters.

Work Order Services

Work order services are used to define the services provided via the job performed at the customer site. These services can have a monetary value determined by the price lists associated with the work order. A given work order can have multiple work order services (Figure 2-7) which are billed on an hourly basis. When a service is selected for the work order, the lookup field on the Work Order Service record under the subgrid is referring to products in the system. These products are categorized as services under the Field Service tab of the Product record.

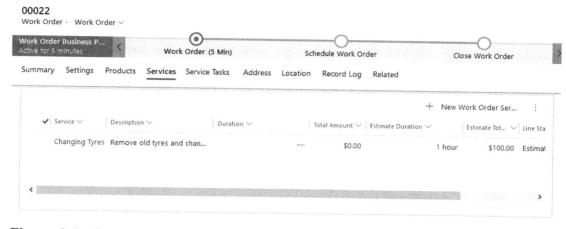

Figure 2-7. *Services tab of the Work Order record*

Just as it can with work order products, the system can automatically create work order services when the work order is created by pulling services from the primary Incident Type record. Like work order products, work order services can also be added to the work order manually. Also, until the Line Status field is not set Used, the service item is not fully utilized. As shown in Figure 2-8, the Work Order Service does not have a warehouse because this is not an inventory item.

Changing Tyres
Work Order Service

General   Estimate Information   Duration & Sale Amount   Service Relates To   Actual Cost   Other   Notes   Related

General			
Service	⊕ Changing Tyres	⚲ Taxable	Yes
⚲ Unit	▨ Hour	Line Status	Estimated

Figure 2-8. *Work Order Service record's Line Status field*

Bookable Resources

A *bookable resource*, also known as a *resource*, can be anything that requires scheduling. The most common types of resources used in Field Service are people and vehicles. For example, field service agents, technicians, etc. can be considered as resources or bookable resources. The type of resource must be set at the point of creating the bookable resource. The following different types of bookable resources are available in Dynamics 365 Field Service:

- *User*: The most common type of resource is the User. This option is used when a system/organizational user requires access to the Dynamics 365 Field Service. If the resource requires access to the Field Service Mobile, the Resource Type must be set to User.

- *Account/Contact*: This option is required if there are external contractors. These resources will not have access to the Field Service Mobile. In such scenarios, external systems can be integrated with the scheduling process.

- *Crew*: This option is useful in scenarios where multiple staff members use vehicles during different shifts. In this scenario, the vehicle becomes the crew header, and the staff members (users, accounts or contacts) are the children of the crew. The crew header can be created to define the shifts of each staff member as resource children. This will be discussed in upcoming chapters.

- *Pool*: This type of resource is required when there is a requirement for managing the capacity of comparable resources. The key feature of this option is that it will not schedule the whole group of resources within the pool.

- *Facility*: This option can be used if building spaces or rooms require scheduling.

- *Equipment*: This option is used if machinery or equipment requires scheduling.

For more information about resources, visit `https://docs.microsoft.com/en-us/dynamics365/field-service/set-up-bookable-resources`.

The resources can be found under the Resources section in the left navigation (Figure 2-9).

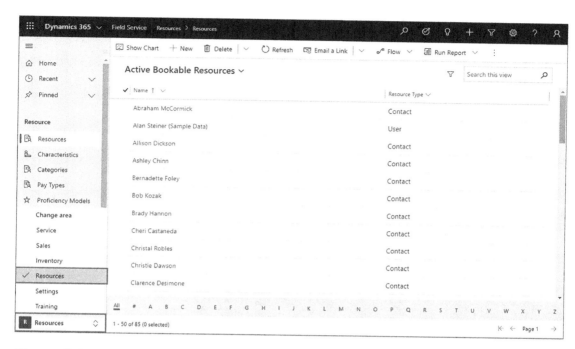

Figure 2-9. *Active Bookable Resources view*

Figure 2-10 shows an example of a bookable resource of type User.

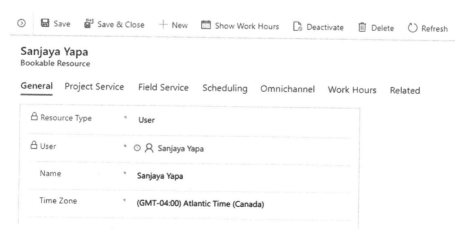

Figure 2-10. *Bookable resource of type User*

To view the possible work hours for a resource, click **Show Work Hours** from the toolbar (Figure 2-11). Click **New** to add new work hours.

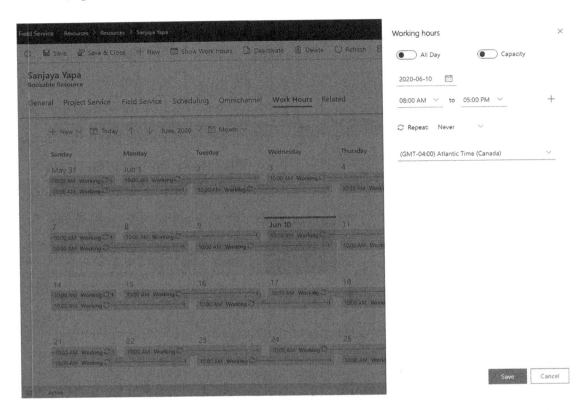

Figure 2-11. *Resource work hours*

For more information, visit https://docs.microsoft.com/en-us/dynamics365/ field-service/set-up-bookable-resources#add-work-hours.

Resource Requirements

When a work order is created, a resource requirement is created automatically. This defines when and where the job should be performed. The resource requirement are located in the Related section of the Work Order record (Figure 2-12). The information within the Resource Requirement record is used for scheduling. This record is the bridge between the resource scheduling and the work order. Some scenarios could require multiple resources—for instance, a field technician and the equipment to perform the work, or perhaps multiple field technicians.

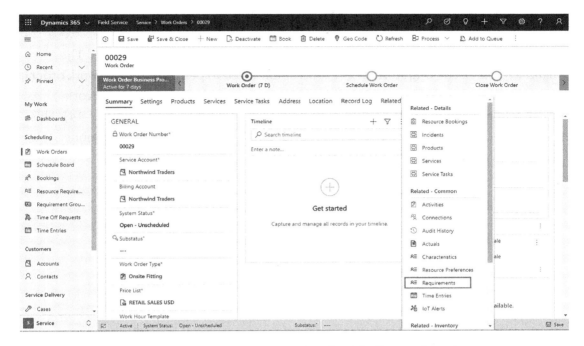

Figure 2-12. *Resource requirements associated with the work order*

The time promised to perform the work and the location details are located under the Scheduling tab of the Resource Requirement record (Figure 2-13).

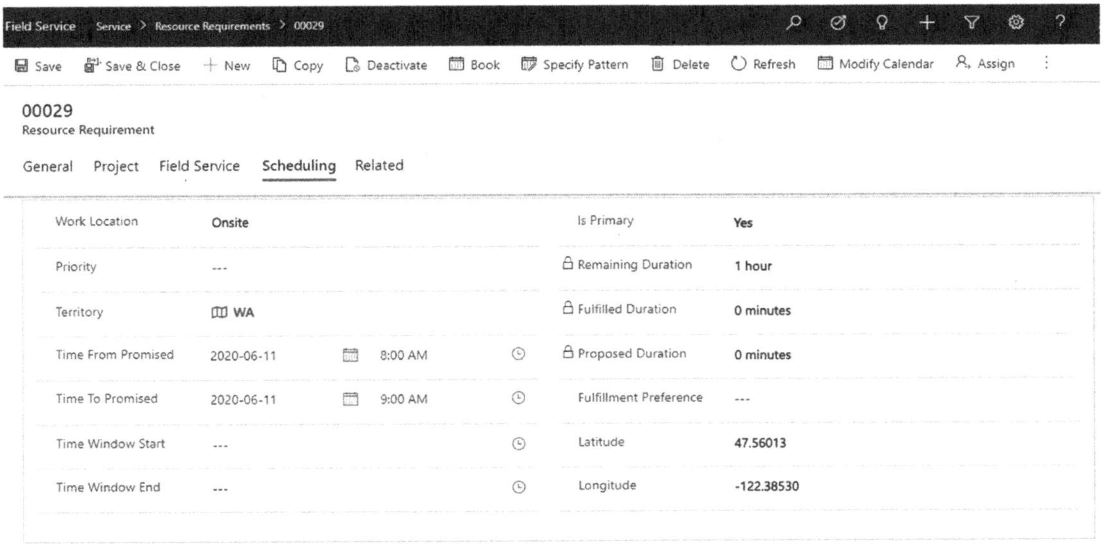

Figure 2-13. *Time promised to complete the work order*

Bookable Resource Bookings

In order to be performed, the job described in the work order needs resources. The *bookable resource booking* stores the resources allocated to perform the job (work order). The work order can contain multiple bookable resource bookings. When the work order is scheduled, the Bookable Resource Booking record is created (Figure 2-14). This ensures that the field staff will get to see the work order in the Field Service Mobile.

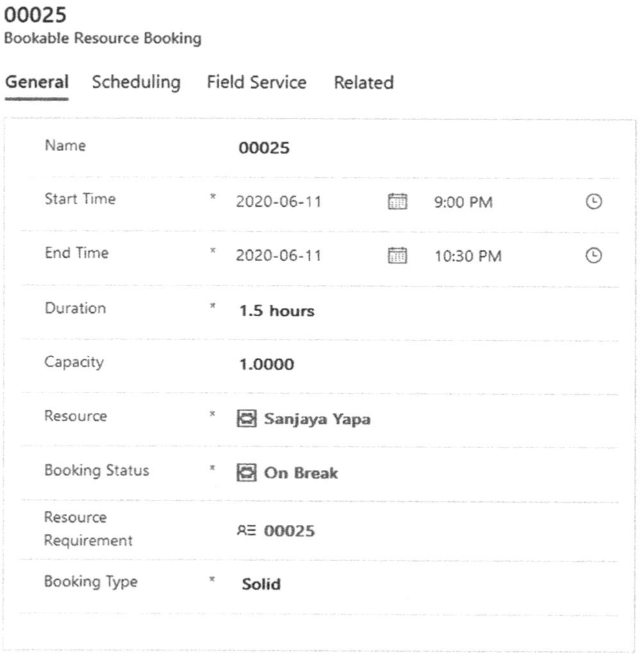

Figure 2-14. *Bookable Resource Booking record*

The field staff can use the Bookable Resource Booking record to update the related work order's system status, which cannot be updated directly. The following options are available in the Booking Status field of the Bookable Resource Booking record:

- *Scheduled*: When the work order is assigned to the resource, the bookable resource booking is created with this status. This means the work order is assigned to the resource and ready for execution.

- *Travelling*: Once the work order is assigned to the resource (technician) and the field staff is notified, the field staff can change the status to Travelling to indicate that the technician is travelling to the incident location.

- *In Progress*: This status indicates that the field staff is attending to the job.

- *On Break*: If the work order takes a long time to complete and the field agent requires a short break, they can change the status to On Break.

- *Completed*: When the work is fully completed, the technician can change the status to Completed. This will trigger a back-end process and put the work order to Open-Completed status and awaiting approval from the supervisor.

The schedule board displays the statuses in different colors (Figure 2-15). When the Booking Status field is changed in the Bookable Resource Booking record, the color of the status changes in the schedule board. This enables supervisors to monitor the workforce closely.

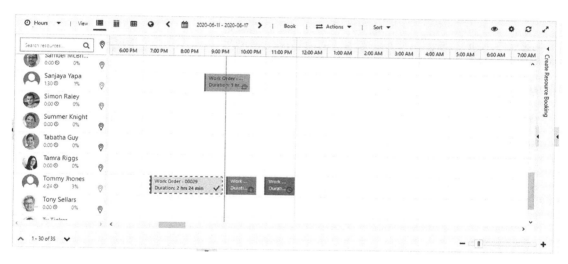

Figure 2-15. *Work orders assigned to resources in different statuses*

Resource Characteristics

Resource characteristics are the talents a bookable resource possesses. There could be scenarios where some jobs require a certification or special license. These can be defined as resource characteristics. The resource characteristics are selected when the work order is created (Figure 2-16).

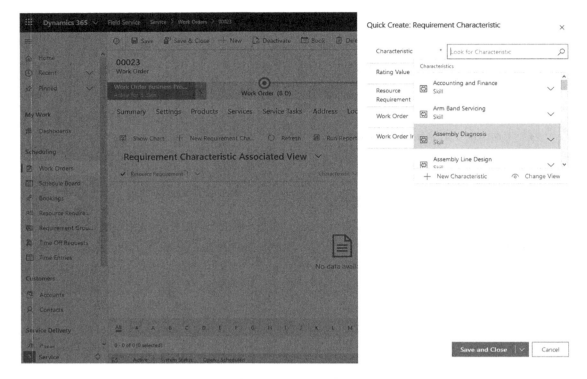

Figure 2-16. *Creating resource characteristics for a work order*

The characteristics also can be defined on the Bookable Resource record (Figure 2-17).

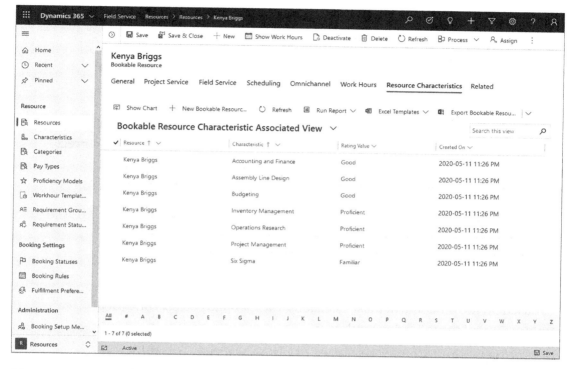

Figure 2-17. *Bookable resource characteristics*

Creating a work order with specific characteristic requirements allows the schedulers/dispatchers to filter the resources with similar characteristics, which simplifies the scheduling process.

Scheduling

Generally, organizations that operate a field staff need to schedule the workforce to provide services or sell products to the doorstep of the customers. There could be a wide range of scheduling scenarios for such organizations. The process of scheduling work and assigning staff could be a daunting task due to various challenges. This will become more challenging if the resources are limited. The scheduling staff behind the scene must have all the vital information to allocate resources to the work and avoid any bad experiences for the customers. The following parameters govern the work schedule process:

- Who is available to deliver the services or items

- When the resources are available

- Who is the best resource to attend to the specific work

- The options if no resources are available

- Whether the customer cancels the request or asks to reschedule it?

- Whether any after-sales visits are required

After finalizing these decisions, the organization must think about the process of scheduling work. The following decisions must be met before choosing the correct avenue:

- The number of field staff available

- The geographical spread of the workforce

- How often the company provides goods and services

- The size of the target audiences

Based on the outcome of these decisions, the company selects one (or a combination) of the following methods:

> *Manual scheduling using the schedule board*: The schedule board is the go-to tool for manually scheduling work orders. It lists all the available resources and unscheduled work. The dispatcher can easily drag and drop the unscheduled work to the available resources. The schedule board offers several ways to schedule work.

> *Semi-automated scheduling using the schedule assistant*: The schedule assistant will suggest the scheduling staff/dispatcher with the available resources and possible time slots of the resource availability. This process is governed by rules such as skills requirements, time window, etc.

> *Fully automated with Resource Schedule Optimization*: This scheduling process can be fully automated using Resource Scheduling Optimization (RSO). This requires additional licenses. Apart from that, if the organization has unique scheduling requirements and rules, they can also customize the auto-scheduling process. For this, a clear set of rules must be defined for the automation to assign the work.

The Schedule Board

In Dynamics 365 Field Service, the schedule board is the playground for dispatching and scheduling staff (Figure 2-18). The schedule board, one of the best features of the solution, is extremely easy to use. The interface allows users to drag and drop jobs in and out from the board. The board also has a map view that shows the resource locations and job locations. The schedule board can be accessed by both Field Service Administrator and Field Service Dispatcher security roles. Resources will have limited access to the schedule board.

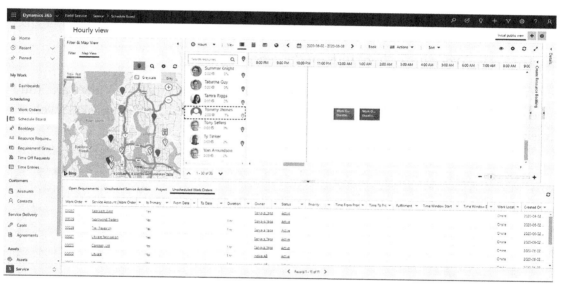

Figure 2-18. *Dynamics 365 Field Service schedule board*

When the schedule board loads, it shows a great deal of information related to scheduling of resources. The middle section displays all the bookings for the resource (Figure 2-19). In each booking, you can see some basic information, such as work order number and duration.

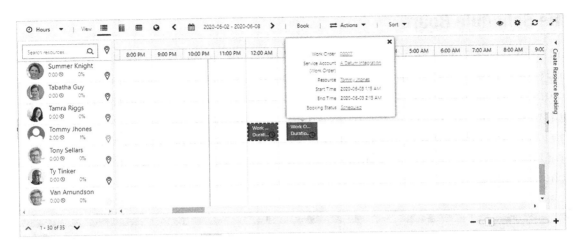

Figure 2-19. *Work order bookings on the schedule board*

When you right-click a resource from the resources list and click the View Card, the schedule board will show information about the selected resource, such as skill levels, time zone, job role, etc. (Figure 2-20).

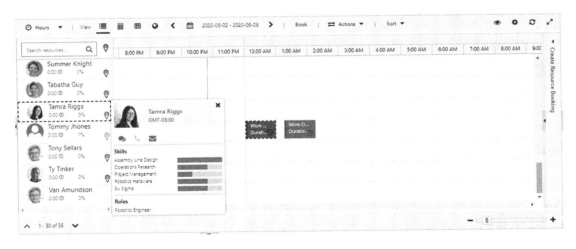

Figure 2-20. *Resource information on the schedule board*

The other interesting feature in the schedule board is the map view. As shown in Figure 2-21, each resource has a map pin next it. This pin can be used to locate the resource on the map.

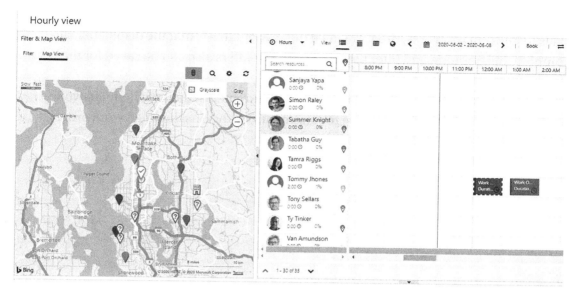

Figure 2-21. *Resource location tracked on the map*

On the map, you can see the unscheduled work order with red pins with question marks. The map view includes a filter pane (Figure 2-22).

Figure 2-22. *Filtering on the schedule board*

You can filter the resources based on various criteria—for example, based on the skills to perform a job or by area. The nice thing about this is that the dispatcher can combine these criteria and filter the resources. The filters also can be saved for the next time.

At the bottom of the schedule board is the requirements and unscheduled work orders pane, which lists the resource requirements for the unscheduled work orders (Figure 2-23).

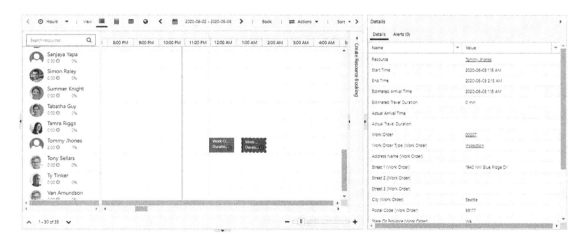

Figure 2-23. *Unscheduled work order view on the schedule board*

The Details pane is on the right side. When a user selects a booking from the main scheduling area, this pane displays additional detail about the booking (Figure 2-24).

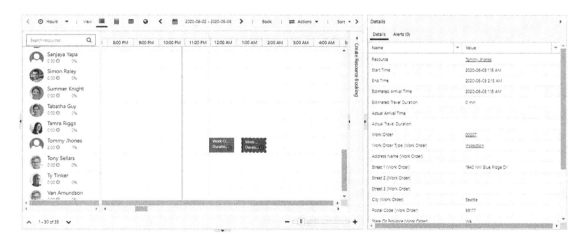

Figure 2-24. *Details pane on the schedule board*

Along the top of the schedule board are different tabs that can display different types of scheduling options based on the territory or type of work (Figure 2-25).

Figure 2-25. *Schedule board views*

When the plus sign is clicked, a window appears that enables you to specify the required tab settings (Figure 2-26).

Figure 2-26. *Tab settings window of the schedule board*

As previously mentioned, a dispatcher can schedule a work order (job) in one of the following ways:

- The dispatcher can select a requirement from the lower resource requirements panel and drag it to the relevant timeslot of the resource.

- Similarly, the dispatcher can expand the map view and drag an unscheduled map pin from the map and assign it so the resource in the center.

- If the dispatcher knows the work order number but does not want to search it from the requirements pane or the map, they can allocate the time slot on the relevant resource and search the work order from the quick search popup. This action will assign the work order to the resource.

Customers and Vendors

Customers and vendors are key aspects of any business. Every business interacts with many customers and vendors. Information a customer and or vendor's account is stored in the Account record, and their contact information is stored in the Contact record.

Accounts

In the Dynamics 365 world, an *account* is an organization that can be interacted for business purposes. In some businesses, an account is an individual, but in the majority of the scenarios, an account represents an organization or a business. Figure 2-27 shows the Account record.

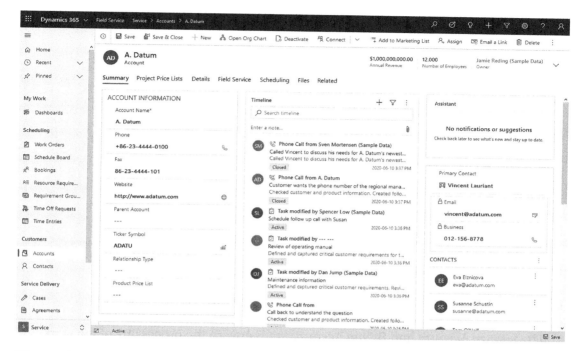

Figure 2-27. *Account record*

The same purpose of representation of the Account entity as a business or an
organization applies in Dynamics 365 Field Service. Accounts are used in many places
in Field Service, but their primary use is with work orders. Accounts include both service
accounts and billing accounts. The service account is where the work is performed, and
the billing account pays for the work (Figure 2-28).

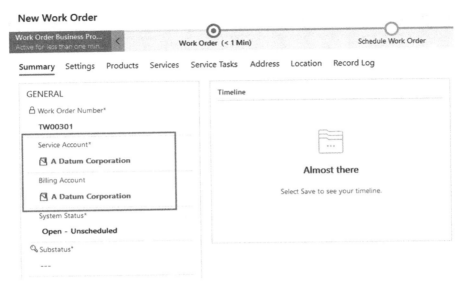

Figure 2-28. *Service and billing accounts in a work order*

The Service Account and Billing Account fields govern the processing of the work order. This is how it happens:

- Out-of-the-box, when the user fills the Service Account field, the Billing Account field is also populated. When the Service Account field is selected, the Billing Account field of the Service Account record is queried; if the field is blank, then the Billing Account field of the work order is filled with the service account selected.

- The tax-exempt status, which determines whether to apply tax on the work order, is defined in the Service Account field. If the field is set to Yes, then the appropriate sales tax code should be selected.

- The Service Account field will also define the service territory of the work order.

- The price list of the work order is copied from the price list of the billing account. The price list is used to determine the price applied for the products and services used in the work order.

- The invoice account is the Billing Account, which is the account listed in the invoice.

Contacts

In Dynamics 365 Customer Engagement, a *contact* is a person representing an organization. In Dynamics 365 Field Service, however, a *contact* can be used as a resource to provide services. This scenario is primarily used when the work is delegated to external contractors. If contact resources are used, there should be a mechanism to delegate the work orders to the external parties and update the work orders as and when they complete the work orders. Otherwise, someone from the back office who has access to Field Service should update the work orders based on the inputs from the contractors. Figure 2-29 shows the Contact record.

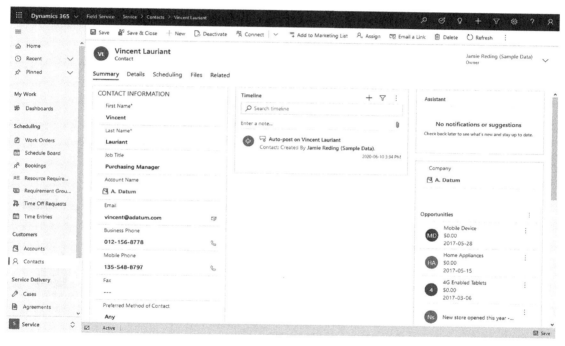

Figure 2-29. *Contact record*

Inventory

This section explains the entities used for managing inventory. These entities play a significant role in work order processing—that is, they hold the inventory required for the field operations. Inventory is stored in a warehouse, transferred between locations, and adjusted on location. The entities and underlying processes described in this section are specifically designed to facilitate such operations. For sophisticated inventory processing, however, other platforms are available, such as Dynamics 365 Finance and Operations, which is Microsoft's enterprise resource planning (ERP) platform.

Warehouses

A *warehouse* is a location where the inventory exists. In the majority of scenarios, warehouses can be geographically spread—that is, different states could have one warehouse or many warehouses. For instance, every state in the country could have a distribution center where all the stock is purchased from the vendors and distributed across the child warehouses, which can be smaller, regional store locations where field staff can replenish inventory to carry out the work assigned to them. Figure 2-30 illustrates a typical warehouse setup.

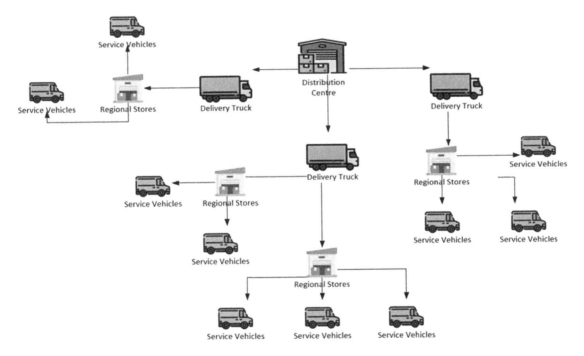

Figure 2-30. *A typical warehouse structure*

This setup can be created easily in Dynamics 365 Field Service. Each location, even a delivery truck and service vehicle, can be set up as a warehouse, allowing you to track the inventory movement between different locations. The warehouse can be considered as a container for the product inventory (Figure 2-31).

Figure 2-31. Warehouse record

Products

Products are items and services that can be sold to the clients. Figure 2-32 shows an example of a Product record. The same record can be used for many work orders. When the product is consumed by a work order, the client is invoiced using the attached price list. Several underlying entities are involved. A product is linked to the work order by work order products and work order services, as explained earlier. The inventory is managed through the product inventory of the associated warehouse. Finally, the price is determined by the price list items that a product or service belongs to.

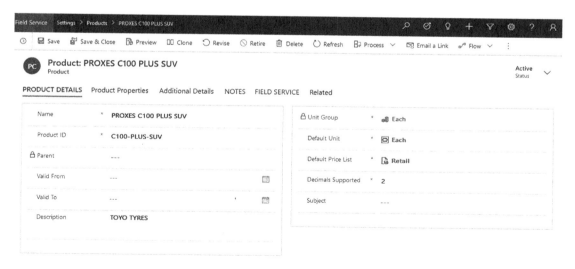

Figure 2-32. Product record

In Field Service, the following three types of products are available out of the box (Figure 2-33):

- *Inventory*: These items have a monetary value and the quantities are tracked in the warehouses.

- *Non-inventory*: These items are not tracked in warehouses and have no monetary value to the business.

- *Service*: These products can be defined as the labor a business can sell to its customers. The quantity is measured in hours or duration of time.

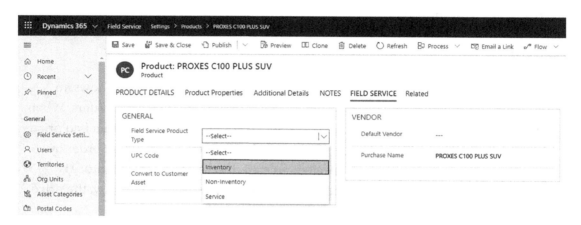

Figure 2-33. *Selecting the product type*

The product type is defined under the Field Service tab of the Product record. Setting this property is essential to segregate the type of work a field operative will be doing. For instance, a field operative might be changing a tire of a car. As explained earlier, the Work Order record includes two separate Products and Services tabs. The inventory items can be added to the work order under the Products tab, and the service items can be added to the work order under the Services tab. You can create a product by navigating to **Field Service ➤ Settings ➤ Product ➤ Add Product**.

Pricing for the product or service is determined by the price lists. Generally, the price list consists of price list items, which define the price for each product or service. Also, there is a property in the Products record called *List Price*. The value defined here will be used if the product is not added to a price list.

Product Inventory

In most field services scenarios where products are sold, the organizations should keep an inventory. As explained in the "Warehouses" section, these inventories are kept in warehouses. The link between the warehouse and the product is established using the Product Inventory record, which dictates a product in a warehouse and the quantity available within that particular warehouse (Figure 2-34).

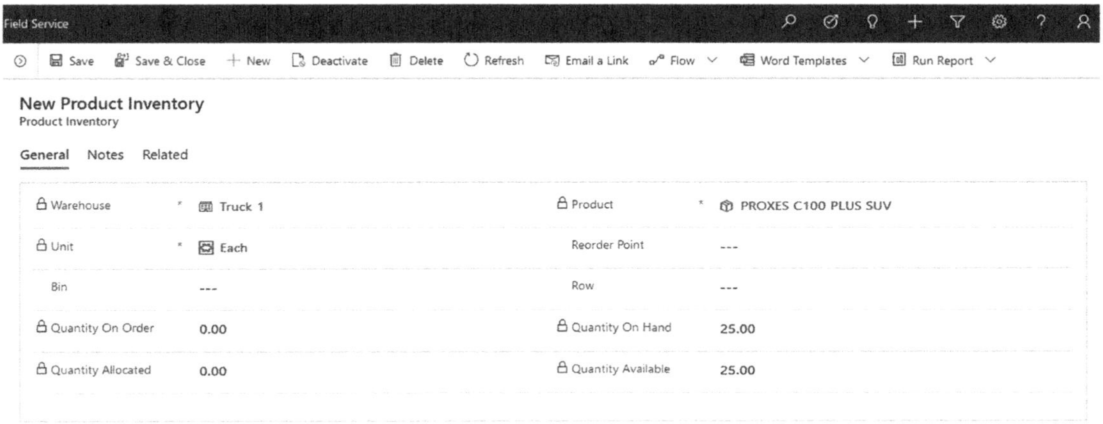

Figure 2-34. *Product Inventory record associated with a warehouse*

Inventory Transfers

Inventory transfers are used to move products between warehouses. An inventory transfer can change the product inventory of each warehouse that is involved in the transfer. One important characteristic of the process is that the inventory flow is one direction per transfer—i.e., from the source to the destination. The most common scenario for an inventory transfer is when a field technician goes to a regional store location (source warehouse) and transfers the items required for the work to their van (destination warehouse). Figure 2-35 shows the Inventory Transfer record.

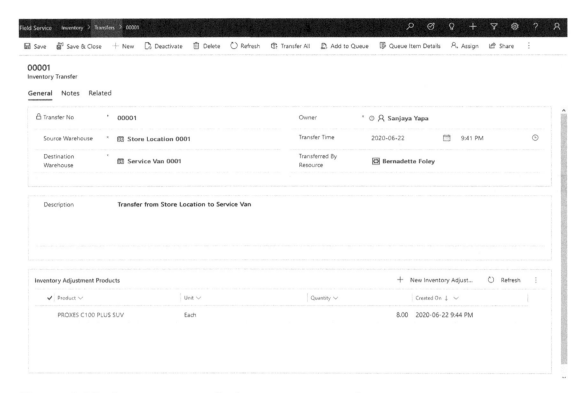

Figure 2-35. *Inventory transfer between two warehouses*

This process can also be used to transfer items between main warehouses/ distribution centers and regional store locations. For instance, an inventory transfer can be initiated from the distribution center, and once the goods are physically transferred to the destination, the transfer can be completed.

An Inventory Adjustment Product record is used to trigger the process. As soon as the user adds an inventory adjustment product, the inventory of the source decreases and the inventory of the destination increases.

Inventory Adjustments

Inventory adjustments allow inventory managers to increment or decrement stock from a given warehouse. This process is best handled by inventory managers, to alter incorrect inventory counts. For instance, if the inventory manager takes a physical count of the items in the warehouse that does not match the count in the system, then they can initiate an inventory adjustment. Another scenario for this process is when setting up a brand new warehouse. Enabling inventory adjustments for the field staff is not advisable, to avoid fraud in the inventory.

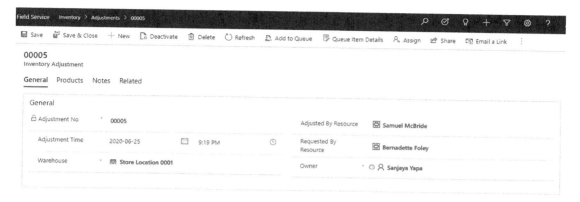

Figure 2-36. *Inventory Adjustment record*

Figure 2-36 shows the Inventory Adjustment record. To add products, go to the **Related** tab and select the products from the menu. On the subgrid, click "New Inventory Adjustment" to add the inventory adjustment product, as shown in Figure 2-37, and then click the **Save and Close** button. The inventory of the selected warehouse will get the update.

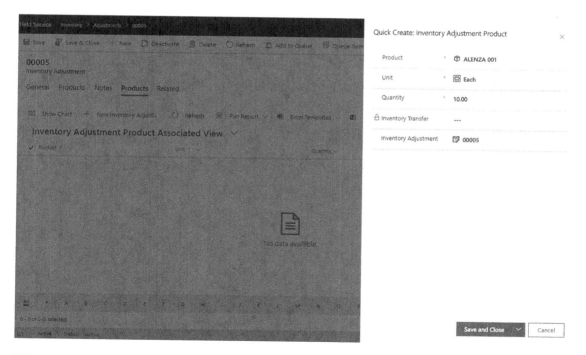

Figure 2-37. *Adding products to the inventory adjustment*

Purchase Orders

Purchase orders can be used to add inventory to warehouses. However, they are better suited for purchasing inventory for the main warehouses. Purchase orders also can be used to buy a specific item to complete a work order. A set of related entities are required to complete the purchase order process. As shown in Figure 2-38, the process is set up as a business process flow.

Figure 2-38. *Purchase Order record and the business process flow*

Purchase Order Products

The Purchase Order Product record holds the products required for the warehouse or the work order (Figure 2-39). The purchase order will be raised to buy the products listed here from the vendors.

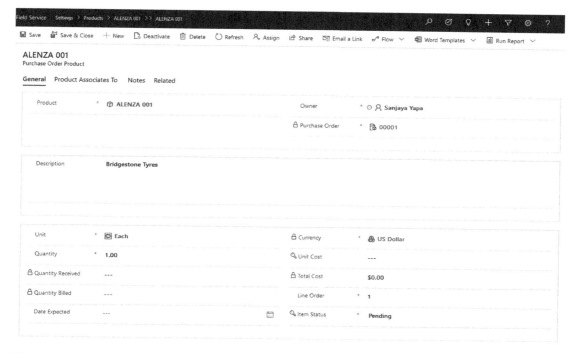

Figure 2-39. *Purchase Order Product Record associated with the purchase order*

Purchase Order Receipts

Purchase order receipts are generated when the location receives the products ordered. A purchase order can have multiple receipts to manage the arrival of goods in different time frames. For instance, if the purchase order is raised to replenish the main warehouse, the products ordered might arrive at the warehouse in different timelines. Figure 2-40 shows the Purchase Order Receipt record.

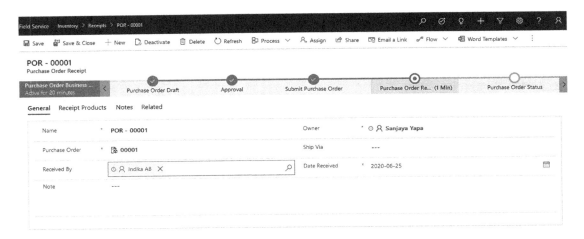

Figure 2-40. *Purchase Order Receipt record*

Purchase Order Receipt Products

The Purchase Order Receipt Products indicate the products received for the purchase order. When the ordered products arrive at the warehouse, the warehouse staff can create the Receipt Product, which indicates the items are received. The Purchase Order status will be changed to Received when all the Purchase Order Receipt Products are added to the receipts (Figure 2-41).

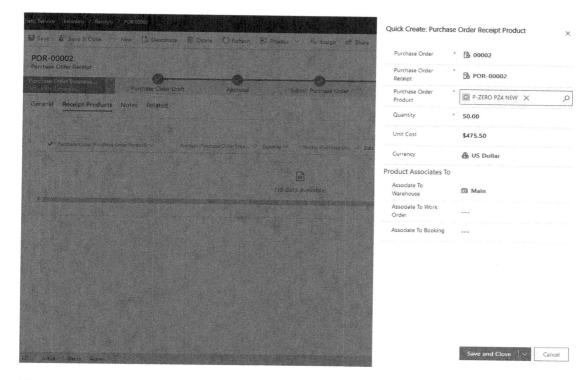

Figure 2-41. *Adding a Purchase Order Receipt Product to the Purchase Order Receipt record*

Purchase Order Bills

Purchase order bills are created to track the invoices received from the vendors. After receiving the inventory for the purchase order, the bill can be raised to include the corresponding invoice received from the vendor (Figure 2-42).

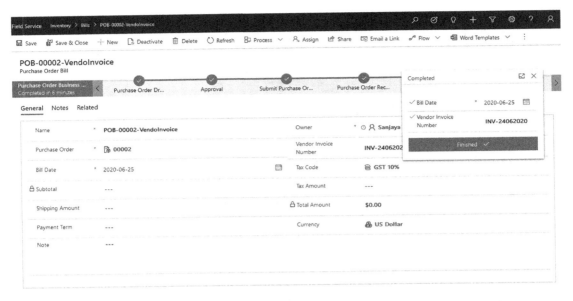

Figure 2-42. *Purchase Order Bill record*

Inventory Journals

Inventory journals are used to record all the inventory transactions in the system. For example, when an item is used from the warehouse to process a work order, an Inventory Journal record is created. An Inventory Journal record is also created for inventory transfers. The primary purpose of this record is to make inventory integration between ERP systems easier.

RMA (Return Merchandise Authorization)

The return merchandise authorization (RMA) process is specifically designed to handle returned items. If an item is malfunctioning or the customer is dissatisfied with an item, it can be returned through the RMA process. The RMA entity holds the details about the return. Optionally, the RMA entity can be associated with a work order. This association will link the price lists, tax codes, and products used in the work order. Click the **Add WO Product** button on the toolbar to add the products associated with the work order (Figure 2-43).

As shown in Figure 2-43, the RMA process involved the following three actions:

- Create RTV

- Return to Warehouse

- Change Asset Ownership

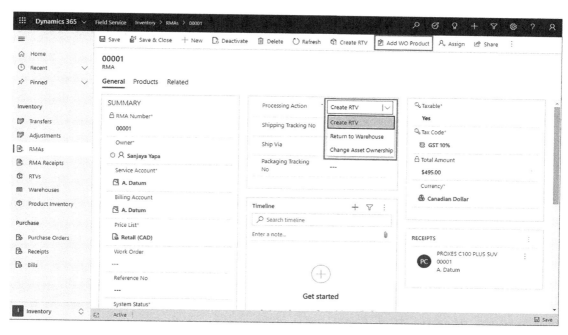

Figure 2-43. *RMA record and the processing actions*

RMA Products

The item returned is created as an *RMA product* associated with the RMA Product record
(Figure 2-44). This record contains information such as where to return the item, the
quantity, the processing action, etc. If the RMA product is associated with a work order,
then most of this information will be synced from the work order products used in the
work order.

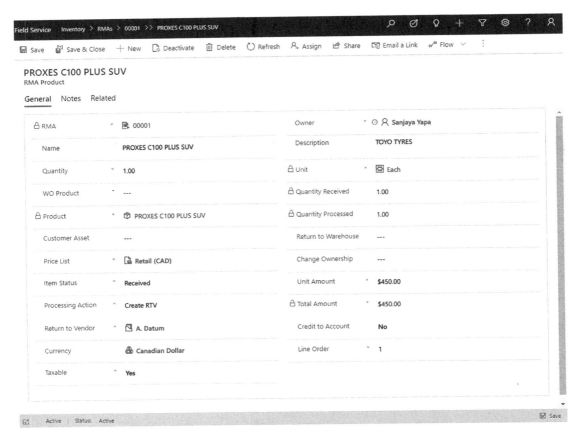

Figure 2-44. RMA Product record

RMA Receipts

An *RMA receipt* is created to track and approve item returns (Figure 2-45). As you can see, the receipt is related to the RMA record. Note, also, the Credit To Customer button on the toolbar. When this option is selected, a credit invoice will be created to match the items added to the receipt.

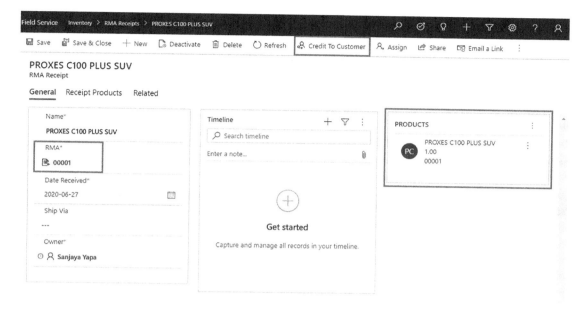

Figure 2-45. *RMA Receipt record*

An RMA receipt also contains the product records associated with the RMA. These products are added to the receipt as RMA receipt products (Figure 2-46).

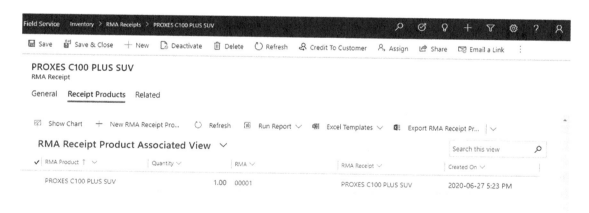

Figure 2-46. *RMA receipt products*

If the products are part of the inventory and the Processing Action of the RMA record is set to Return to Warehouse, then the inventory will be adjusted.

RTV (Return to Vendor)

The return to vendor (RTV) process is suitable in scenarios where the returned items are sent back directly to the vendor. The RTV record holds the information for this process. The returned items will not be added to the inventory. When the RMA is created, you can specify to create an RTV in the Processing Action field. Once the products are received, click the Create RTV button on the toolbar to create the RTV record. We will look at this process in detail later in the book.

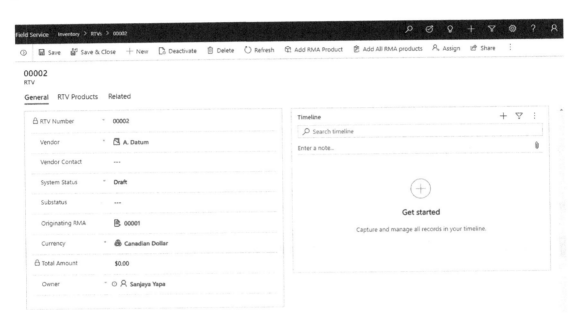

Figure 2-47. *RTV record created for RMA*

As shown in Figure 2-47, the RTV is related to the RMA that is specified in the Originating RMA field.

RTV Products

Under the RTV Products tab, you can add the products associated with the RMA, which will become the RTV products. Note the following two options on the toolbar (Figure 2-48):

Add RMA Product: Use this option if the RMA has multiple products and only one may need to be returned to the vendor.

Add All RMA Products: Use this option if the RMA has one or more records and all should be returned to the vendor.

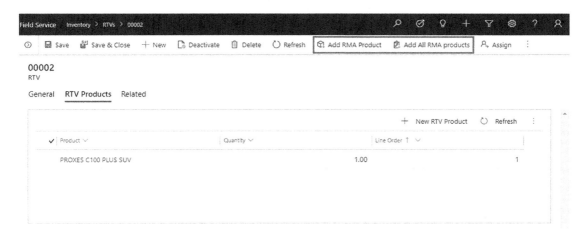

Figure 2-48. *RTV products associated with the RTV record*

Introduction to Field Service Mobile Configuration

Administrators and developers can use App Designer to configure the Field Service Mobile based on the requirements of the business (Figure 2-49).

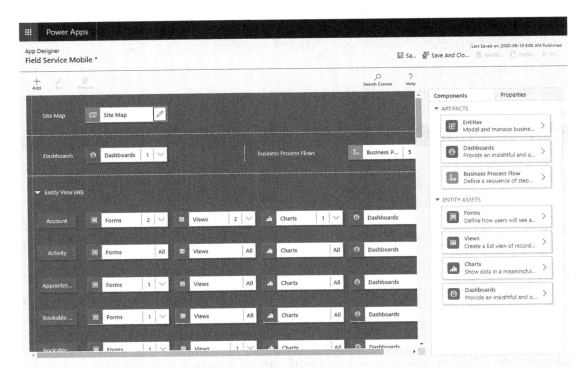

Figure 2-49. *App Designer for Field Service Mobile*

Sitemap Designer

Locate the Field Service Mobile under the My Apps section, and then open App Designer. You can use Sitemap Designer to edit the navigation of the Field Service Mobile based on the entities exposed to the users.

Here, we will be adding inventory transfers to the Field Service Mobile for the field agents. We also will add a link to the warehouses to view their content.

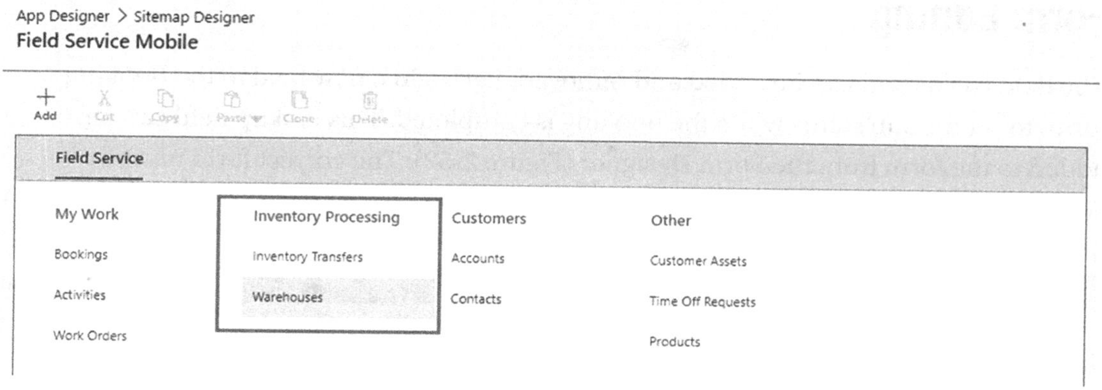

App Designer > Sitemap Designer
Field Service Mobile

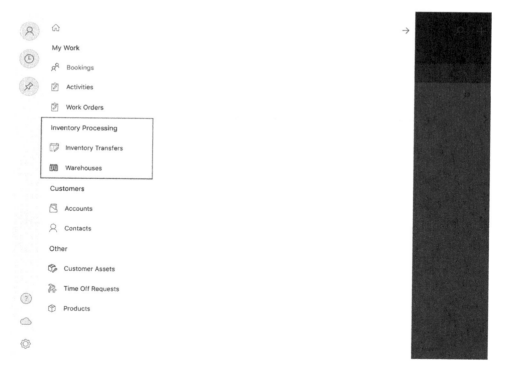

Figure 2-50. *Adding a new group and a subsection to the Field Service Mobile navigation*

Save and publish the changes, and then refresh the Field Service Mobile. The navigation is updated for processing inventory transfers and viewing inventory within the warehouses.

Figure 2-51. *Field Service Mobile navigation updated*

Form Editing

The fields on a form can be added and removed. Let's add a new field to the Booking form, to set the sub status when the booking is completed. This lookup field can be added to the form from the Form Designer (Figure 2-52). The correct form must be selected to edit.

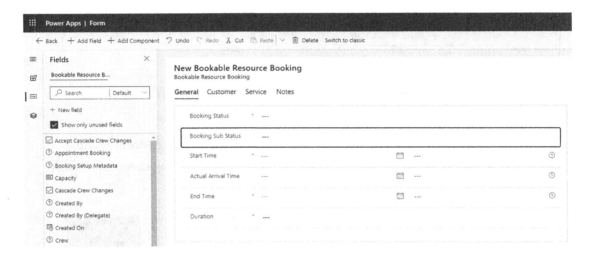

Figure 2-52. *Adding fields to the form used in Field Service Mobile app*

As shown in Figure 2-53, the new field appears on the mobile form.

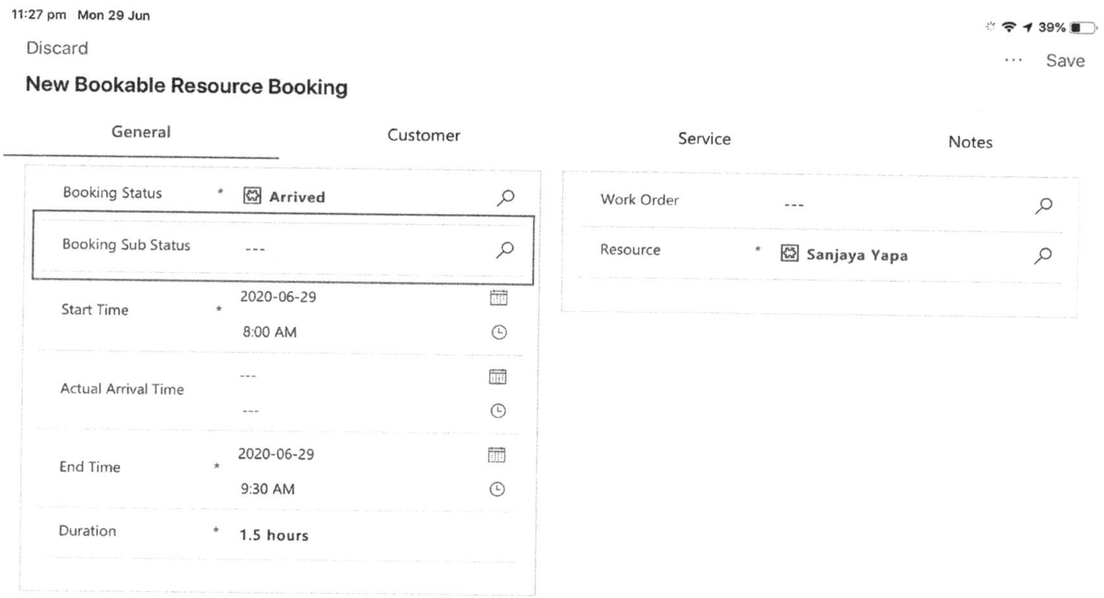

Figure 2-53. *Field Service Mobile form with the new file's Booking Sub Status field*

The app is built as a model-driven app, and different controls in the Power Apps control framework can be used in the forms (Figure 2-54).

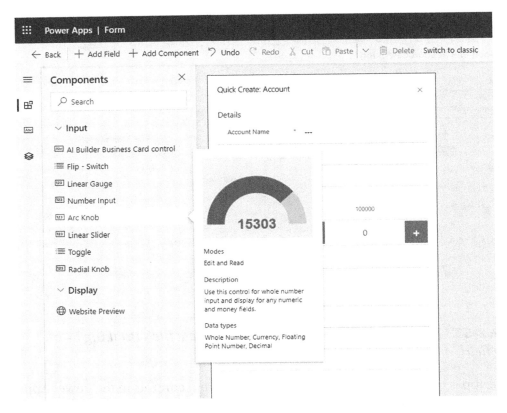

Figure 2-54. *Power Apps components*

The Quick Create form of the account entity has two such controls (Figure 2-55).

Figure 2-55. *Account entity's Quick Create form with Power Apps controls*

Business Rules

Business rules can be used with the Field Service Mobile to makes it easier to do validations without the need to write JavaScript code. For instance, the Bookable Resource Booking form includes a Booking Sub Status field that is visible only when the Booking Status field is set to Completed. This is, of course, a business rule defined in the bookable resource booking. As shown in Figure 2-56, the field displays when the Booking Status changed to Completed.

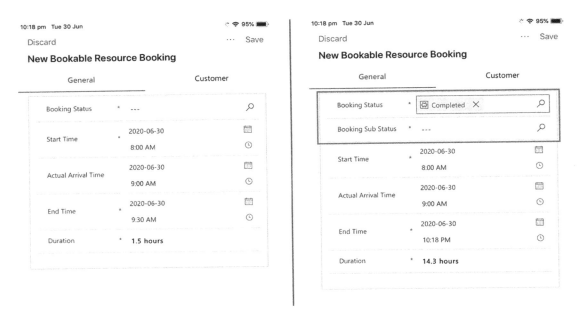

Figure 2-56. *Business rules in the Field Service Mobile app*

Offline Data Synchronization

Even though mobile networks are improving and becoming more geographically widespread, some areas have either faulty service or no service at all. When field technicians are working in basements or underground parking lots, they usually won't have service—but are still expected to complete his work. Dynamics 365 Field Service is the ideal application because of its offline capabilities. It is capable of storing the subset of data in the mobile device so that technicians can continue to work when there is no service.

The thing to note here is that the entire set of data does not have to be downloaded for every device. The profile can be configured and the criteria filtered to limit the amount of data downloaded to the device. Navigate to **Settings→Mobile Offline** and select **Field Service Mobile – Offline Profile** (Figure 2-57).

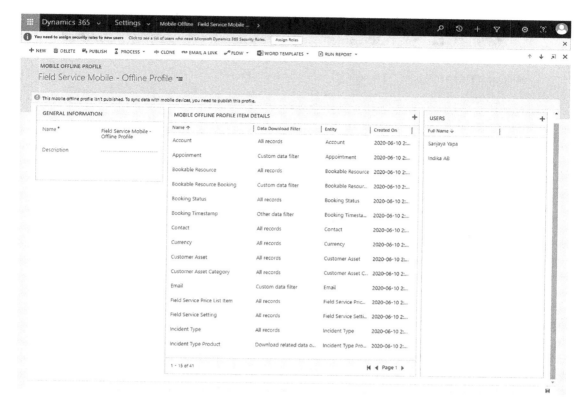

Figure 2-57. *Field Service Mobile - Offline Profile*

You can use custom filters to limit the data set size. Open the required entity within the **Mobile Offline Profile Item Details** pane (Figure 2-57). As shown in Figure 2-58, click **Data Download Filter** and select **Custom Data Filter**.

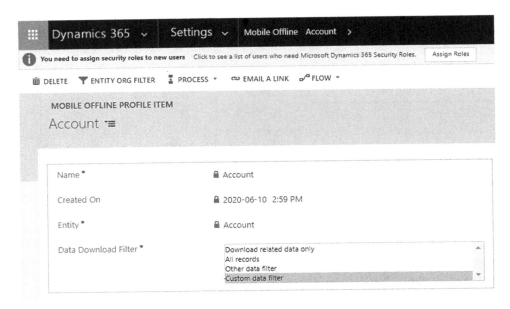

Figure 2-58. *Custom data filter for Mobile Offline Profile Item*

Click **Define Filter Rule**. The **Define Profile Item Entity Filter** window will appear. You can define the filter criteria, for example, to load the accounts owned by the current user (Figure 2-59).

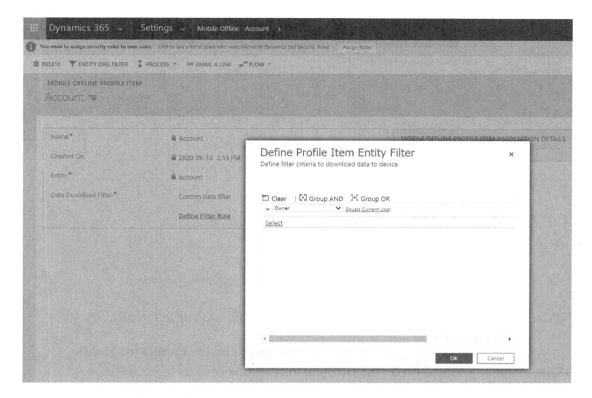

Figure 2-59. *Define Profile Item Entity Filter for the Account Entity*

You also can add new entities to the list of **Mobile Offline Profile Item Details** pane (Figure 2-57). Simply click the + on the top-right corner of the section.

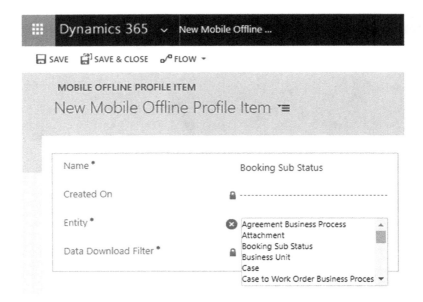

Figure 2-60. *Adding a new entity to the Mobile Offline Profile Details*

For custom entities, the **Enable for Unified Client** and the **Enable for Mobile Offline** must be enabled under the **Outlook and Mobile** section of the solution. Otherwise, the entity will not be listed in the **Entity** dropdown list (Figure 2-60). For more information, visit `https://docs.microsoft.com/en-us/dynamics365/field-service/mobile-2020-power-platform#configure-offline-data-and-sync-filters`.

Field Service Security

Out of the box, Dynamics 365 Field Service comes with a predefined set of *security roles* specific to the solution. These roles are designed to grant access to the entities unique to the solution. A Field Service user must have at least one security role in order to access the application. Predefined *field security profiles* are also provided out of the box. Field security profiles define which fields end users can edit.

The following security roles are available:

> *Field Service – Administrator*: The users assigned with this security role have full access to all the entities specific to Field Service. This role has full CRUD capabilities to the entities in the application. Only IT administrators or service managers should be granted this access.

Field Service – Resource: This security role should be used to grant access to the users who will be operating in the field to provide services to the customers. The role has limited read-write capabilities, but they are sufficient for executing the fieldwork.

Field Service – Salesperson: Sometimes field operatives may want to access the leads, opportunities, and quotes. Those users should be assigned with this role.

Field Service – Dispatcher: Call center operatives who will be creating and assigning work orders to the field staff should be given this role. This role has limited CRUD capabilities but possesses enough access to perform scheduling tasks.

Field Service – Inventory Purchase: This security role is designed for inventory managers and grant access to the inventory-related entities of the Field Service solution. Users with this security role can process purchase orders, inventory retunes, etc. This role also has limited CRUD capabilities to the inventory-related entities.

Note   These security roles will also grant users access to the Field Service Mobile. For instance, field service operatives who are granted the Field Service – Resource role can use the Field Service Mobile to complete the work assigned to them.

Figure 2-61 illustrates the list of security roles under the Security section of the application.

Security Roles

Business Unit: tyreworx1000

  New | | | X | More Actions ▾

☐	Name ↑	Business Unit
	Export Customizations (Solution Checker)	tyreworx1000
☑	Field Service - Administrator	tyreworx1000
☑	Field Service - Dispatcher	tyreworx1000
☑	Field Service - Inventory Purchase	tyreworx1000
☑	Field Service - Resource	tyreworx1000
☑	Field Service - Salesperson	tyreworx1000

Figure 2-61. *Out-of-the-box Field Service security roles*

In order to be granted access to Field Service, a user must have both a security role and a field security profile. A field security profile corresponds to each security role (Figure 2-62):

Field Security Profiles

  New | | | X | More Actions ▾

☐	Name ↑	Modified On	Description
☑	Field Service - Administrator	2020-05-11 10:34 PM	
☑	Field Service - Dispatcher	2020-05-11 10:34 PM	
☑	Field Service - Inventory Purch...	2020-05-11 10:34 PM	
☑	Field Service - Resource	2020-05-11 10:34 PM	

Figure 2-62. *Out-of-the-box field security profiles*

The best practice is to keep these out-of-the-box security roles as they are and create copies of them. This enables you to extend the security roles without spoiling the core security roles. If you want to start over, you still can use the core roles. Most of the time, the solution might require a few additional custom entities to meet the unique requirements of the business. By extending these security roles, you can grant users access to these custom entities. In a scenario where you have multiple security roles cloned from the original roles, you could use the Role Updater of XrmToolBox to easily update the roles and grant access to entities.

Note   XrmToolBox is a Windows application that connects to the Common Data Service for Apps (CDS/Dataflex). XrmToolBox includes different tools to make Dynamics 365 Customer Engagement customizations and configuration easy. You can download XrmToolBox from `www.xrmtoolbox.com/`.

For example, you can copy the Field Service Resource role for two different business domains, such as wholesale and retail. First, copy the security roles by selecting the role to be copied and selecting **Copy Role** from the **More Actions** drop-down list (Figure 2-63).

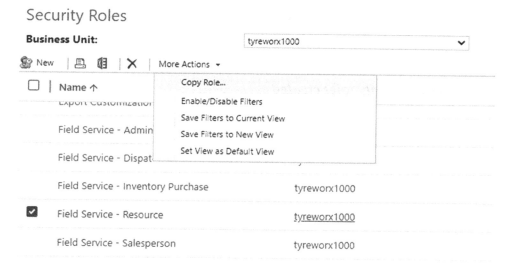

Figure 2-63. *Copying security roles*

Next, give appropriate names for the user roles. As you can see, you can copy multiple security roles (Figure 2-64).

Security Roles

Business Unit: tyreworx1000 ⌄

🐵 New | 🖻 🗐 | ✕ | More Actions ▾

☐	Name ↑		Business Unit
	Export Customizations (Solution Checker)		tyreworx1000
	Field Service - Administrator		tyreworx1000
	Field Service - Dispatcher		tyreworx1000
	Field Service - Inventory Purchase		tyreworx1000
	Field Service - Resource		tyreworx1000
☑	Field Service - Resource - Retail Technician		tyreworx1000
	Field Service - Salesperson		tyreworx1000
☑	Field Service - Salesperson - Sales Rep		tyreworx1000
	Forecast manager		tyreworx1000

Figure 2-64. *New security roles created*

After creating the security roles, open XrmToolBox, load Role Updater (Figure 2-65), and then click **Load Roles and Privileges**. The tool will load all the security roles available.

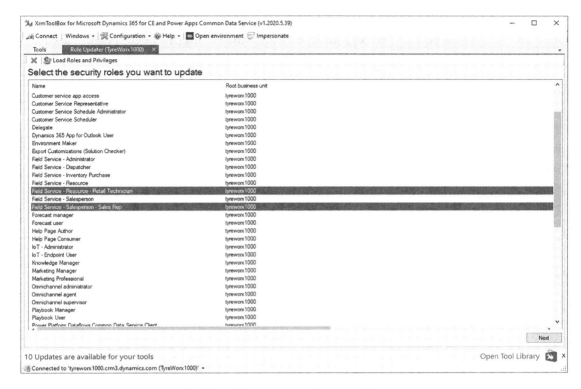

Figure 2-65. *Security roles listed in XrmToolBox Role Updater*

Select the security role to update and then click **Next** (Figure 2-66).

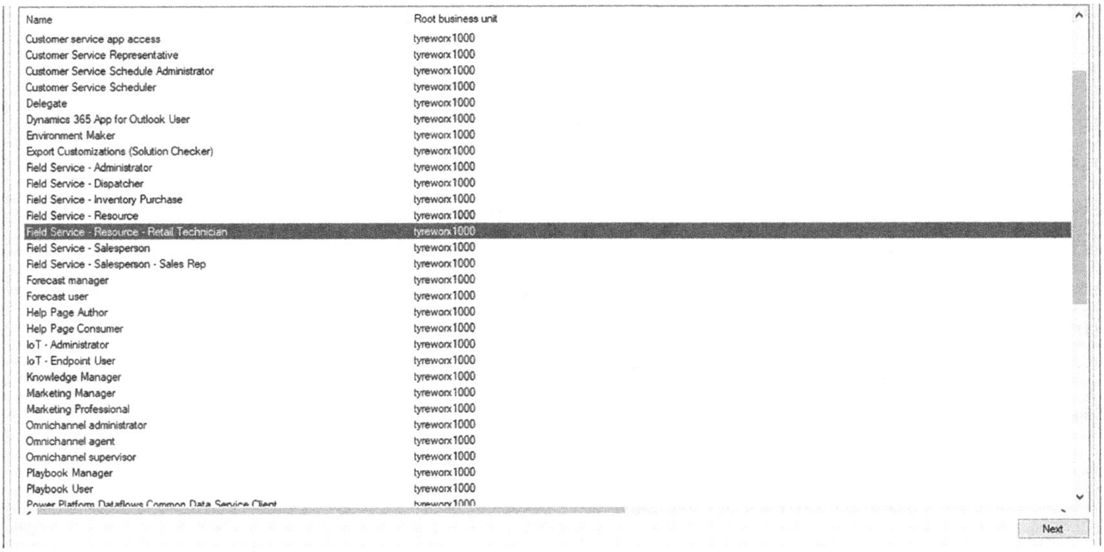

Figure 2-66. *Selecting a security role to edit*

On the next screen, you can select the entities and grant privileges. The nice thing about this tool is that you can select multiple entities and grant privileges (Figure 2-67).

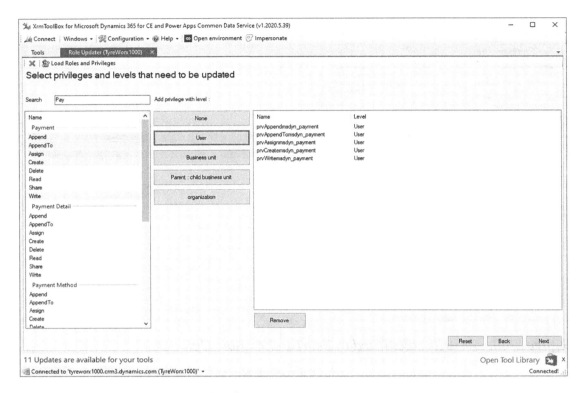

Figure 2-67. *Granting user-level access to an entity*

In different scenarios, users must be given a combination of security roles. For instance, the field staff must be given the Field Service-Resource security role if they are using the Field Service Mobile. If the field staff is allowed to receive products to complete the work orders requested from a third-party vendor, then they should be granted Field Service – Inventory Purchase role as well. Basically, before individuals are granted access to the application, it is highly advised that they be segregated into their respective functional areas.

As shown in Figure 2-68, when a user is granted only Field Service-Resource – Field Technician access, they cannot access prospects (leads).

USER ▾
Tommy Jhones ▾☰

ⓘ This record won't be processed by server-side synchronization or the Email Router until its primary email address has been approved by the system administrator.
ⓘ The information provided in this form is viewable by the entire organization.
ⓘ This user's information is managed by Office 365. To edit this information visit the User Administration section of the Office 365 Portal.

Role Associated View ▾

Manage Roles | 🖳 🗐 | Remove Roles | More Actions ▾

☐	Name ↑	Business Unit	
☐	Field Service - Resource - Retail Technician	tyreworx1000	
	Sales, Enterprise app access	tyreworx1000	

Figure 2-68. *User assigned the Field Service - Resource - Retail Technician role*

As shown in Figure 2-69, when the user is logged into the Field Service Mobile, they do not have access to the prospects (leads).

Figure 2-69. *Field Service Mobile access based on the security roles assigned*

To give the user access to the prospects, you should assign the user with the specific roles (Figure 2-70).

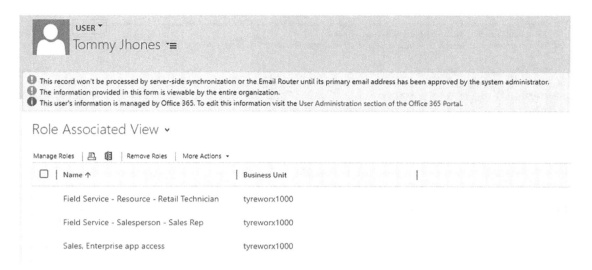

Figure 2-70. *A user granted with Filed Service - Salesperson - Sales Rep security role*

When the user logs into the Field Service Mobile and expands the navigation, they can see the Prospect section in the navigation (Figure 2-71). This allows them to create new a new prospect or update an existing prospect's details.

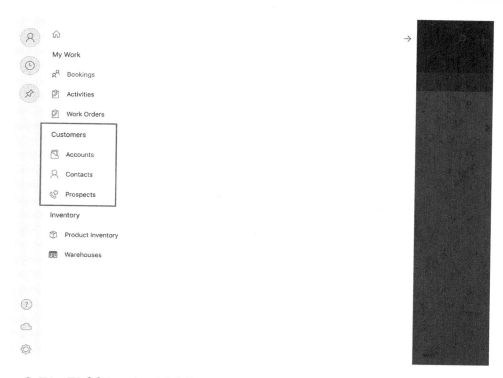

Figure 2-71. Field Service Mobile navigation after assigning more privileges

Summary

This chapter looked at the basic building blocks of Dynamics 365 Field Service. The majority of the chapter explained the entities within the solution. We also looked at how to configure the Field Service Mobile for field operations. Finally, we looked at setting up security for Dynamics 365 Field Service. The remaining chapters dive into setting up the sample scenario to give you a practical understanding of how to configure and customize the application.

CHAPTER 3

Work Orders and Scheduling

Creating work orders and scheduling work orders are two vital processes in Dynamics 365 Field Service. In order to create and schedule work orders in different ways, you need to configure the system with multiple settings and master data as prerequisites.

This chapter uses examples of retail and wholesale business scenarios in the field to explain the work order and the scheduling processes in Field Service. The initial sections describe the common and most important prerequisites for any field service system, such as service accounts, billing accounts, price lists, Universal Resourcing Schedule settings, bookable resources, and geocoding configurations.

The creation of work orders with different settings and master data will enable you to better understand the practical usage of the work order, its attributes, and the associated record types. Work orders can be scheduled in a few different ways in Field Service, and this chapter covers the most useful scheduling methods.

The chapter also provides usage examples of crews, another special type of bookable resource. The latter part of the chapter describes receiving work order notifications in the Field Service app installed in different types of mobile devices and operating systems. Finally, you will be able to design a basic model application for your own requirements using Dynamics 365 Field Service.

Prerequisites for Creating Work Orders
Service Accounts

A *service account* represents the account that receives the service in the work order.

Service accounts can be in multiple locations to receive the service. For example, a taxi service can consist of different accounts in multiple locations that need onsite services (Figure 3-1).

© Sanjaya Yapa and Indika Abayarathne 2021
S. Yapa and I. Abayarathne, *Dynamics 365 Field Service*, https://doi.org/10.1007/978-1-4842-6408-9_3

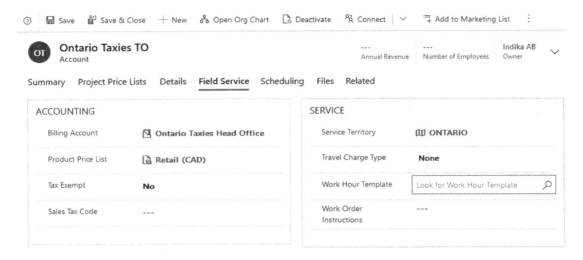

Figure 3-1. *Service account Field Service tab settings*

Billing Accounts

A *billing account* represents the account that receives the invoice for the work order.

Billing accounts are useful when work orders are created for different service accounts but the billing or the invoices are handled under one account. For example, a taxi service can have different service accounts located in multiple locations but only one billing account for handling payments (Figure 3-2). Relationship between Product, Pricelist, Pricelist Items and Work Order is shown under Figure 3-3.

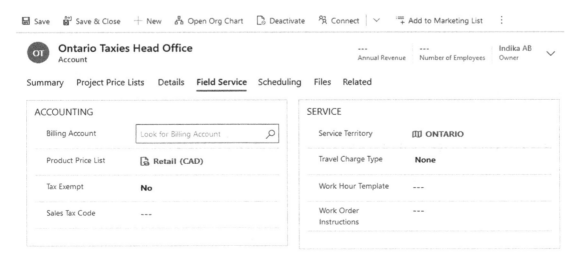

Figure 3-2. *Billing account Field Service tab settings*

If a billing account for a work order is unavailable, the service account serves as the billing account by default.

Price Lists

A *price list* contains prices for all the products and services that can be billed through the work orders. Each price list includes a time duration so that the invoices of work orders will have different prices depending on the date of the work performed. Price lists can be defined in the account under the Field Service tab.

The following two scenarios can happen related to service and billing accounts:

- *Both the service and billing accounts are available*: In this scenario, the price list of the billing account will be populated automatically on the work order when the billing account is filled.

- *Only the service account is available*: In this scenario, the price list on the work order record will be used.

The same tire product is sold at different prices for retail and wholesale customers. Also, the tire prices and the services are different in each state, as every state has different taxes. The currency for all the price lists is Canadian Dollars (CAD). In order to satisfy these requirements, the system needs multiple price lists—both retail and wholesale— for each state. Each price list will include multiple price list items for each product.

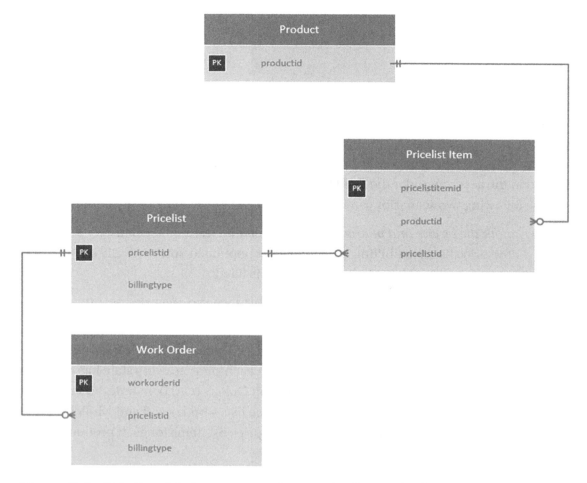

Figure 3-3. *Relationship between products, price lists, price list items, and work orders*

The TyreWorx example uses only two price lists, Retail and Wholesale. When a work order is created, the correct price list should be selected according to the retail or wholesale purpose. The price or the total amount for the work order is automatically calculated from the system for the products and services according to the price list.

Billing Method

A billing method's global option set can be used to categorize price lists and work orders. The global option set now includes Retail and Wholesale options (Figure 3-4 and Figure 3-5, respectively). The same global option set is used to identify the type of the work order.

Retail (CAD)
Price List

General   Role prices   Role price markups   Category prices   Price List Items   Territory

Name	*	**Retail (CAD)**
🔒 Context	*	**Sales**
Start Date		2020-07-01 📅
End Date		2021-06-30 📅
🔒 Currency	*	🪙 Canadian Dollar
🔒 Time Unit		🕐 Hour
Billing Method		**Retail**

Figure 3-4. *Retail price list settings*

Wholesale (CAD)
Price List

General   Role prices   Role price markups   Category prices   Price List Items   Territory

Name	*	**Wholesale (CAD)**
🔒 Context	*	**Sales**
Start Date		2020-07-01 📅
End Date		2021-06-30 📅
🔒 Currency	*	🪙 Canadian Dollar
🔒 Time Unit		🕐 Hour
Billing Method		**Wholesale**

Figure 3-5. *Wholesale price list settings*

Retail Price List

Retail price list items contain retail prices for products for a given period of time (Figure 3-6). Price list items can contain different discounts for each product. A good example of the retail discounts or the product bundle offering is the "Buy Three Get One Free" package that tire retailers often offer.

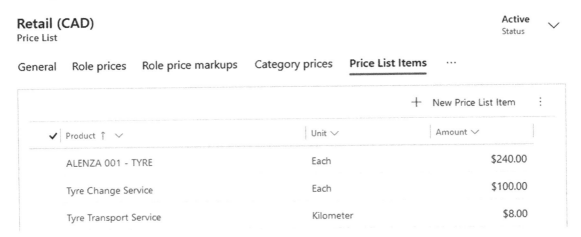

Figure 3-6. *Retail price list items*

Wholesale Price List

Wholesale price list items contain wholesale prices for products for a given period of time (Figure 3-7). Price list items can contain different discounts for each product unit. Wholesale prices usually vary based on the number of products in each unit.

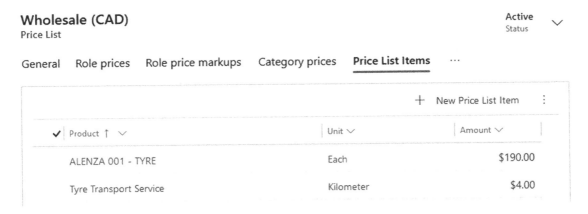

Figure 3-7. *Wholesale price list items*

Configuring URS for Field Service

Unified Resource Scheduling

Dynamics 365 Field Service uses Universal Resource Scheduling (URS) to allocate resources to work orders. URS enables Field Service to assign technicians and equipment to location-specific jobs, as well as tasks, known as work orders, as they are available. Figure 3-8 shows both the Field Service apps and Resource Scheduling app in Dynamics 365.

Figure 3-8. *Resource Scheduling app and Field Service apps*

URS needs to be configured before its scheduling features can be used in the Field Service app. Once URS is configured, users can schedule resources from the following four areas:

- Work orders

- Requirements

- Schedule board

- Resource Scheduling Optimization (RSO)

Enabling Work Orders for Scheduling

To access the scheduling settings, select Resource Scheduling→Settings→Administrati on. The following settings can be adjusted (Figure 3-9):

- Enable Resource Scheduling for Entities

- Scheduling Parameters

- Modify Schedule Board Settings

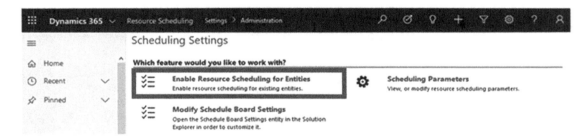

Figure 3-9. *Scheduling settings*

When Field Service is installed or a Field Service environment is set up, a work order entity is enabled for resource scheduling. If resource scheduling features are needed for other entities, they can be enabled using the same entity. Figure 3-10 shows enabling resource scheduling for a new entity (left) as well as the entities already enabled (right). Scheduling parameters can be set using the option shown under Figure 3-11.

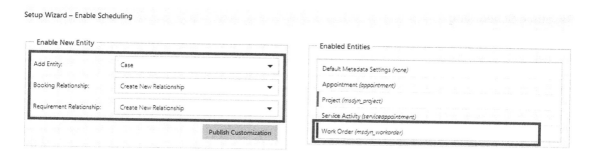

Figure 3-10. *Enabling resource scheduling for entities*

Before creating work orders and scheduling resources, you need to set some parameters. Figure 3-12 shows different options under Sheduling Parameters screen.

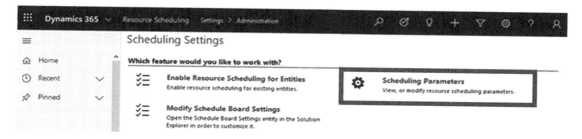

Figure 3-11. *Setting for scheduling parameters*

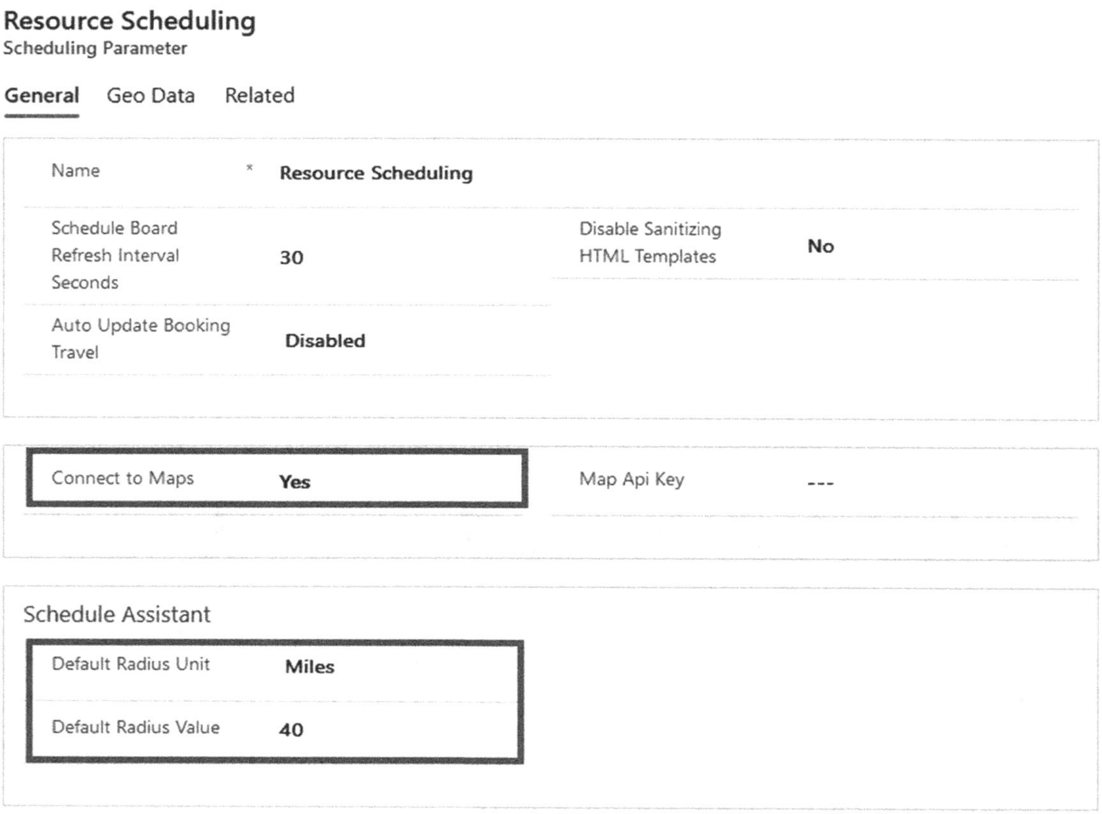

Resource Scheduling
Scheduling Parameter

General   Geo Data   Related

Name	*	**Resource Scheduling**	
Schedule Board Refresh Interval Seconds	**30**	Disable Sanitizing HTML Templates	**No**
Auto Update Booking Travel	**Disabled**		

Connect to Maps	**Yes**	Map Api Key	---

Schedule Assistant

Default Radius Unit	**Miles**
Default Radius Value	**40**

Figure 3-12.   *Scheduling Parameter settings*

Adding Bookable Resources

Bookable resources are playing an important role in field service. In order to assign jobs, bookable resources need to be available in the area. Figure 3-13 shows a bookable resource and its warehouse information.

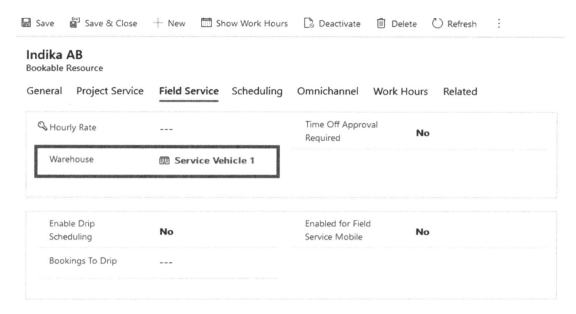

Figure 3-13. *Field Service settings for bookable resources*

Configuring Geocoding

Once the Geocoding is added, the system can attempt to locate the address and populate longitude and latitude of the address.

Field Service
Field Service Setting

| Work Order / Booking | RMA | RTV | Agreement | Purchase | Inventory | **Other** | ... |

Entity Number Length	5		Enable Address Suggestions	**Yes**	
Auto Allocate Estimated Products	**No**		Product Cost Order	**Current/Standard**	
Auto Geo Code Addresses	**Yes**		Use Enhanced Background Processing	**No**	

Figure 3-14. *Enabling geocoding*

Creating Work Orders

Work orders can originate from cases, sales opportunities, or agreements. Most commonly, a case can result in performing a job described by a work order. The attributes of the work order job and the information related to the job—such as products, services, service tasks, and so forth—can be added manually.

Incident types are defined to differentiate job types. Each incident type consists of different attributes and related information to perform each job. These incident types can act as a work order template. A work order created using an incident type will inherit all the job-related attributes and related information from the incident type and that information came through the template can be modified as required.

Creating Work Orders for a Retail Business

The Billing Method option helps to categorize work orders as Retail or Wholesale. The Billing Method option also relates to the price list. The products and services sold under the work order will be billed based on the selected price list in the work order.

Although the TyreWorx example uses only one retail price, every financial year could contain a retail price list. Figure 3-15 shows a Work Order with retail pricelist.

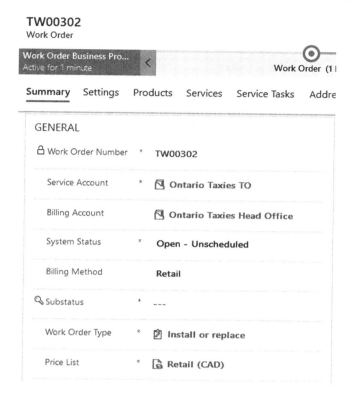

Figure 3-15. *Creating a work order for a retail business*

Creating Work Orders for a Wholesale Business

Wholesale work orders are created to schedule dispatching tires to stores in different locations at wholesale prices. The TyreWorx example uses only one wholesale price list, and the wholesale prices are less than the retail prices. In the real world, however, almost every financial year might contain a separate wholesale price list. Figure 3-16 shows a Work Order with a wholesale pricelist.

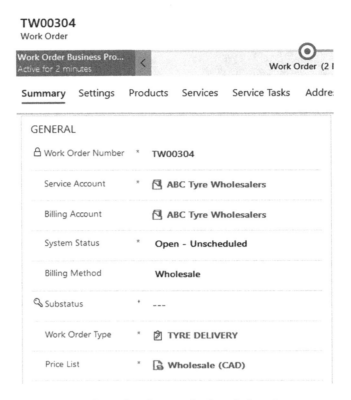

Figure 3-16. *Creating a work order for a wholesale business*

Adding Products and Services

Inventory products and services needed to perform the job are listed under the Products tab (Figure 3-17). If the work order has products and services under the incident type selected, the system automatically adds products and services to the work order. The users creating the work order also can manually add products and services.

The estimated total amount is calculated based on the price list selected in the Summary tab. The same product or the service amount will get different values, as the price list items have different values under each price lists, such as Retail, Wholesale, etc.

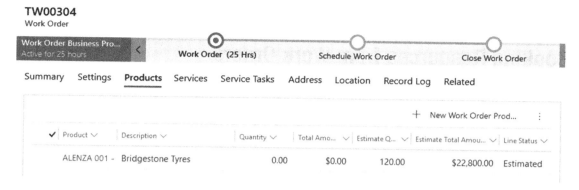

Figure 3-17. *Adding products to a work order*

Adding Location Information

The work order scheduler can add the location information using Bing Maps. Bing Maps enables users to find the exact location using different views, such as Road, Aerial, etc. Figure 3-18 shows an example of a Location tab for a work order.

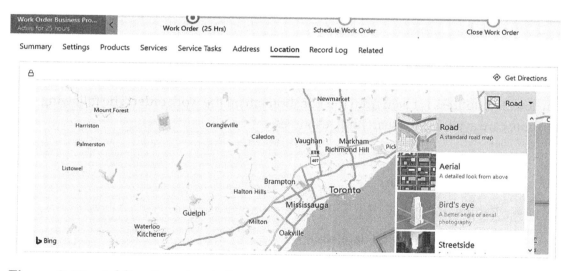

Figure 3-18. *Adding location information using Bing Maps*

Scheduling Work Orders

Booking Resources from Work Orders

Most of the time, resources are assigned from work orders. Figure 3-19 shows both a work order and the schedule assistant that pops up when the Book button is clicked.

Figure 3-19. *Scheduling from work orders*

Schedule assistant filters are used to find the suitable resource to be allocated. The location address is taken from the Location tab on the work order. The following attributes are available for searching resources:

- Work location type

- Available duration

- Radius

- Search start and end date/time

- Characters

- Roles

- Territories

- Resource types

- Business resources

Once all the resources are listed, users can select any resource from the list. The system shows the following data based on the user's availability:

- Start date/time

- Estimated arrival date/time

- End date/time

- Booking status

- Distance

- Travel time

Clicking Book will schedule the booking, whereas clicking Book & Exit will schedule the booking and quit the scheduling assistant window.

Booking Resources from Requirements

Resources can also be scheduled from the resource requirement level under each work order. When the work order contains multiple requirements, all the requirements should be booked separately. Figure 3-20 shows the Book button on the Work Order form for booking resources.

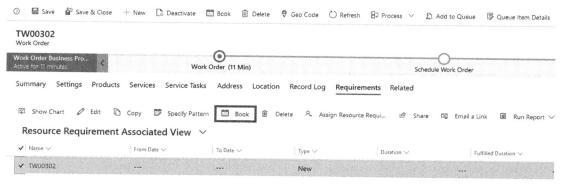

Figure 3-20.   *Scheduling from resource requirements*

Schedule Board

The schedule board enables users to see all the open work orders and requirements needed to schedule. The bottom pane of the schedule board lists all the open or unscheduled work orders (Figure 3-21).

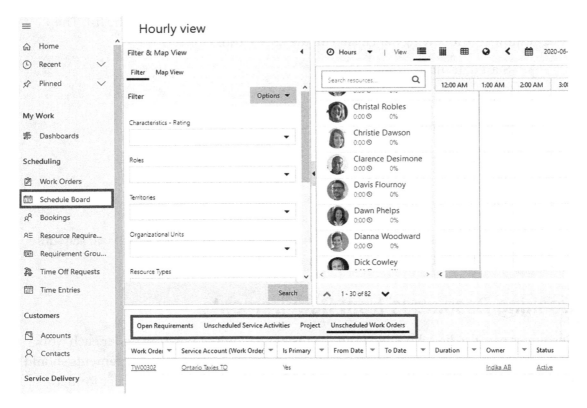

Figure 3-21. *Scheduling from the schedule board*

Using Crews to Schedule Work Orders

Crews are another resource type that consist of multiple resources to perform a job. Some work orders need more than one resource, depending on the skills and the equipment required to perform the job. Using crews, the scheduler can assign multiple resources to one job at once. Without crews, schedulers would need to assign individual tasks to individual resources, which takes time due to the availability of the resources.

Dynamics 365 Field Service functionalities can make a set of resources available anytime of the day by using crews. A service crew can consist of multiple resources available at different times of the day and on different days of the week.

For example, a service crew can contain a vehicle and a set of resources during the day, and the same crew can contain another set of resources during the night with the same vehicle. However, the crew is available at any time during the day to schedule a work order.

A crew record includes two main settings : Crew Strategy and Start and End Locations.

Crew Strategy includes the following three options:

- *Cascade and Accept Cascade Completely:* In this strategy, usually one resource can manage all the work in a job using equipment.

- *Crew Leader Management*: When multiple resources are performing a job, one designated resource can manage the work during the job.

- *Crew Member-Self Management*: This strategy is useful when multiple resources are performing different parts of a job and bill separately.

The schedule will be changed based on which Crew Strategy option is selected.

The Start and End Locations settings are important when scheduling work orders. The scheduler will consider the resources' location settings and scheduled job sites when a new work order is scheduled. The following settings are available:

- *Location Agnostic*: In this approach, resources usually perform their day-to-day work remotely. With this option, scheduling doesn't consider the location where the resource is located in order to visit the new job site.

- *Resource Address*: The scheduler will consider the resource's address to be their personal address when scheduling the work orders.

- *Organizational Unit Address*: With this option, the bookable resource starts or ends with the company location.

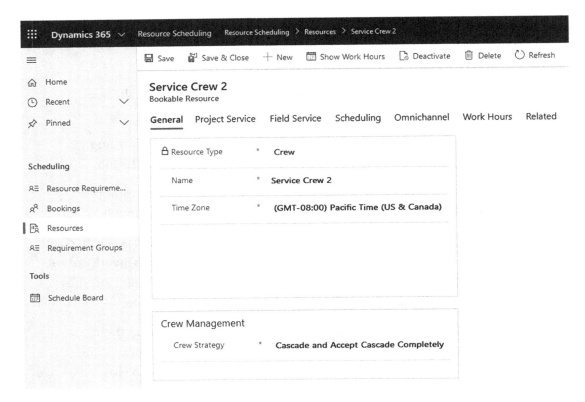

Figure 3-22. *Creating a new Crew*

Figure 3-22 shows a screen of creating new crew. Resources of the crew can be added under the Resource's Children tab in the crew record (Figure 3-23). Different crew members can work at different times of the day so that a crew member is always available.

With a crew a vehicle can be available 24X7 for multiple field technicians to use in different time slots during the day. Even you can configure the resources to use the vehicle in particular days of a given month.

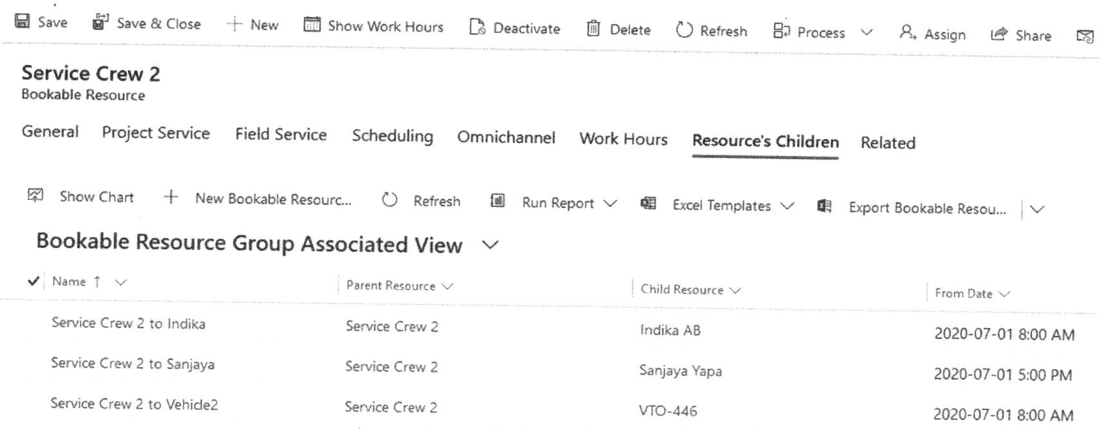

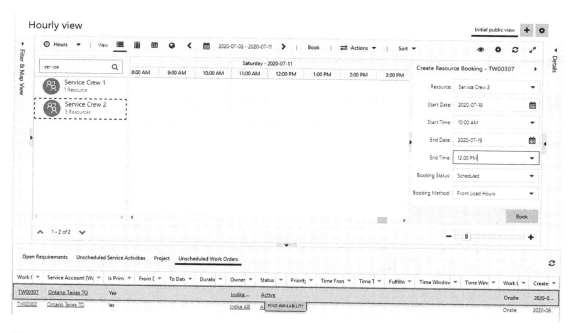

Figure 3-23. *Adding resource children to the crew*

The schedule board can be used to assign a work order to a service crew. According to the time selected, the field service scheduler automatically assigns the work to the available crew members. Figure 3-24 shows booking a service crew for a work order.

Figure 3-24. *Booking a service crew for unscheduled work orders*

Once the work order is scheduled with a crew, the schedule board shows the allocated time and the resources (Figure 3-25). Because the job has been scheduled on a weekend, only one resource has been assigned to the work.

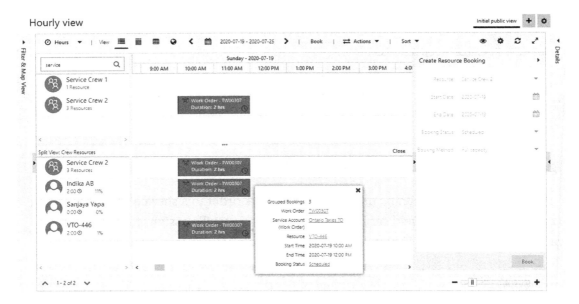

Figure 3-25. *Split view of a crew resource allocation*

Work Order and Resource Allocation

In the previous sections of the chapter, we described individual components and features associated with the scheduling process. In this section, we are going to provide a holistic view of resource allocations around the work order.

Any person or piece of equipment that can work on a job is stored under bookable resources. For example, one technician is a one bookable resource record. Bookable resource groups (such as crews) are also bookable resources. A bookable resource of the crew resource type can have one or more child resources. Figure 3-26 shows the relationship between bookable resources and the resource children.

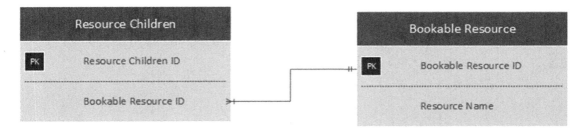

Figure 3-26. *Relationship between bookable resources and resource children*

One job under a work order can be completed by one or more resources, which are allocated under resource requirement records. Figure 3-27 shows the relationship between work orders and the resource requirements.

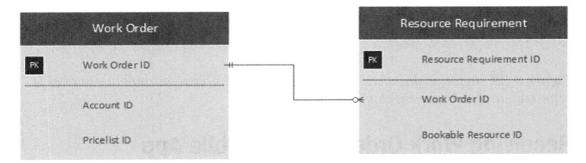

Figure 3-27. *Relationship between work orders and resource requirements*

Resource requirement records are created for each bookable resource that are required to perform the job. If any service crew is involved in performing the job, resource requirements are created for the crew and for all the resource children in the crew. Figure 3-28 shows the relationship between work orders, resource requirements, bookable resources, and resource children.

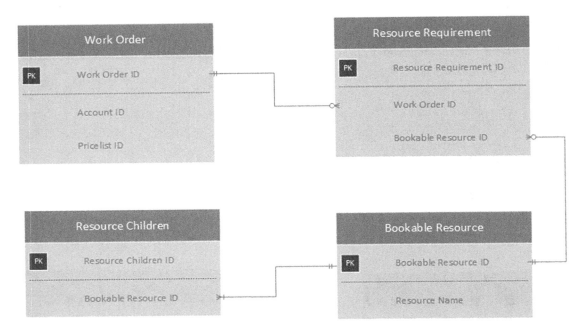

Figure 3-28. *Relationship between work orders, resource requirements, bookable resources, and resource children*

Receiving Work Orders in the Mobile App

Once the job is assigned to the relevant resources (under a crew or individually), the job appears on the Field Service mobile app of the resource (Figure 3-29). Under My Open Resource Bookings, all the scheduled jobs are shown in one of three views: Month, Week, and Day.

Figure 3-29. *Bookings received to the Field Service mobile app (Android tablet)*

The same set of bookings can appear in different landscapes. Figure 3-30 shows the Month view. The Month view is ideal for recurring bookings. (Chapter 4 covers recurring bookings in greater detail.)

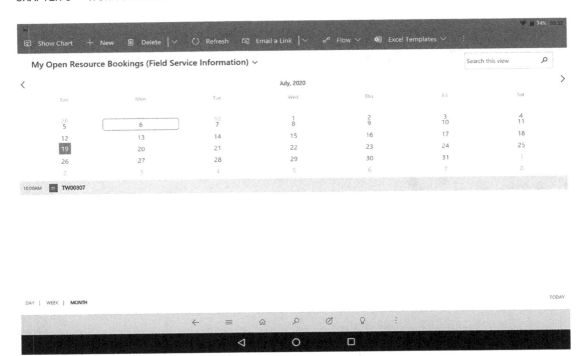

Figure 3-30. *The Month view on an Android tablet*

The user can change the view to Day to track daily bookings (Figure 3-31). In the TyreWorx example, most of the retail work is assigned daily; therefore, the ideal view for the retail business is the Day view.

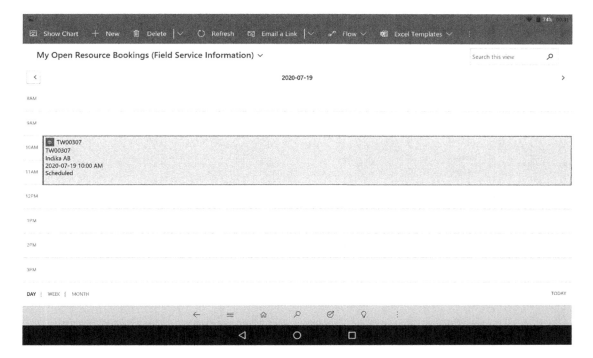

Figure 3-31. *The Day view on an Android tablet*

When the booking is opened, the Booking Status is Scheduled (Figure 3-32). After completing the work order, the user should be change the setting to Complete.

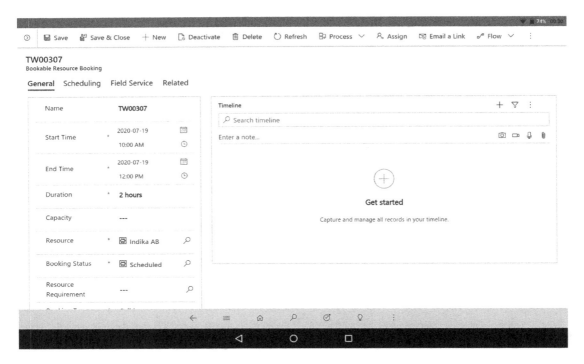

Figure 3-32. *Individual work order booking view on an Android tablet*

Summary

This chapter started by configuring the Field Service app and creating master data as prerequisites. Then we created work orders and scheduled them in different ways to show the Field Service capabilities with sample scenarios. Finally, we looked at how to find work orders using mobile devices. The next chapter explains agreements in Dynamics 365 Field Service.

CHAPTER 4

Agreements

This chapter looks at the concept of agreements in Dynamics 365 Field Service. Agreements are used to generate work orders and invoices automatically. A few prerequisites are required to generate records automatically, which this chapter discusses in detail. Agreements are primarily used to generate work orders for future work, such as sales visits to wholesale customers, maintenance work, etc. These types of work could occur daily, weekly, biweekly, monthly, quarterly, or yearly. Agreements also can be created manually and uploaded in bulk. This chapter discusses both methods.

Creating Agreements Manually

Agreements consists of the following records, which act as the configuration for generating work orders:

- Agreement

- Agreement Booking Setup

- Agreement Booking Date

Figure 4-1 illustrates the process of generating work orders automatically.

© Sanjaya Yapa and Indika Abayarathne 2021
S. Yapa and I. Abayarathne, *Dynamics 365 Field Service*, https://doi.org/10.1007/978-1-4842-6408-9_4

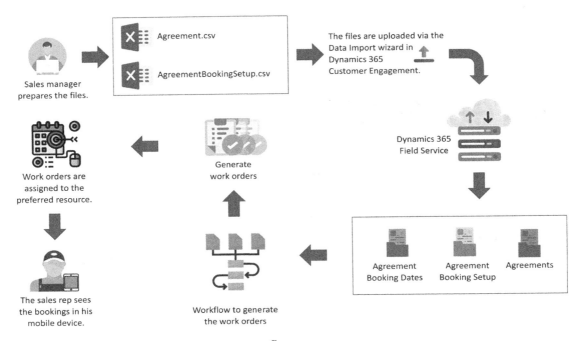

Figure 4-1. *Agreement setup process flow*

As shown in Figure 4-1, the sales manager will create the two Excel files that contain the data to set up the agreements. Once the agreements are ready, they will be uploaded via the Data Import wizard. Next, the Agreements, Agreement Booking Setup, and the Agreement Booking Date records are created. Then, a background workflow will trigger based on the settings defined in the records, and the work orders will be created. Several entities are involved to facilitate this process. Figure 4-2 illustrates the relationships between these entities.

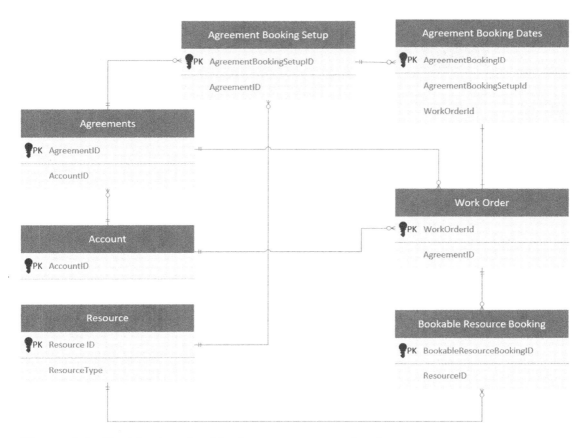

Figure 4-2. *Entities involved in the agreement upload process*

The Agreement Record

The Agreement record contains the agreement's primary information, such as the billing account, service account, price list, sales tax, start and end dates, etc. (Figure 4-3).

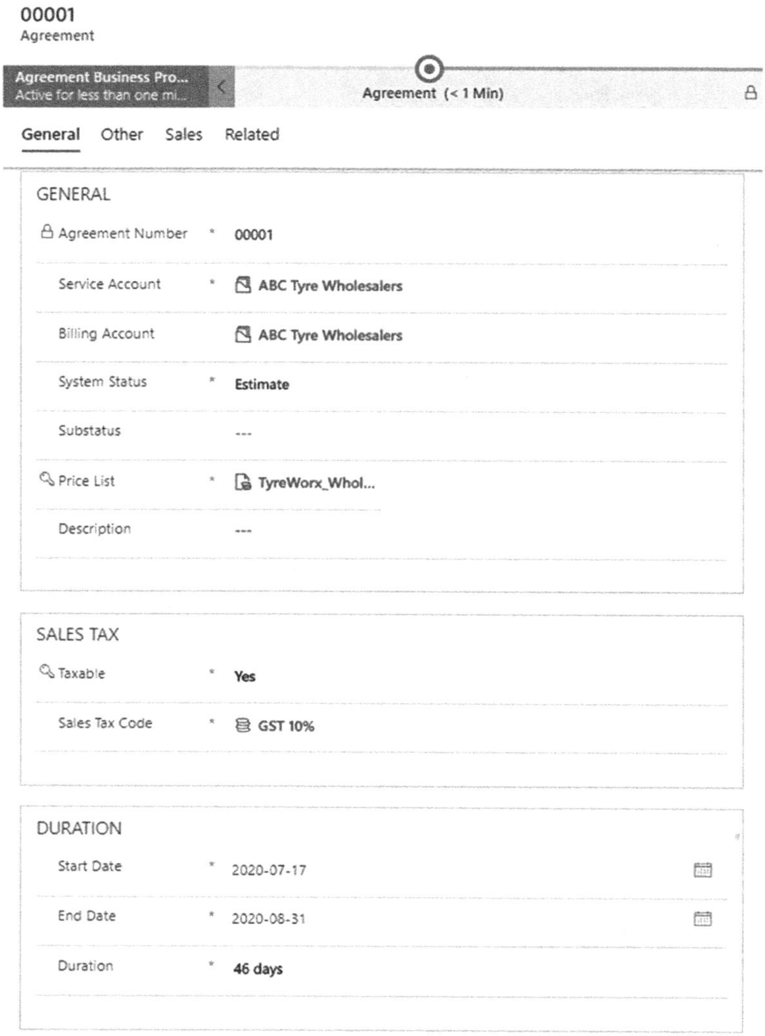

00001
Agreement

Agreement Business Pro...
Active for less than one mi...   <   ⊙ Agreement (< 1 Min)   🔒

General   Other   Sales   Related

GENERAL

🔒 Agreement Number   *   00001

Service Account   *   🗄 ABC Tyre Wholesalers

Billing Account   🗄 ABC Tyre Wholesalers

System Status   *   Estimate

Substatus   ---

🔍 Price List   *   🗄 TyreWorx_Whol...

Description   ---

SALES TAX

🔍 Taxable   *   Yes

Sales Tax Code   *   🗄 GST 10%

DURATION

Start Date   *   2020-07-17   📅

End Date   *   2020-08-31   📅

Duration   *   46 days

Figure 4-3. *The Agreement record and its mandatory fields*

In this example, a TyreWorx sales rep will visit a specific customer from July 17th 2020 to August 31st 2020. During these visits, the sales rep will replenish the customer with new inventory. For this, he will raise an invoice and mail it to the customer. The business process flow makes it very easy to set up all the required information for the agreement. First, let's set the primary information for the agreement.

As shown in Figure 4-4, the Duration section of the record has a field called Duration, which will be the number of days between the Start Date and the End Date. This is an auto-calculated field.

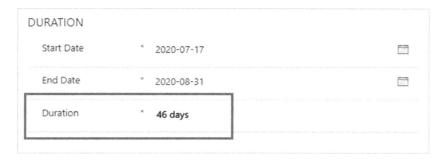

Figure 4-4. *The duration for start and end dates are auto-calculated*

The other important thing to remember here is the *System Status* field. The drop-down field has four values: Estimate, Active, Expired, and Cancelled. At this point, the Status is Estimate, meaning that it is still being prepared.

Note   To set the Agreement Number format, select **Settings ➤ Field Service Settings**, open the **Field Service** record, and then navigate to **Agreement** tab. Several configuration settings are available to determine the behavior of the process (Figure 4-3). If the requirement is to generate the work orders automatically, then set the **Auto Generate Work Order for Agreement Booking** to **Yes** (Figure 4-5).

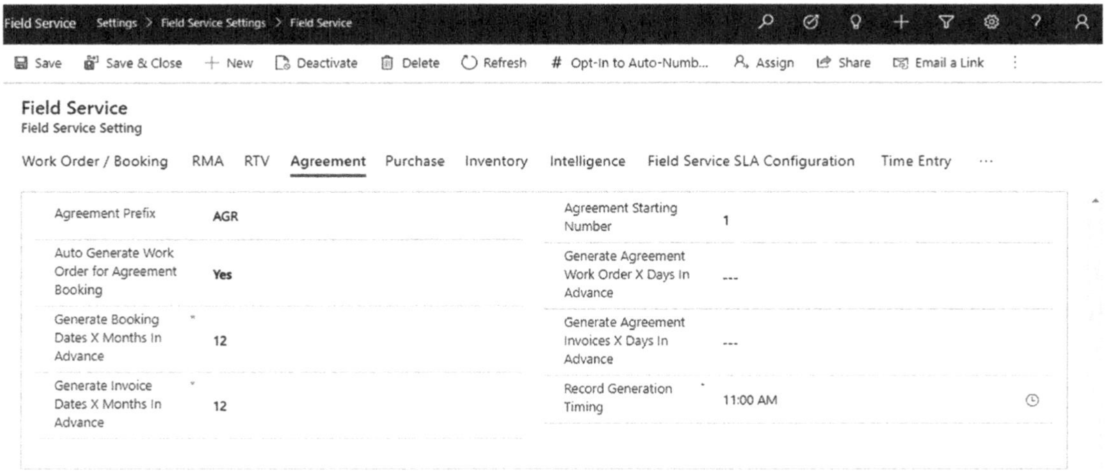

Figure 4-5. *Agreement settings under Field Service Setting*

The Agreement Booking Setup Record

The Agreement Booking Setup record is a related record to the Agreement record. The Agreement Booking Setup record defines the type of activity performed and the frequency or the recurrence of the activity. The record will be a template for the work orders generated by the system. On the business process flow, click **Next Stage** (Figure 4-6). This step will expand to add the Agreement Booking Setup.

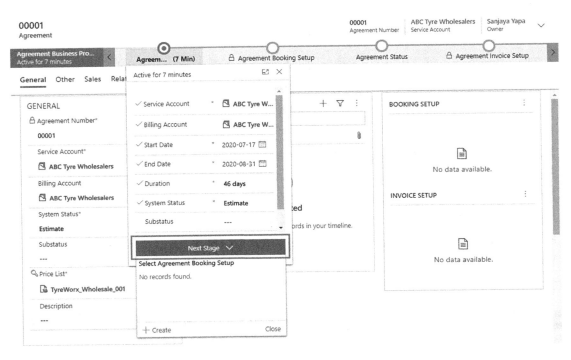

Figure 4-6. *Initiating the agreement booking setup from the business process flow*

The Agreement Booking Setup record includes specific tasks the individual is doing, the products involved, and the services provided. As shown in Figure 4-7, Product, Services, and Service Tasks sub-grids record this information.

Figure 4-7. *Agreement booking setup created and linked to the agreement*

For example, assume that a sales rep for TyreWorx can sell only a specific set of tires. These tires can be listed under the Products tab (Figure 4-8). When the work orders for the sales rep are generated, the work orders will contain the specified tires. This does not mean that they cannot add additional products to the work order. If there is a requirement to limit adding more products except for the defined products list, then security roles should be used to revoke the Create rights from the work order products.

ABC Wholesale - Weekly Visits
Agreement Booking Setup

Agreement Business Pro...	Agreement	Agreement Booking ... (9 Min)	Agreement Status	Agreement Invoice S...	Activate Agreement
Active for 33 minutes					

General   **Products**   Services   Service Tasks   Related

+ New Agreement Booki...   ↻ Refresh   :

✓	Name ∨	Line Order ↑ ∨	Quantity ∨	Agreement ∨	Agreement Booking Setup ∨	Created On ∨
	ALENZA 001 - TYRE	1	10.00	00001	ABC Wholesale - Weekly Visits	2020-07-14 11:10 ...
	AZENIS FK510 - TYRE	2	8.00	00001	ABC Wholesale - Weekly Visits	2020-07-14 11:11 ...
	CINTURATO P1 - TYRE	3	10.00	00001	ABC Wholesale - Weekly Visits	2020-07-14 11:12 ...
	CT50AS - TYRE	4	7.00	00001	ABC Wholesale - Weekly Visits	2020-07-14 11:12 ...

1 - 4 of 5 (0 selected) |← ← Page 1 →

Figure 4-8. *The list of products that will be associated with the work order*

Because this is a wholesale process, the sales rep will not provide any services. However, management wants each sales rep to perform a specific task at the customer site. This can be defined under the Service Tasks tab (Figure 4-9).

ABC Wholesale - Weekly Visits
Agreement Booking Setup

Agreement Business Pro...	Agreement	Agreement Booking ... (26 Min)	Agreement Status	Agreement Invoice S...	Activate Agreement
Active for 50 minutes					

General   Products   Services   **Service Tasks**   Related

+ New Agreement Booki...   ↻ Refresh   :

✓	Name ∨	Line Order ↑ ∨	Task Type ∨	Description ∨	Agreement ∨	Agreement Booking Setup ∨	Created On ∨
	Inventory Counting	1	Inventory Counting	---	00001	ABC Wholesale - Weekly Visits	2020-07-14 ...
	Replenished stock	2	Replenished stock	---	00001	ABC Wholesale - Weekly Visits	2020-07-14 ...
	Issue Invoice	3	Issue Invoice	---	00001	ABC Wholesale - Weekly Visits	2020-07-14 ...
	Collect Payment	4	Collect Payment	---	00001	ABC Wholesale - Weekly Visits	2020-07-14 ...

Figure 4-9. *The list of service tasks that will be executed with the work order*

The Summary section under the General tab includes a reference to the Agreement, and the Name can be set to an Auto Number (Figure 4-10).

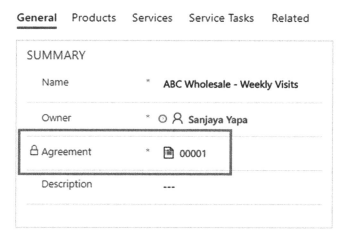

General   Products   Services   Service Tasks   Related

SUMMARY

Name	*	ABC Wholesale - Weekly Visits
Owner	*	○ ⨂ Sanjaya Yapa
🔒 Agreement	*	📄 00001
Description		---

Figure 4-10. *Reference to the Agreement record*

Under the Work Order Settings section, set the following settings (Figure 4-11).

WORK ORDER SETTINGS

Auto Generate Work Order	*	Yes
Work Order Type	*	📋 TYRE
Generate Work Order Days In Advance		1
Priority		---
Work Order Summary		---
Work Location		Onsite

Figure 4-11. *Work order settings in the agreement booking setup*

- Set the **Auto Generate Work Order** to **Yes** so that the system will automatically generate the work orders. The system will generate the work orders on a rolling basis. If this setting is set to No, the work orders must be created manually.

- For this example, set the **Generate Work Orders Day in Advance** to **1**. This setting imposes the number of days in advance the work order will be generated. In this case, the work order will be generated one day before the day of the visit. If a value is not specified in this field, the work order will be generated on the expected day of the sales visit and at the record generation time defined at the agreement level.

Note   When the work order is generated, the System Status field will be set to Open-Unscheduled, which means the work orders must be scheduled manually. To make things easier, this can be automated in the Booking Settings section.

The Booking Settings section has some important settings. For the TyreWorx scenario, a typical Agreement Booking Setup record would look something like the one shown in Figure 4-12.

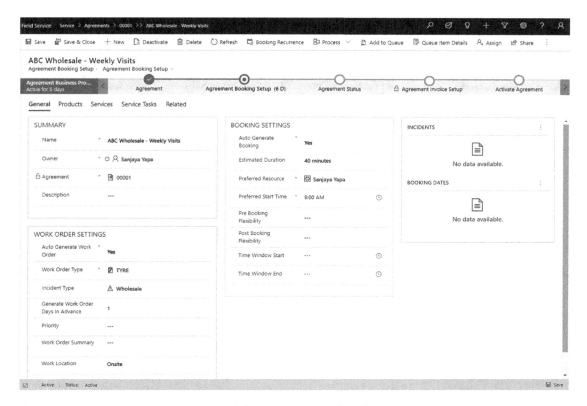

Figure 4-12. *Booking settings of the agreement booking setup*

- Set the **Auto Generate Booking** to **Yes** so that the system will generate the booking dates and will use those booking dates to assign the work order generated to the preferred resource. If this is set to No, then the work order should be scheduled manually.

- **Preferred Resource** is the sales rep visiting the customer site. All work orders generated will be booked for this resource.

- **Estimated Duration** is the time the sales rep will be spending at the customer site for sales activities.

- **Preferred Start Time** defines the time when the sales rep expects to start their visit at the customer site.

For the TyreWorx sales visits, the preceding settings are adequate. To learn more about the other settings, visit https://docs.microsoft.com/en-us/dynamics365/ field-service/set-up-customer-agreements#booking-settings.

Once these settings are configured, set the booking recurrence to define how often the sales visits should occur (Figure 4-13).

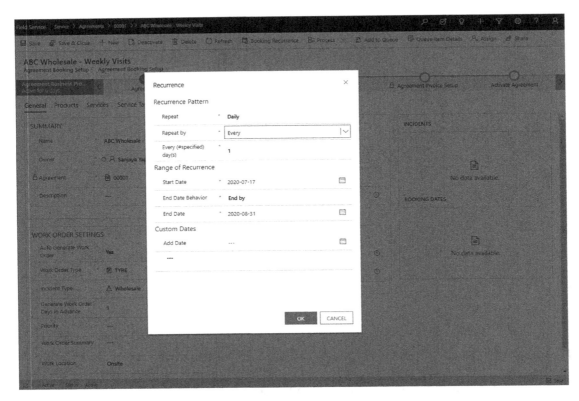

Figure 4-13. *Booking Recurrence setup*

This feature allows for the creation of recurrence patterns relevant to the business—for this example, three weekdays every week. Notice that the start and end dates are auto-populated based on the start and end dates defined at the agreement level. That is, all the work orders will be generated and scheduled between the dates defined in these fields.

You can determine the recurrence pattern that is most suitable for your customers (Figure 4-14). Some customers might not require frequent visits.

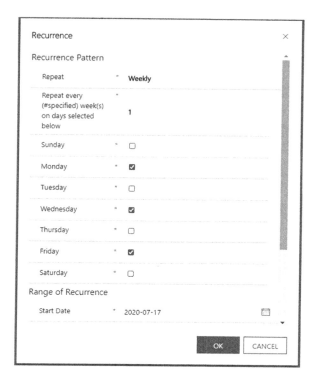

Figure 4-14. *Recurrence settings for weekly visits*

Note The Booking Recurrence settings are stored as an XML entry in the Agreement Booking Setup record (Figure 4-15). This is important because this XML should be generated when agreements are uploaded in bulk.

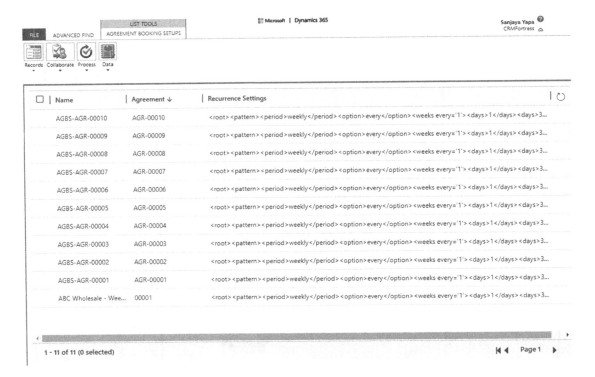

Figure 4-15. Booking Recurrence XML view

The Agreement Booking Date Record

Agreement booking dates will be generated for the Recurrence Settings defined in the Agreement Booking Setup record. These will be used by the system to generate and assign the work orders to the resource specified in the agreement booking setup. This process will trigger only when the Status field in the Agreement record is set to Active (Figure 4-16).

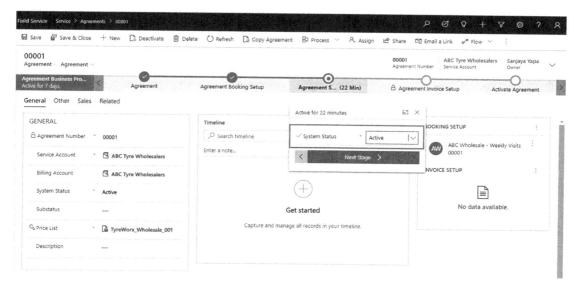

Figure 4-16. *Changing the agreement status to Active from the business process flow*

Once the business process flow is completed, the list of agreement booking dates will be generated for this setup (Figure 4-17).

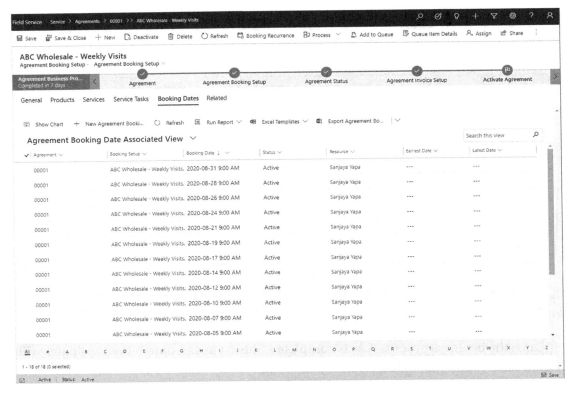

Figure 4-17. *Agreement booking dates generated for the agreement*

As shown in Figure 4-18, when the work order gets generated for the booking date, the Work Order field will get updated. This will also have a reference to the agreement.

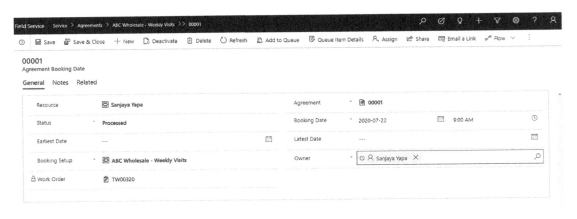

Figure 4-18. *Agreement Booking Date record*

Also, the Status field of the Agreement Booking Date record will be changed to Processed once the work order is generated. This will prevent the system from generating the work order twice for the same booking date.

You also can generate the work orders manually. This option is useful in scenarios where the Auto Generate Work Order field is set to No. In such situations, you will need to open each Agreement Booking Date record and execute the Generate Work Order command. Or, you could select multiple records and execute the command (Figure 4-19).

Figure 4-19. *Generating a work order manually for the agreement booking dates*

As shown in Figure 4-20, on the Field Service Mobile, the work order shows the products associated with the agreement booking setup. This is a summary view of the associated products, which means this customer is purchasing only this set of products.

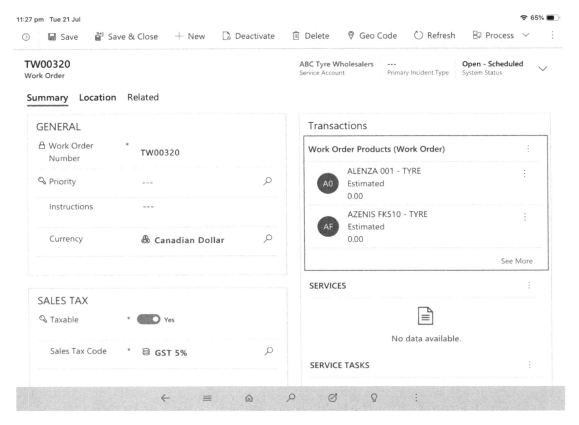

Figure 4-20. *Summary view of the products associated with the work order*

Under the Related tab, you can find a more detailed view of the products associated with the work order (Figure 4-21). Remember, these are the products we defined under the Products tab of the Agreement Booking Setup record.

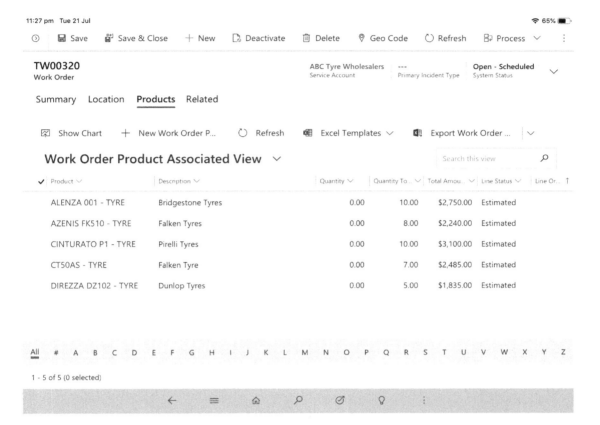

Figure 4-21. *Detailed view of the products associated with the work order*

Notice that the price for each item is calculated but still in the estimated state. The system will calculate the estimated total amount, as shown in the Total section of the Work Order record (Figure 4-22). The final total amounts will be calculated when the work order is fully processed. We discuss processing these work orders in more detail later in the book.

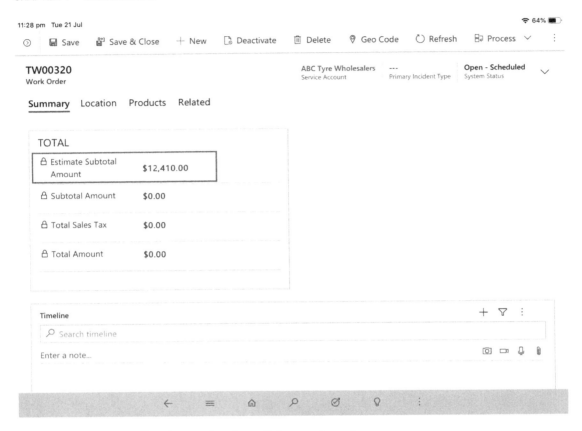

Figure 4-22. *Total estimated price of the work order*

The service tasks associated with the agreement booking setup will also be available under Service Tasks defined in the generated Work Order (Figure 4-23). A more detailed view of the service tasks is available under the Related tab of the Work Order record.

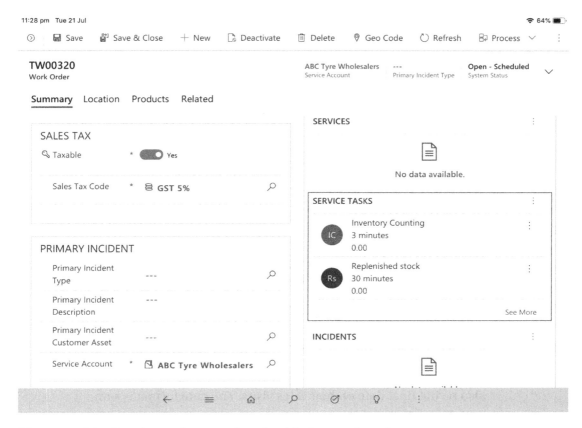

Figure 4-23. *Service tasks associated with the work order*

At this point, all the basic information required to process the work order when the sale rep visits the customer is ready. The sales rep can add additional products, services, or service tasks to the work order.

Bulk Upload Agreements

There could be scenarios in which several hundreds of customers require frequent sales visits. Creating all the agreements one by one manually is time consuming and error-prone. For this exercise, we will be using the Data Import feature of Dynamics 365 Customer Engagement. Two CSV files are required for this process.

1. The first CSV file is used to import the agreements. The file should contain the following fields:

- *Agreement Number*: This is the next agreement number in the sequence. That is, if there is already an agreement with Agreement Number 0001, then you need to start the number with 0002 in your file.

- *Service Account*: This is the customer who requires the service. In the TyreWorx scenario, this will be the wholesale customer.

- *Billing Account*: This is the customer who will be invoiced. In the TyreWorx scenario, it will be the same as the service account.

- *System Status*: The system status of the agreement should be set to Active so that the work orders will be auto-generated.

- *Start Date*: This is the agreement's start date. For TyreWorx, it will be the start date of their sales visits. On the import file, the date format should be MM/DD/YYYY.

- *End Date*: This is the agreement's end date. For TyreWorx, it will also be the final date of their sales visits. The date format is same as the Start Date field.

- *Duration*: The duration is calculated by using the following formula:

  Minutes × Number of Billable Hours × Number of Days Between the Start and End Dates (for example, $60 \times 8 \times 30 = 14400$)

- *Price List*: This is the price list that is used for work order processing. Different price lists can be assigned to different customers.

- *Taxable*: This dictates whether the work order will be taxable.

- *Sales Tax Code*: If the Taxable field is set to Yes, then the sales tax code defined in the system should be provided.

- *Service Territory*: This is optional, but if the sales operation is dispersed geographically, then this should be defined. In the TyreWorx scenario, the sales operations are distributed geographically.

  Once the file is created, it should look like Figure 4-24.

	A	B	C	D	E	F	G	H	I	J
1	Agreement Number	Service Account	Billing Account	System St	Start Date	End Date	Duration	Price List	Taxable	Sales Tax Code
2	AGR-00001	Avalon Tyre Centre Ltd	Avalon Tyre Centre Ltd	Active	7/20/2020	8/31/2020	14400	TyreWorx_Wholesale_001	Yes	GST 5%
3	AGR-00002	Supreme Tyres Limited Limited	Supreme Tyres Limited Limited	Active	7/20/2020	8/31/2020	14400	TyreWorx_Wholesale_002	Yes	GST 5%
4	AGR-00003	Bridgestone Tyre House	Bridgestone Tyre House	Active	7/20/2020	8/31/2020	14400	TyreWorx_Wholesale_003	Yes	GST 5%
5	AGR-00004	CAD Tyre Dealers	CAD Tyre Dealers	Active	7/20/2020	8/31/2020	14400	TyreWorx_Wholesale_004	Yes	GST 5%
6	AGR-00005	Highway Tyres	Highway Tyres	Active	7/20/2020	8/31/2020	14400	TyreWorx_Wholesale_005	Yes	GST 5%
7	AGR-00006	Village Tyre Store	Village Tyre Store	Active	7/20/2020	8/31/2020	14400	TyreWorx_Wholesale_006	Yes	GST 5%
8	AGR-00007	Davidson Automotive	Davidson Automotive	Active	7/20/2020	8/31/2020	14400	TyreWorx_Wholesale_007	Yes	GST 5%
9	AGR-00008	Tyre Champions Pvt Ltd	Tyre Champions Pvt Ltd	Active	7/20/2020	8/31/2020	14400	TyreWorx_Wholesale_008	Yes	GST 5%
10	AGR-00009	Tyre Workshop Ltd	Tyre Workshop Ltd	Active	7/20/2020	8/31/2020	14400	TyreWorx_Wholesale_009	Yes	GST 5%
11	AGR-00010	Out Door Tyres	Out Door Tyres	Active	7/20/2020	8/31/2020	14400	TyreWorx_Wholesale_010	Yes	GST 5%

Figure 4-24. *Agreement file format*

2. The second CSV file is used to import the agreement booking setup. The file should contain the following fields:

- *Name*: This is the name of the agreement booking setup.

- *Agreement Number*: This is the agreement number in the Agreement record that will be used to link the agreement and the agreement booking setup.

- *Auto Generate Booking*: Set this to Yes to auto-generate the booking and assign the work order to the preferred resource. For the TyreWorx scenario, this field is set to Yes.

- *Auto Generate Work Order*: Set this field to Yes to auto-generate the work order. The TyreWorx work orders for should be auto-generated.

- *Estimated Duration*: This is the estimated time the sales rep will be spending at a sales visit.

- *Preferred Resource*: This is the name of the sales rep. This should contain the bookable resource name.

- *Preferred Start Time*: This is the preferred time the sales rep will be visiting the customer.

- *Work Order Type*: This is the work order type. For TyreWorx, this field will be Tyre Sales.

- *Incident Type*: You can use different incident types for different customers in scenarios where specific products are being sold or when there are customer-specific service tasks. When uploading agreements as a file, there is no easy way to specify the products, services, and service tasks for the work orders. Instead, incident types can be used, and products, services and service tasks can be defined, so that when the work order gets created, this information will be available. TyreWorx will be using wholesale incident types.

- *Generate Work Order Days in Advance*: This is the number of days in advance the work order should get generated.

- *Recurrence Settings*: This field is used to set the recurrence settings. The only drawback is that the Customer Engagement system wants this to be submitted as an XML entry. Here are some examples of creating recurrence settings with XML.

3. The following XML is used to create recurrence settings for every weekday on a weekly basis. The days tag represents the day of the week. In this setting, it is from Monday to Friday.

```
<root>
    <pattern>
        <period>weekly</period>
        <option>every</option>
        <weeks every='1'>
            <days>1</days>
            <days>2</days>
            <days>3</days>
            <days>4</days>
            <days>5</days>
        </weeks>
    </pattern>
    <range>
        <start>7/22/2020</start>
        <option>endBy</option>
        <end>8/31/2020</end>
```

```
    </range>
    <datas/>
</root>
```

The following XML is used to create recurrence settings for Tuesday and Thursday on weekly basis:

```
<root>
    <pattern>
        <period>weekly</period>
        <option>every</option>
        <weeks every='1'>
            <days>2</days>
            <days>4</days>
        </weeks>
    </pattern>
    <range>
        <start>7/22/2020</start>
        <option>endBy</option>
        <end>8/31/2020</end>
    </range>
    <datas/>
</root>
```

The following XML is used to create recurrence settings for twice a month for a period of one year:

```
<root>
    <pattern>
        <period>monthly</period>
        <option>every</option>
        <months every='1'>
            <day>7</day>
            <day>21</day>
        </months>
    </pattern>
    <range>
```

```
        <start>8/01/2020</start>
        <option>endBy</option>
        <end>7/31/2021</end>
    </range>
    <datas/>
</root>
```

When the agreement booking setup CSV file is completed, it should look like Figure 4-25.

	A	B	C	D	E	F	G	H	I	J	K	L	M
1	Name	Agreement	Auto Generat	Auto Generat	Estimate	Preferred Resource	Preferred Start Time	Work Order Type	Incident Type	Generate	Recurrence Settings		
2	AGBS-AGR-00001	AGR-00001	Yes	Yes	60	Tony Richards	07/20/2020 8:00:00 AM	Tyre	Wholesale	1	<root><pattern><period>weekly</period>		
3	AGBS-AGR-00002	AGR-00002	Yes	Yes	60	Tony Richards	07/20/2020 9:30:00 AM	Tyre	Wholesale	1	<root><pattern><period>weekly</period>		
4	AGBS-AGR-00003	AGR-00003	Yes	Yes	60	Sam Peters	07/20/2020 9:00:00 AM	Tyre	Wholesale	1	<root><pattern><period>weekly</period>		
5	AGBS-AGR-00004	AGR-00004	Yes	Yes	60	Tony Richards	07/20/2020 11:00:00 AI	Tyre	Wholesale	1	<root><pattern><period>weekly</period>		
6	AGBS-AGR-00005	AGR-00005	Yes	Yes	60	Sam Peters	07/20/2020 10:30:00 A	Tyre	Wholesale	1	<root><pattern><period>weekly</period>		
7	AGBS-AGR-00006	AGR-00006	Yes	Yes	60	Tony Richards	07/20/2020 1:00:00 PM	Tyre	Wholesale	1	<root><pattern><period>weekly</period>		
8	AGBS-AGR-00007	AGR-00007	Yes	Yes	60	Sam Peters	07/20/2020 12:00:00 P	Tyre	Wholesale	1	<root><pattern><period>weekly</period>		
9	AGBS-AGR-00008	AGR-00008	Yes	Yes	60	Sam Peters	07/20/2020 1:30:00 PM	Tyre	Wholesale	1	<root><pattern><period>weekly</period>		
10	AGBS-AGR-00009	AGR-00009	Yes	Yes	60	Sam Peters	07/20/2020 3:00:00 PM	Tyre	Wholesale	1	<root><pattern><period>weekly</period>		
11	AGBS-AGR-00010	AGR-00010	Yes	Yes	60	Tony Richards	07/20/2020 2:30:00 PM	Tyre	Wholesale	1	<root><pattern><period>weekly</period>		

Figure 4-25. *Agreement booking setup CSV file*

Importing the Files

The next step is to import the CSV files into the system, as follows:

1. Compress both files into one ZIP folder. This enables you to map and import both files together (Figure 4-26).

☐ Name	Date modified	Type	Size
AgreementBookingSetup	19/07/2020 9:18 PM	Microsoft Excel C...	4 KB
Agreements	19/07/2020 9:23 PM	Microsoft Excel C...	2 KB
WholesaleAgreementSetup	20/07/2020 4:57 PM	Compressed (zipp...	2 KB

Figure 4-26. *The CSV files compressed for importing*

2. Navigate to the **Data Management** section under the **Advanced Settings**. Select the **Import** option (Figure 4-27).

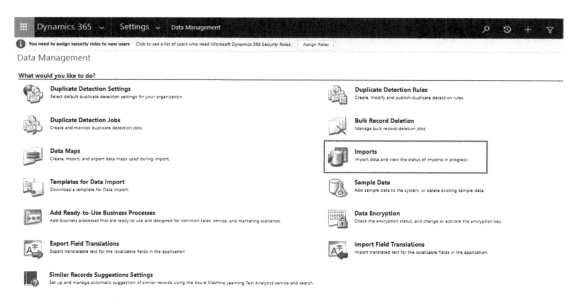

Figure 4-27.   The Imports option under Data Management

3.   Click the **Import Data** option from the toolbar (Figure 4-28). This
will load the Data Import Wizard.

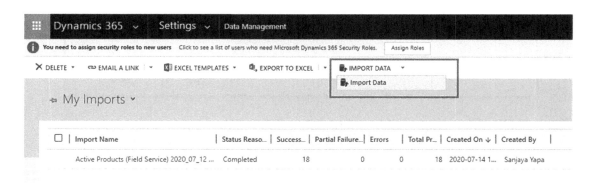

Figure 4-28.   Initiating the data import process

4.   Select the file from the file system and click **Next** (Figure 4-29).

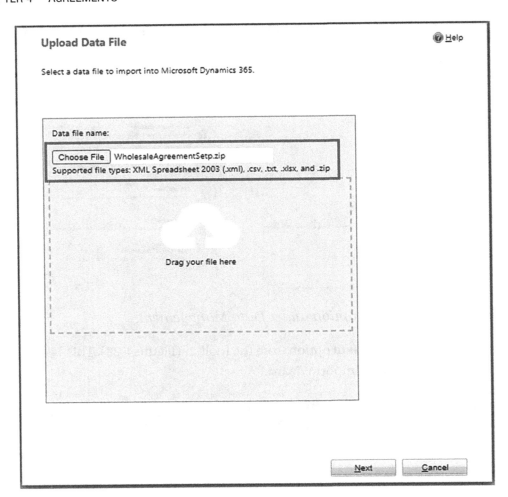

Figure 4-29. *Choosing the file to import*

5. Leave the **File Upload Summary** as it is for the context of this example (Figure 4-30). Click **Next**.

Review File Upload Summary   ⓘ Help

The following data will be imported into Microsoft Dynamics 365.

ⓘ 2 files found in the WholesaleAgreementSetp.zip file.

File Name	Size
AgreementBookingSetup.csv	4 KB
Agreements.csv	2 KB

◢ Delimiter Settings

Select the field and data delimiters. If there is more than one file, these
delimiters will be applied to all files that you want to import.

| Field delimiter: | Comma (,) | ⌄ |
| Data delimiter: | Quotation mark (") | ⌄ |

☑ First row contains column headings

| Back | Next | Cancel |

Figure 4-30. Upload summary and delimiter settings

6. Because this is a new data import, the Select Data Map step can be
    skipped. However, if the data map from the previous imports were
    saved, this would be the step to select the data map. We do not
    have a saved data map at this point, so simply click **Next** to move
    to the next step (Figure 4-31).

Figure 4-31. *Selecting an existing data map*

7. Map the two files to the two entities—i.e., map the Agreement file
    to the Agreement entity and the Agreement Booking Setup file to
    the Agreement Booking Setup entity (Figure 4-32).

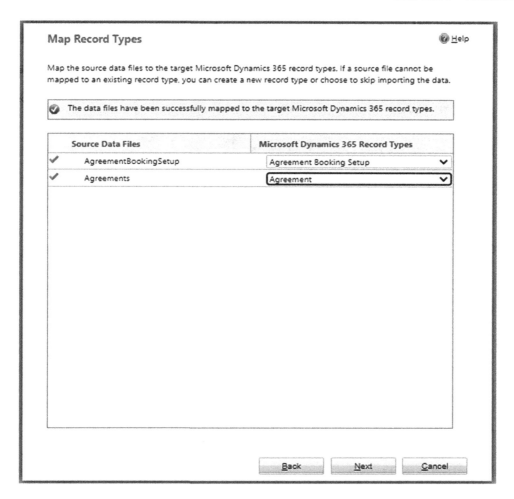

Figure 4-32. *Mapping record types to the files*

8. The next step is to map the fields. As you can see, the Agreement entity fields are already mapped with the fields in the file. For the Agreement Booking Setup entity, there is one field to map, which should be done manually. If the wizard cannot determine a mapping field, it will show the unmapped field with an exclamation mark. In this scenario, all the fields are automatically mapped (Figure 4-33).

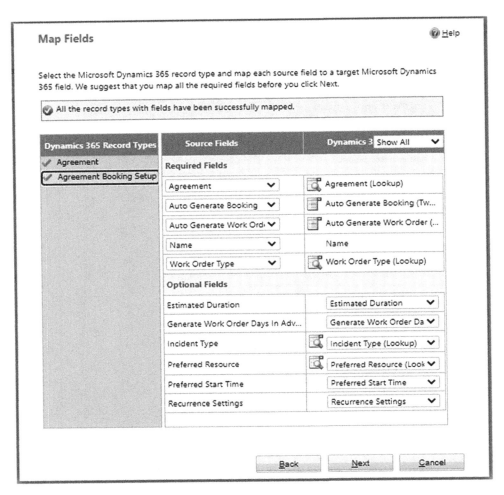

Figure 4-33. *Mapping fields with the columns in the files*

9. Click **Next** on the **Review** page and the **Review Settings and Import Data** page, save the data map by providing a name, and then hit **Submit** (Figure 4-34).

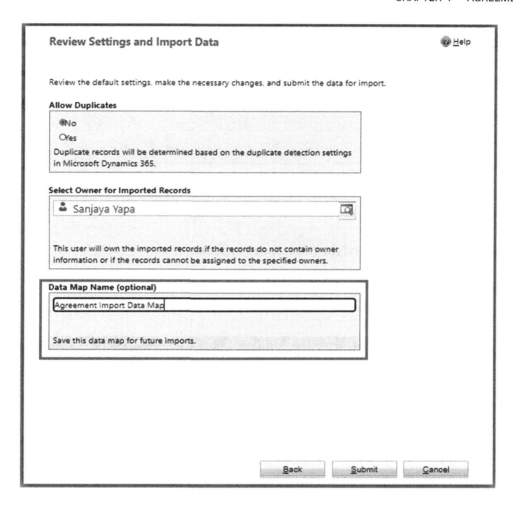

Figure 4-34. *Reviewing the settings and saving the data map*

10. On the final screen, click **OK** to continue. The files will be submitted to Data Import process of Dynamics 365 CE (Figure 4-35).

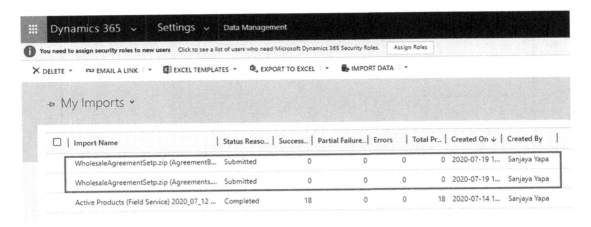

Figure 4-35. *Files submitted for the import process*

11. Once the files are successfully uploaded, the import status will be changed to **Completed** (Figure 4-36).

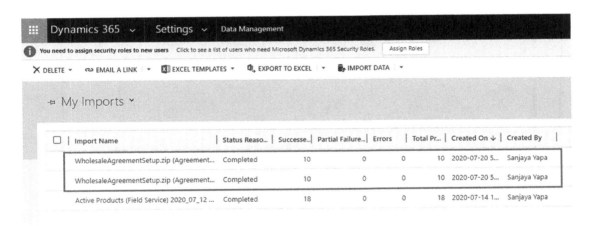

Figure 4-36. *File import completed*

12. Navigate to the **Active Agreements** view. All the imported agreements are listed (Figure 4-37).

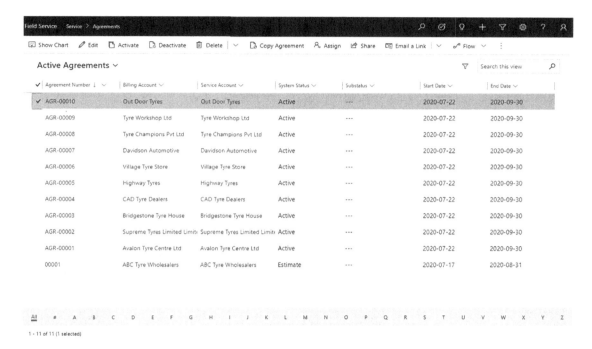

Figure 4-37. *Agreements created in the system*

13. Open one of the agreements. You can see the information submitted via the file is in the record. Under the **Booking Setup** section, you can see the Agreement Booking Set is also created and mapped with the agreement (Figure 4-38).

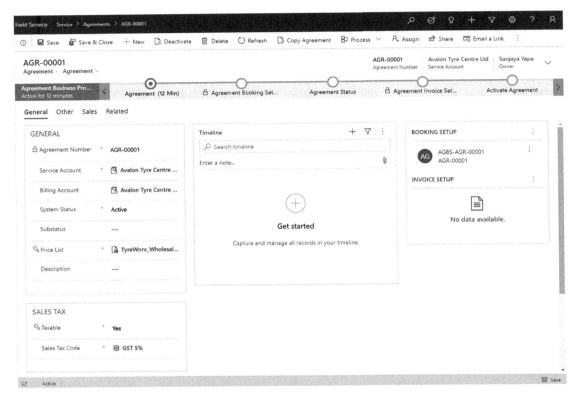

Figure 4-38. *Agreement record created from the data import*

14. Open the Agreement Booking Setup record linked to the agreement.
     As you can see, the agreement booking dates are created and linked
     with the agreement booking setup (Figure 4-39). These records
     were created based on Recurrence Settings XML.

```
<root>
    <pattern>
        <period>weekly</period>
        <option>every</option>
        <weeks every='1'>
            <days>1</days>
            <days>3</days>
            <days>5</days>
        </weeks>
    </pattern>
```

```
<range>
    <start>7/22/2020</start>
    <option>endBy</option>
    <end>9/30/2020</end>
</range>
<datas/>
</root>
```

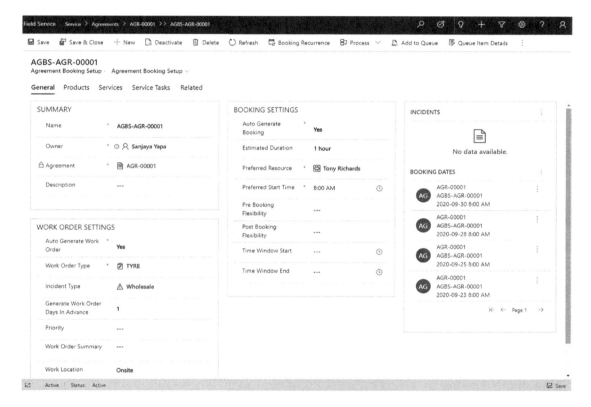

Figure 4-39. *Agreement booking setup created from the data imported*

15. Open one of the Agreement Booking Date records. The Work
    Order link is still empty (Figure 4-40). This link will be filled only
    when the work order is generated based on the settings defined in
    the Agreement Booking Setup record.

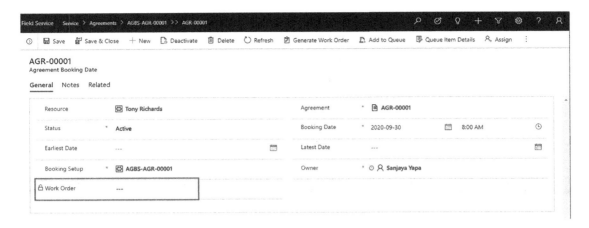

Figure 4-40. *Agreement Booking Date record before generating the related work order*

16. The work order is generated and attached to the Agreement Booking Date record. Notice that the **Status** has changed from **Active** to **Processed** (Figure 4-41).

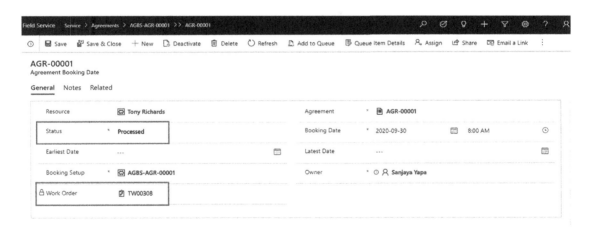

Figure 4-41. *Agreement Booking Date record after the work order is generated*

As explained earlier, the work order(s) is now booked and assigned to the resource. When the scheduling staff navigates to the schedule board, the work orders for the customer sales visits are assigned to the resource (Figure 4-42).

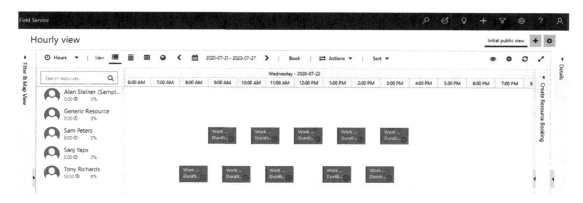

Figure 4-42. *Work orders generated and booked on the schedule board*

When the sales rep logs into the Field Service Mobile, they can see the bookings for customer visits (Figure 4-43).

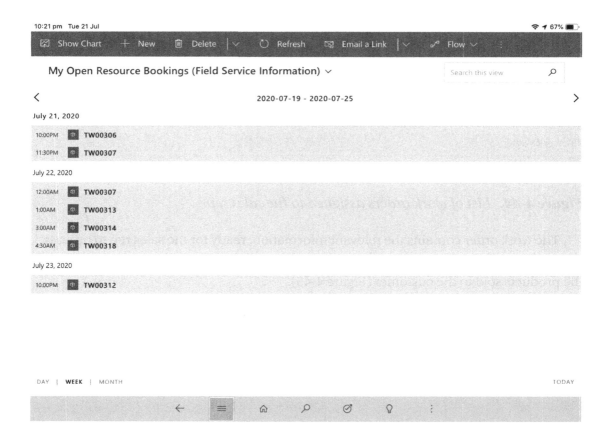

Figure 4-43. *Bookings on the mobile device assigned to the sales rep*

When navigates to the work orders related to the planned visits can be seen (Figure 4-44).

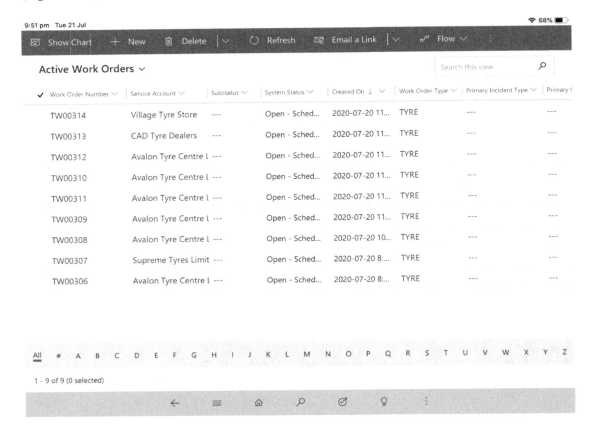

Figure 4-44. *List of work orders assigned to the sales rep*

The work order contains the relevant information, ready for the sales rep to process the work order at the client site. Now when the sales rep visits the customer, they can add the products sold to the customer (Figure 4-45).

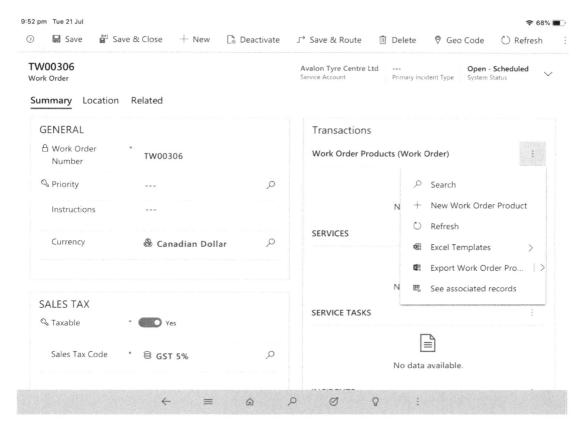

Figure 4-45. *Work order on the Field Service Mobile, ready for processing by the sales rep*

Chapter 7 explains the work order processing in greater detail.

Summary

This chapter discussed the two methods for creating work orders for recurring services. We looked at how to create agreements, agreement booking setups, and agreement booking dates by following the out-of-the box business process flow. The second part of the chapter explained how to apply this process for multiple customers.

CHAPTER 5

Setting Up Inventory

Setting up inventory and pricing products are important tasks in Field Service. Chapter 2 introduced most of the Field Service entities and features. In this chapter, we are going to set up the product catalog, warehouses, and their inventories for TyreWorx. The product catalog is a sales feature that Field Service uses for billing purpose. The product catalog explains unit groups, products and services, and product bundles, including prices, discounts, and taxes. In addition, warehouses and inventories are set up for the products in the product catalog.

TyreWorx uses only a few unit groups, products, and product bundles. The two main price lists are for the company's retail and wholesale businesses. Multiple tax codes have been defined due to multiple Canadian tax codes. Multiple warehouses and delivery and service vehicles are used according to the structure described in Chapter 2. The Field Service app is used onsite, including in the warehouses.

Setting Up Products and Services

This section focuses on setting up the product catalog and the service catalog that the field technicians will use during their daily field operations. Some jobs (work orders) will involve either selling tires or offering services, and some jobs will involve both. Chapter 7 discusses the utilization of these products and services in detail.

Product Catalogs

A product catalog is a collection of products and their prices, including any discount information. Field Service extends the product catalog and the price list usage by adding them to the work orders.

© Sanjaya Yapa and Indika Abayarathne 2021
S. Yapa and I. Abayarathne, *Dynamics 365 Field Service*, https://doi.org/10.1007/978-1-4842-6408-9_5

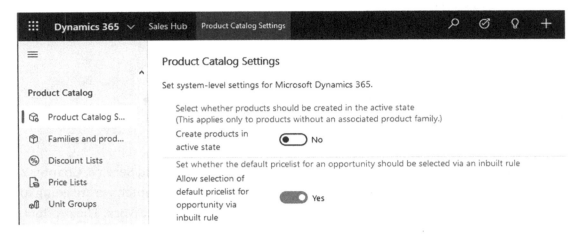

Figure 5-1. Product catalog settings and Product catalog menu

Unit Groups

Unit groups are useful when products are sold and billed in different quantities. Units can be any measurement to quantify products or services based on their attributes. Consider time as a unit, for example. An "hour" could represent the minimum unit of time; a "day" could represent a unit comprising eight hours; and a "week" could represent five units of days. Figure 5-2 shows an example of a unit group with two units.

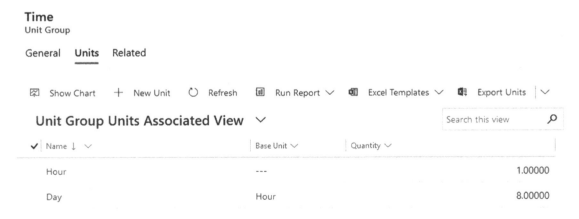

Figure 5-2. Time unit group

TyreWorx use two main unit groups for sales and labor. Tires are the main inventory product and are sold as single products and as sets. One set contains four tires. In order to achieve this business requirement, TyreWorx created a separate unit group (called Tyre Group) that contains two units. As shown in Figure 5-3, the base unit is named Each which means a single tyre, and another unit is named Set and which means 4 tyres. As you can see from Figure 5-3, the base unit for Set of tyres is Each. This means the set contains 4 tyres each. Figure 5-5 shows the field service tab on the product main form.

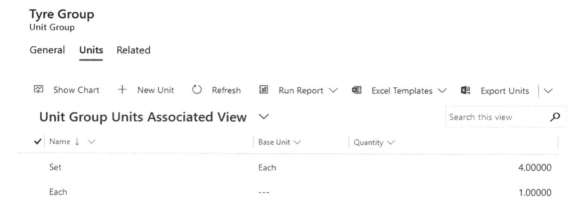

Figure 5-3. *Tyre unit group*

Products

Products are tangible items that are used in work orders to perform the job. Two types of products are available in Field Service: inventory and non-inventory. Products can be priced individually and as bundles. For example, one tire can be sold to a customer at a retail price and four tires (or a one tire set) can be sold at a bundle price under the same retail price list. Sample products and services appear under the Products and Services subsections (Figure 5-4).

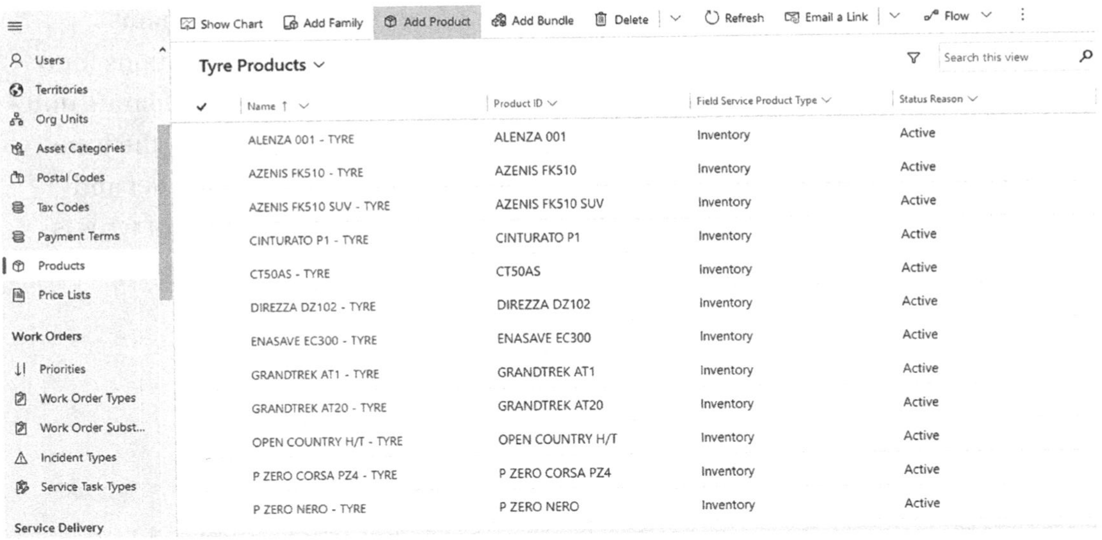

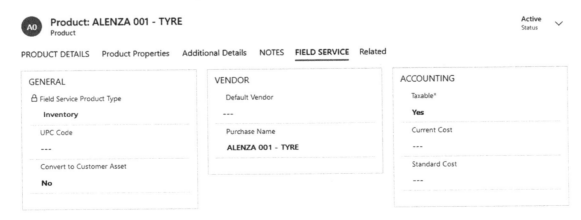

Figure 5-4. *Products list*

Inventory: Products are usually selected as Inventory when the
product has a high value or can be sold to the customer as a
primary item during the job. In our scenario, tires are inventory
items and can be sold as a primary item in a work order.

Non-inventory: This product type represents products with low
value and which are used as supportive or non-primary products.
Examples include stickers to identify tires and resealable ties.
TyreWorx field technicians can give away tire pressure checkers to
customers who buy a set of four tires.

Figure 5-5. *Field Service tab on product main form*

Services

Services are the labor involved in performing the job described in the work order. They are usually measured in time units. Examples include repairing a punctured tire and changing a set of tires. Figure 5-6 shows a service item in the TyreWorx product catalog.

Figure 5-6. *A service item in the TyreWorx product catalog*

As shown in Figure 5-6, the only major difference between the services and the inventory and non-inventory products is the Field Service Product Type field, which is set to Service. TyreWorx services include repairing punctured tires, rotating tires, jump-starting vehicles, and so forth. Services are mainly measured using units in the time groups.

Product Bundles

Multiple products can be billed and sold as bundles. One bundle can have different types of products in different quantities. An example of a bundle is a gift pack. A gift pack can include multiple products and is cheaper than the total cost of products sold individually. This is one of the key features required by the TyreWorx business because the nature of the primary product they sell. That is, 99% of the time, TyreWorx sells tires either as a bundle of two tires or as a bundle of four tires. Figure 5-7 shows multiple products in one bundle.

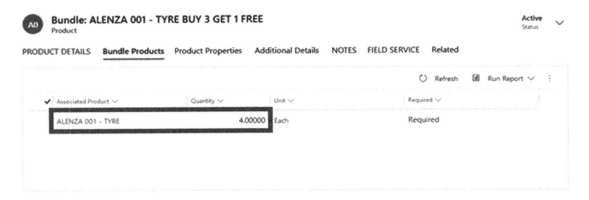

Figure 5-7. *Multiple products under a bundle product*

A product bundle is also an inventory product. Bundles have the same attributes as individual products. Figure 5-8 shows the Field Service tab on a bundle product's main form.

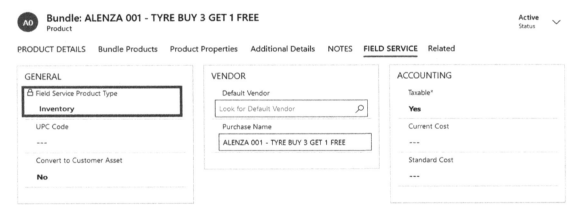

Figure 5-8. *Field Service tab on bundle product's main form*

The primary difference between using one product and a bundle product is that when the bundle is sold, the quantity defined in the bundle will be used in warehouse stock calculations and in invoices.

Setting Up Price Lists
Price Lists

In TyreWorx, the prices of products and services are categorized into two price lists, retail and wholesale. These price lists contain prices for different units of the products and services in a specific currency and in a specific date range. Price List records primarily include Name, Currency, Start Date, and End Date.

TyreWorx revises their retail and wholesale price lists every financial year. Figure 5-9 shows a retail price list for the financial year 2020/2021, and Figure 5-10 shows a wholesale price list. Price lists are important when creating work orders, as the invoice details are generated based on the selected price list under the work order. Agreements are generated using predefined price lists under the customer contacts. Chapter 4 discussed agreements in greater detail.

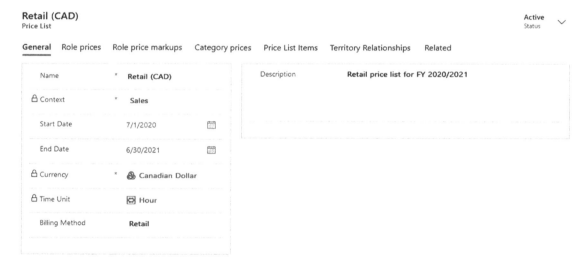

Figure 5-9. *Retail price list main form*

Name: This helps to identify the price list.

Currency: Prices can have in different currencies, such as Canadian Dollar (CAD), US Dollar (USD), Australian Dollar (AUD), etc. All the price list items are listed in the selected currency on the price list.

Start Date: Prices will be effective from the start date on the price list.

End Date: Prices will be effective until the end date on the price list.

The start and end dates can be defined according to a purpose, such as financial year or promotional time period.

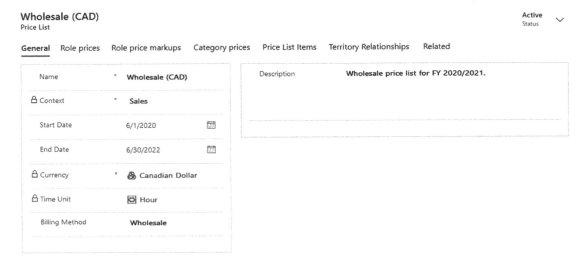

Figure 5-10.   *Wholesale price list main form*

Multiple active price lists can be available within a same time period. For example, for the same set of products and services in the same financial year, TyreWorx offers multiple price lists for citizens and non-citizens and for members and non-members. TyreWorx also varies the prices for the same products and services among the different Canadian provinces.

Custom fields can be added to the price list to differentiate the price lists according to specific requirements. TyreWorx uses the Billing Method custom field to identify retail and wholesale prices for the same products and services.

Price List Items

One price list contains multiple price list items for different units of different products and services. Price list item records generally include the price list, the product, the product's unit, the currency, and the discount list. Figure 5-11 shows some examples of prices of the same product or service under different price list years.

TyreWorx uses two different price lists in a financial year. The same product has two different prices in each price list. For example, one ALENZA 001 – TYRE product is sold to retail customers for $280.00 in one price list item, whereas the same product is sold to wholesale customers for $270.00 in another price list item. One set of four ALENZA 001 – TYRE products is priced at $720 in another price list item under the same retail price list. Figure 5-12 shows a list of price list items and and Figure 5-16 shows one of the sample price list items.

Product/Service	Unit	2020		2021	
		Retail	Wholesale	Retail	Wholesale
ALENZA 001 - TYRE	Each	$280.00	$270.00	$290.00	$275.00
ALENZA 001 - TYRE (Bundle of 4)	Each	$720.00		$750.00	
Tyre Puncher Repair	Each	$150.00		$165.00	

Figure 5-11. *Product prices*

Retail (CAD)
Price List

Active
Status

General   Role prices   Role price markups   Category prices   **Price List Items**   Territory Relationships   Related

+ New Price List Item   :

✓	Product ↑ ∨	Unit ∨	Amount ∨
	ALENZA 001 - TYRE	Each	$280.00
	AZENIS FK510 - TYRE	Each	$285.00
	CINTURATO P1 - TYRE	Each	$315.00
	CT50AS - TYRE	Each	$360.00
	DIREZZA DZ102 - TYRE	Each	$370.00
	ENASAVE EC300 - TYRE	Each	$400.00
	GRANDTREK AT1 - TYRE	Each	$410.00
	PROXES C100 PLUS SUV - TYRE	Each	$300.00

Figure 5-12. *Retail price list items*

Figure 5-13 shows the main form of the TyreWorx retail price list item. Price list item main form with the relevant price list.

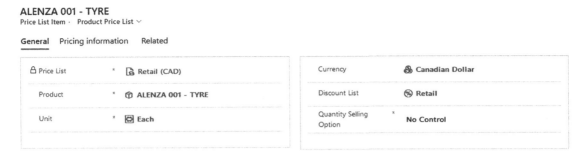

ALENZA 001 - TYRE
Price List Item · Product Price List ∨

General   Pricing information   Related

🔒 Price List	*	🔖 Retail (CAD)	Currency	🪙 Canadian Dollar
Product	*	🔷 ALENZA 001 - TYRE	Discount List	🔖 Retail
Unit	*	▣ Each	Quantity Selling Option	* No Control

Figure 5-13. *Price list item main form*

Price List: This is the relevant price list reference for the price list item.

Product: This is the product or service in the product catalog. It also can be a product bundle, such as a gift pack containing different products in one pack.

Unit: Products can be priced for different units, such as individual items, sets of items, pallets, boxes of items, etc.

Currency: This should be same as the parent price list's currency.

Discount List: Multiple discounts lists can be applied to the price list item. With this feature, only selected price list items for selected products can have discounts.

The Relationship Between Work Orders and the Product Catalog

It is important to understand the relationship between work orders and the product catalog. Work orders can contain multiple products and one price list. TyreWorx work orders contain tire products and tire services under work order products.

A work order contains invoice product items. Invoice product items pull unit prices from price list items according to the unit groups and according to the price list.

Figure 5-14 shows the high-level relationship between work orders and the product catalog-related entities.

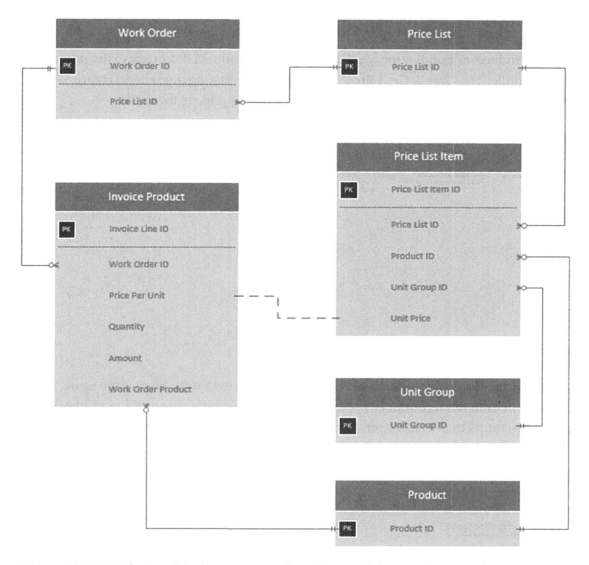

Figure 5-14. Relationship between work orders and the product catalog

Discounts

Businesses offer discounts in different ways, including direct discounts and indirect discounts. This section describes the discount-related features offered by Power Platform.

Discounts Through Bundles

Selling products as bundles for special rates will offer indirect discounts to the products in the bundle. The "Buy 3, Get 1 Free" offer is common among tire sellers (Figure 5-15). In this scenario, four tires are sold in one bundle for the price of three tires.

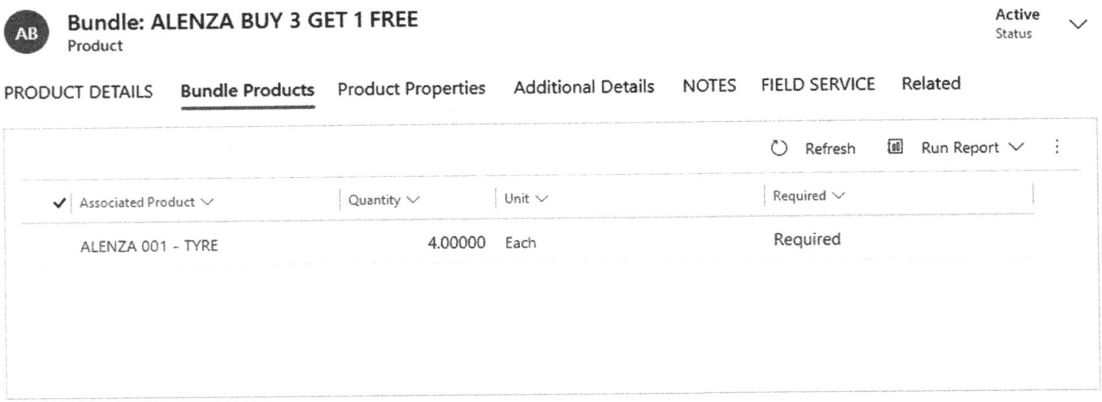

Figure 5-15. *Discount option via product bundles*

The price for a bundle product is usually lower than that for buying the same quantity of individual products. Promotions through bundles are another method of giving discounts to the customer. Price list items can be created from the price list. Figure 5-16 shows a price when buying 4 tyres together.

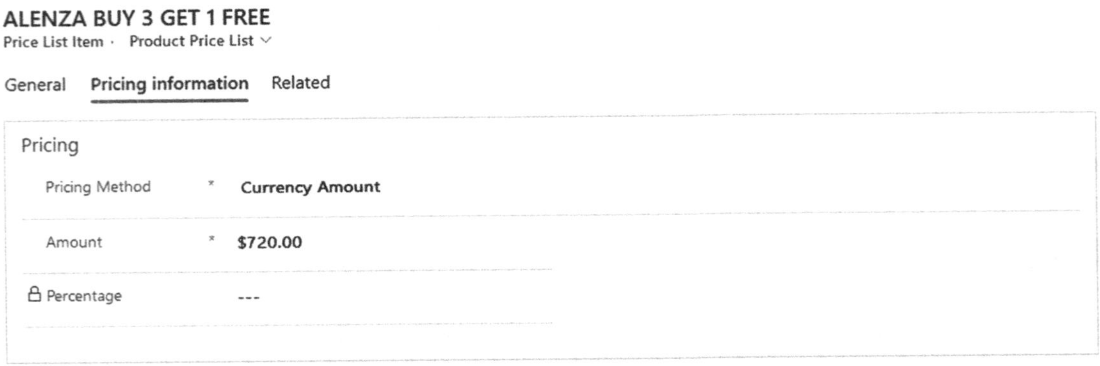

Figure 5-16. *Pricing information of a product bundle on a price list item*

Discount Lists

A discount list is an out-of-the-box feature in Power Platform. Two types of discounts can be configured: percentage-based and amount-based.

TyreWorx offers percentage-based discounts to retail customers and amount-based discounts to wholesale customers.

Discount lists can be created by selecting **Settings ➤ Product Catalog ➤ Discount Lists ➤ New**. Figure 5-17 shows a new form of a retail dicount list.

> *Percentage*: Discounts are calculated on a percentage basis for different quantities of purchase.
>
> *Amount*: Discounts are calculated on an amount basis for different quantities of purchase.

Retail
Discount List

General   Related

Name	* Retail	🔒 Type	Percentage

Description
Retail discount list

Figure 5-17. *New retail discount list form*

Figure 5-18 shows a discount list with two percentage-based discounts. When the product quantity is from 4 to 6, a 5% discount is offered. When the product quantity is from 7 to 8 products, a 7% discount is offered.

Figure 5-18. *Discount layers under the retail price list*

One price list item can have only one discount. Figure 5-19 shows a price list item form with a discount list. The main fields on the price list item form are Price List, Product, Unit, Currency, and Discount List.

Figure 5-19. *Retail price list in a price list item*

The wholesale discount list shown in Figure 5-20 contains two amount-based discounts: $15 when the product quantity is from 101 to 200, and $25 when the product quantity is from 201 to 300.

Wholesale
Discount List

General   **Discounts**   Related

⧉ Show Chart   + New Discount   ○ Refresh   ▣ Run Report ⌄   ▦ Excel Templates ⌄   ▥ Export Discounts | ⌄

Discount Associated View ⌄

Search this view   ⌕

✓	Percentage ↑ ⌄	Amount ⌄	Begin Quantity ⌄	End Quantity ⌄
	---	$15.00	101.00000	200.00000
	---	$25.00	201.00000	300.00000

Figure 5-20. *Wholesale discount layers*

Taxes

Taxes are a vital part of invoicing in any sales process. Every country uses a different tax model, and the model can vary within the same country, from state to state or province to province. The tax can be applied from one simple tax code to different tax layers, such as tax on tax. Figure 5-21 shows a CRM form for a one tax code.

TyreWorx must adhere to the tax layers defined in each province of Canada. Some provinces have only one single tax layer for selling products and services, whereas other provinces have two tax layers. The tax type and tax percentage different, too. Figure 5-22 explains tax codes using few examples on different provinces use tax layers.

Tax Codes

Dynamics 365 Customer Engagement enables you to set up tax codes. The number of tax codes varies based on the requirements. You can add tax codes by clicking **New** under **Settings ➤ Tax Codes**.

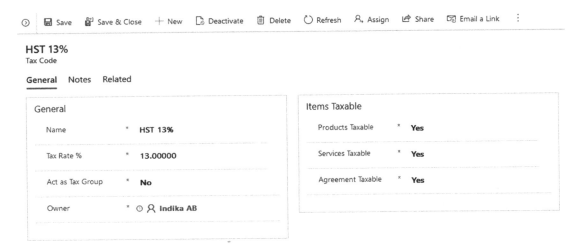

Figure 5-21. *Creating a new tax code*

The Tax Code record includes the following fields:

Name: Helps to clearly identify the tax code.

Tax Rate %: The tax value as a decimal value.

Act as a Tax Group: When multiple taxes are applied, the tax code can be defined as a tax group. A value of No means the tax code acts as a simple tax with one rate.

Products Taxable: A value of Yes means the products in the work order are taxable.

Services Taxable: A value of Yes means the services in the work order are taxable.

Agreement Taxable: A value of Yes means the agreements generated are taxable.

Tax Groups

Many countries, states, and provinces apply multiple taxes. In Canada, one province can have one or more tax types with different rates. Figure 5-22 shows examples of tax types and tax rates in few different Canadian provinces. GST: Goods and Services Tax. HST: Harmonized Sales Tax. PST: Provincial Sales Tax.

Province	Type	PST	GST	HST	Total Tax Rate
Alberta	GST		5%		5%
British Columbia	GST + PST	7%	5%		12%
Ontario	HST			13%	13%

Figure 5-22. *Tax types and rates*

In order to achieve the preceding scenario, the system needs some business rules. Having different tax codes in each state results in having different prices for the same product after taxes. The following high-level set of business rules can be used to determine the tax for each invoice generated under the work orders:

1. Province-based sales territories are defined in the system (e.g., ALBERTA).

2. Tax codes and tax groups are allocated to each sales territory (e.g., GST to ALBERTA).

3. Work orders are created under different sales territories, which are based on the province (e.g., ALBERTA Territory).

4. Work order types are defined as taxable so that the Taxable field value will be automatically set to Yes when the work order type is selected.

5. The invoice for the work order calculates the tax according to the tax code under the sales territory (e.g., Invoice INV-XXXX pick GST as the tax code).

In order to facilitate the sample requirement in the book, Dynamics 365 Field Service has a feature called *tax groups*. In one tax group, multiple tax code detail records can be available.

You can create a tax group by clicking **New** under **Settings ➤ Tax Codes**. In the Tax Code record, set the **Act as Tax Group** field to **Yes** to define the tax code as a tax group (Figure 5-23).

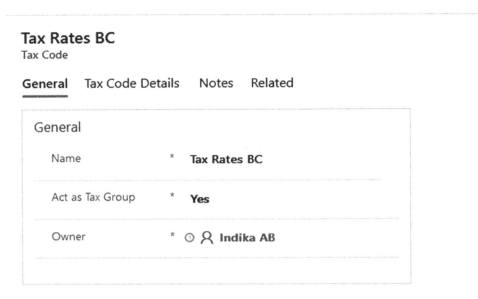

Figure 5-23. *Tax group main form*

The Tax Code Details tab of the Tax Code record contains multiple tax code detail records (Figure 5-24). Tax code detail records are listed according to the Line Order field under each tax group. Figure 5-25 shows the main form of a tax code detail record.

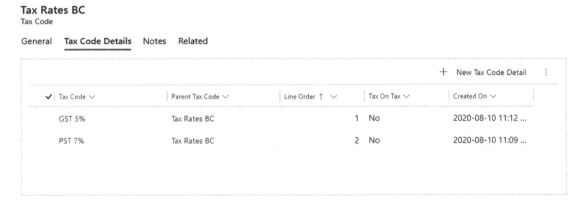

Figure 5-24. *Tax codes under a tax group*

The Tax Code Details tab contains following fields:

> *Tax Code*: Reference to a tax code record.

> *Parent Tax Code*: The parent tax group.

Line Order: This is the sequence of the tax rates. The line order cannot be duplicated within the same tax group.

Tax On Tax:

When the field value is Yes, the tax applies on top of previous tax value on the line order sequence. For example, the tax rate in line order 1 applies first and then the tax rate in line order 2 applies on top of the total value.

When the field value is No, all the tax applies on the work order amount. According to Figure 5-24, the total tax rate on the work order amount is 12%.

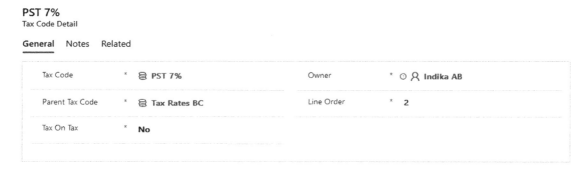

Figure 5-25. *Tax Code Detail main form*

In Dynamics 365 Field Service, tax is applied on the work order. Tax can be applied only when a work order type's Taxable field value is Yes. Sometimes, however, a business is exempted from taxes. The following high-level set of business rules can be used to exempt a work order from taxes: Also, Figure 5-26 shows an example for a tax code used in a work order.

- Province-based sales territories are defined in the system (e.g., ALBERTA).

- Tax codes and tax groups are allocated to each sales territory (e.g., GST to ALBERTA).

- Work orders are created under different province-based sales territories (e.g., ALBERTA Territory).

- Work order types are defined as taxable so that the Taxable field value on the work order, will be automatically set to Yes when the work order type is selected.

- Optional: Non-taxable work order types can be set up.

- The Taxable field value can be set to No. (If it automatically sets to Yes)

- Although the sales territory associates with a tax code, the invoice for the work order doesn't calculate the tax as the work order is not taxable (e.g., Invoice INV-XXXX doesn't pick any tax code).

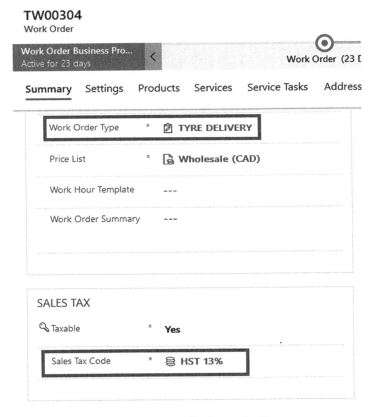

Figure 5-26. *Tax code used in a work order's main form*

Setting Up Warehouses

A warehouse is a physical location or a vehicle with an inventory. Figure 5-27 shows primary information of a warehouse record. An inventory transfer is the process to move products from one warehouse to another. Inventory can be transferred from a warehouse located in a building to a transfer truck and from a delivery truck to another warehouse location.

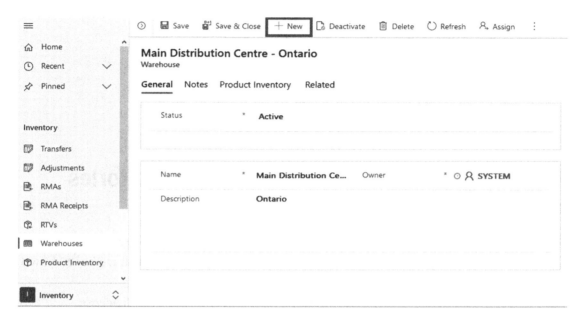

Figure 5-27. *General tab of a warehouse record*

You can create warehouses by selecting **Inventory ➤ Warehouses ➤ New**.

Few warehouse records have been created as master records according to the warehouse structure defined in ***Figure 2-30. A typical warehouse structure*** under Chapter 2.

Product Inventories

Each warehouse maintains an inventory and the inventory products. Their quantity counts are shown under the Product Inventory Associated View (Figure 5-28). One product inventory record is maintained for one product in each unit. This enables users to easily gain an understanding of the product quantities. For example, one product can exist as an individual product for sale under one product inventory record, such as sold as each unit. Also, if a bundle of products is sold together, there will be another product inventory record for them, such as a four-tire bundle in one product inventory record.

Main Distribution Centre - Ontario
Warehouse

General   Notes   **Product Inventory**   Related

⊠ Show Chart   + New Product Inventory   ↻ Refresh   ▣ Run Report ⌄   ▦ Excel Templates ⌄   ▣ Export Product Invent... | ⌄

Product Inventory Associated View ⌄   Search this view   ⌕

✓	Warehouse ⌄	Product ▽ ⌄	Quantity A... ↓ ⌄	Quantity On H... ⌄	Quantity On Or... ⌄	Quantity Alloc... ⌄	Reorder Point ⌄
	Main Distribution Centre - Ontaı	ALENZA 001 - TYRE	1,000.00	1,000.00	0.00	0.00	---
	Main Distribution Centre - Ontaı	GRANDTREK AT20 - TYRE	1,000.00	1,000.00	0.00	0.00	---
	Main Distribution Centre - Ontaı	PROXES C1S - TYRE	1,000.00	1,000.00	0.00	0.00	---
	Main Distribution Centre - Ontaı	DIREZZA DZ102 - TYRE	500.00	500.00	0.00	0.00	---
	Main Distribution Centre - Ontaı	ENASAVE EC300 - TYRE	400.00	400.00	0.00	0.00	---

Figure 5-28. *Product inventory under a warehouse*

Accessing Warehouses and Product Inventories from the Mobile App

The Field Service mobile app can be configured to show inventory-related features. Warehouses, Inventory Transfers, Inventory adjustments and Products have been shown under Inventory menu for the TyreWorx requirements.

Users of the Field Service mobile app must be granted permission to access warehouses and product inventories. Figure 5-29 shows the Warehouses menu on a tablet.

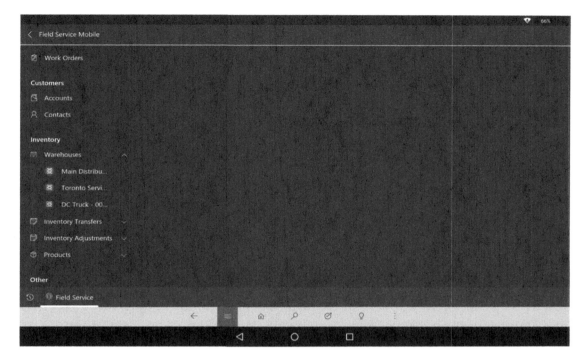

Figure 5-29. *Warehouses menu on a tablet*

Figure 5-30 shows a list of active warehouses under the Warehouses menu in the Field Service mobile app. The default columns in the Active Warehouses view are Name, Description, and Created On.

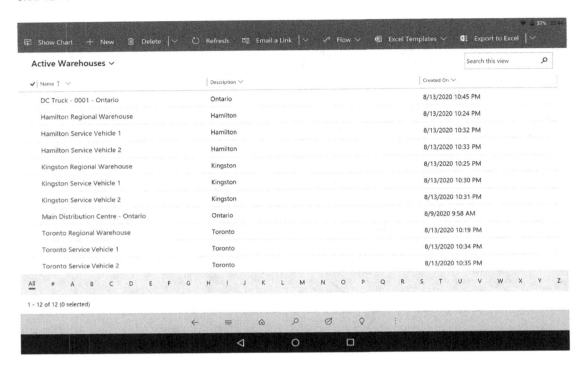

Figure 5-30. *Active Warehouses view on a tablet*

Filtering Warehouses in the Tablet App

Different views of warehouses can be created and made available in Field Service mobile app. Field Service mobile app facilitates changing views as configured in the mobile app. Figure 5-31 shows all the regional warehouses operated by TyreWorx.

Data filtering is important due to the following reasons:

- Users can be allocated only to relevant filters. For example, Ontario users will see only Ontario warehouses.

- It optimizes the screen usage by showing only relevant data.

- It increases user satisfaction by reducing clicks.

- It provides easy navigation for users.

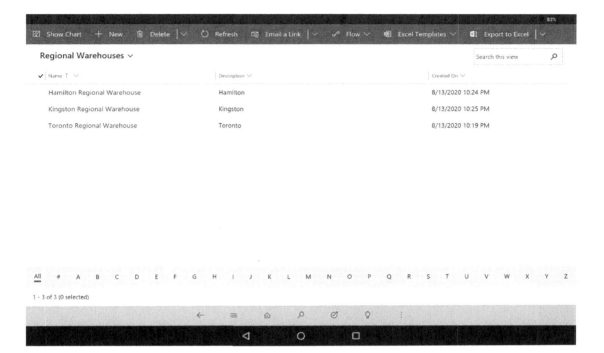

Figure 5-31. *Regional Warehouses view on a tablet*

The Kingston warehouses and service vehicles can be filtered as shown in Figure 5-32. Both locations and service vehicles act as warehouses because both locations and service vehicles maintain inventories.

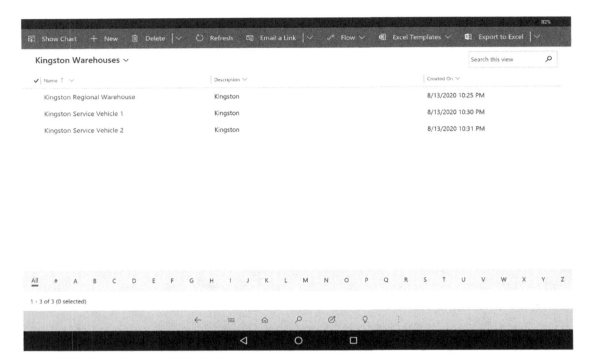

Figure 5-32. *Kingston regional warehouses list in Field Service tablet app in tablet*

Displaying Products in the Tablet App

Tire products are listed under the Tyre Products view (Figure 5-33). Multiple views are available under the products.

Figure 5-33. *Tyre Products view on a tablet*

Transferring Inventories in the Tablet App

Figure 5-34 shows an inventory transfer product under an inventory transfer record on an Android tablet. Inventory transfer records are used when moving stock from one warehouse to another. TyreWorx has selected to transfer 120 ALENZA tires from one warehouse to another warehouse.

Chapter 6 discusses inventory transfers in detail .

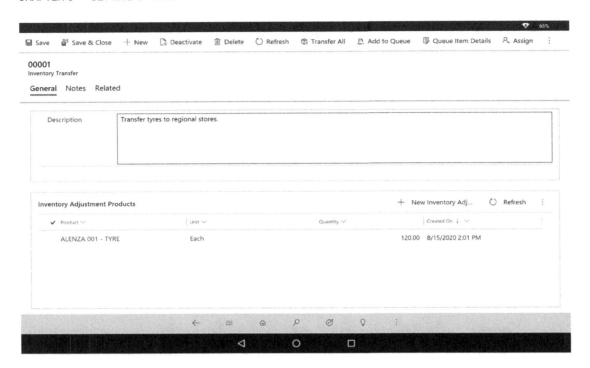

Figure 5-34. *Transferring inventory products on a tablet*

Figure 5-35 shows an inventory transfer on an Android tablet. TyreWorx relies heavily on inventory transfers as part of their onsite process.

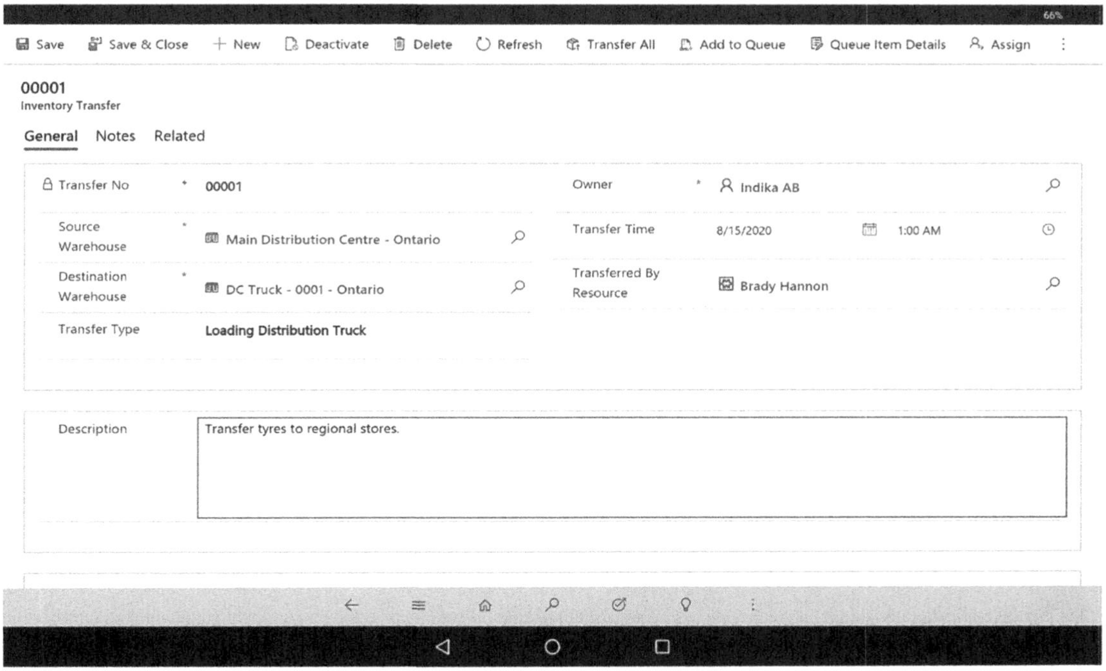

Figure 5-35. *Inventory transfer main form on a tablet*

Figure 5-36 shows an example of multiple products created for an inventory adjustment. Inventory adjustment record is a reprentation of a change happen to any product quantity in an inventory.

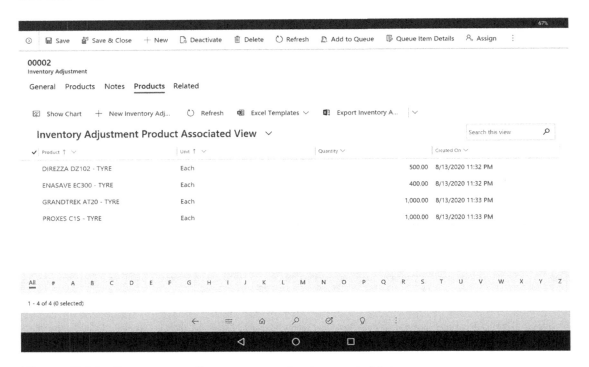

Figure 5-36. *Inventory adjustment products on a tablet*

Summary

This chapter discussed warehouses and their related features. Warehouse and product catalog entities and areas, identified as core entities in Chapter 2, were discussed in more detail. Practical usage scenarios of product catalogs include unit groups, products, product bundles, price lists, and discounts. The chapter also discussed setting up warehouses and inventory in the web client and in the Field Service mobile app. The next chapter discusses all the main processes of inventory movements .

CHAPTER 6

Inventory Movement

Tracking inventory movement is essential for businesses like TyreWorx. They need to keep track of the inventory moving in and out of their warehouses. Also, when processing work orders in both their retail and wholesale businesses, they must know the amount of inventory consumed. Although Dynamics 365 Field Service is not a sophisticated inventory management system, it offers everything required to manage and track inventory. This chapter looks at the inventory movement capabilities of Dynamics 365 Field Service only.

For the TyreWorx business, inventory transfers are used to transfer items among warehouses. Warehouse managers use purchase orders to order new items to the main distribution centers. Some situations call for warehouse managers to use the RMA (return merchandise authorization) and RTV (return to vendor) processes. The out-of-the-box processes suffice in most scenarios, but sometimes they have to be extended. In such situations, Power Automate flows play a crucial role. This chapter includes an example.

Processing Inventory Transfers in the Field

As explained in Chapter 5, TyreWorx has a network of warehouses. They also consider the service vehicles and sales trucks as moving warehouses. Tires are moving between these numerous warehouses daily. Following are some of the scenarios:

- The main distribution center for each province is responsible for distributing tires to all the warehouses via the distribution trucks.

- Every morning, the distribution trucks are loaded with tires and sent to various suburbs within the province where each suburb has a regional warehouse. The distribution truck replenishes the inventory of the regional warehouse.

- Every morning, the service vehicles in the suburbs visit the regional warehouse and are filled with new tires.

- The sales reps fill their sales trucks with new tires from the main distribution center before heading out to the wholesale customers.

Moving Inventory

This section discusses how inventory moves from the main distribution center to the destination and how inventory items are transferred to the final destination of the chain. Let's start at the main distribution center, where distribution trucks are loaded with tyres. Figure 6-1 shows the current stock levels of the Main Distribution Centre.

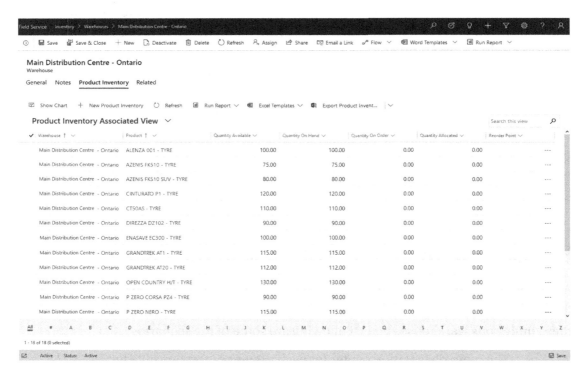

Figure 6-1. *Main distribution center stock levels*

The TyreWorx warehouse staff will be handling this process. To start the process, an Inventory Transfer record is created (Figure 6-2). The source warehouse is the distribution center and the destination warehouse is the distribution truck.

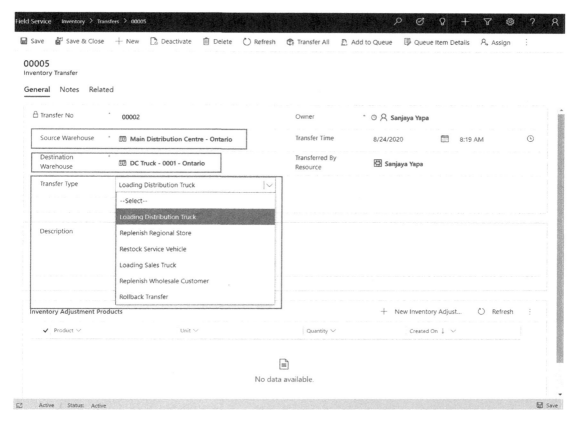

Figure 6-2.   *New Inventory Transfer record*

Because multiple inventory transfers from different locations occur daily, it is important to categorize these transfers. For that, a Transfer Type field is used (Figure 6-2). This is a custom field added to the Inventory Transfer record.

Next, the warehouse staff uses the Inventory Adjustment Product Quick Create form to add the products to the inventory transfer. (Figure 6-3).

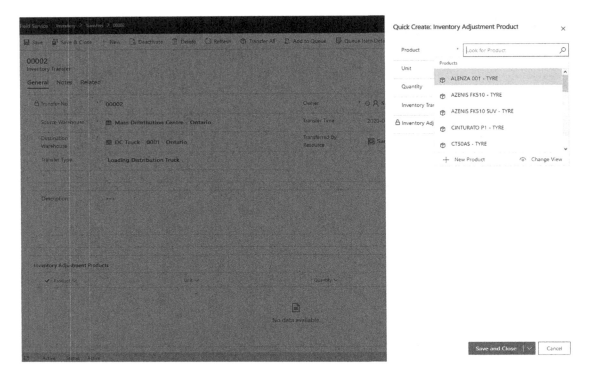

Figure 6-3. *Adding products to the inventory transfer*

On the Quick Create form, the staff specifies the product, unit, and quantity to transfer. Note that this record will be linked with the inventory transfer. The Inventory Adjustment field is filled only when inventory adjustments are performed. After completing the Quick Create form, the staff clicks Save and Close or Save & Create New to continue adding items to the transfer (Figure 6-4).

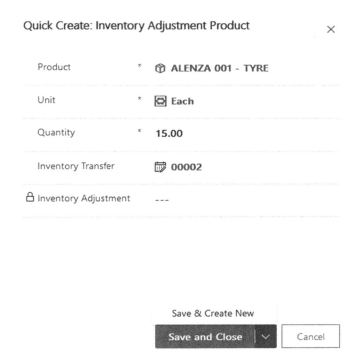

Figure 6-4. *Inventory Adjustment Product Quick Create form*

As shown in Figure 6-5, the products are added to the transfer under the Inventory Adjustment Products sub-grid (Figure 6-5).

Figure 6-5. *Inventory adjustment products added to the inventory transfer*

As soon as a product is added to the transfer, the inventory of source and the destination gets updated. That is, inventory at the source warehouse (the distribution center) will decrease (Figure 6-6).

Main Distribution Centre - Ontario
Warehouse

General   Notes   **Product Inventory**   Related

🗠 Show Chart   ✐ Edit   ▢ Activate   ▢ Deactivate   🗑 Delete Product Invent...   🗠 Email a Link   🖩 Run Report ∨

Product Inventory Associated View ∨

✓ Warehouse ↑ ∨	Product ↑ ∨	Quantity Available ∨	Quantity On Hand ∨	Quantity On Order ∨	Quantity Allocated ∨	Reorder Point ∨
✓ Main Distribution Centre - O	ALENZA 001 - TYRE	85.00	85.00	0.00	0.00	---
✓ Main Distribution Centre - O	AZENIS FK510 - TYRE	65.00	65.00	0.00	0.00	---
✓ Main Distribution Centre - O	AZENIS FK510 SUV - TYRE	65.00	65.00	0.00	0.00	---
✓ Main Distribution Centre - O	CINTURATO P1 - TYRE	108.00	108.00	0.00	0.00	---
Main Distribution Centre - O	CT50AS - TYRE	110.00	110.00	0.00	0.00	---
Main Distribution Centre - O	DIREZZA DZ102 - TYRE	90.00	90.00	0.00	0.00	---
Main Distribution Centre - O	ENASAVE EC300 - TYRE	100.00	100.00	0.00	0.00	---
Main Distribution Centre - O	GRANDTREK AT1 - TYRE	115.00	115.00	0.00	0.00	---

Figure 6-6. *Inventory changes at the source warehouse*

The inventory at the destination (the truck) will be increased; or, if the product does not exist in the product inventory of the Warehouse record, it will be added (Figure 6-7).

DC Truck - 0001 - Ontario
Warehouse

General   Notes   **Product Inventory**   Related

🗠 Show Chart   + New Product Inventory   ↻ Refresh   ▣ Run Report ∨   ▦ Excel Templates ∨   ▥ Export Product Invent... | ∨

Product Inventory Associated View ∨   🔎

✓ Warehouse ↑ ∨	Product ↑ ∨	Quantity Available ∨	Quantity On Hand ∨	Quantity On Order ∨	Quantity Allocated ∨	Reorder Point ∨
DC Truck - 0001 - Ontario	ALENZA 001 - TYRE	15.00	15.00	0.00	0.00	---
DC Truck - 0001 - Ontario	AZENIS FK510 - TYRE	10.00	10.00	0.00	0.00	---
DC Truck - 0001 - Ontario	AZENIS FK510 SUV - TYRE	15.00	15.00	0.00	0.00	---
DC Truck - 0001 - Ontario	CINTURATO P1 - TYRE	12.00	12.00	0.00	0.00	---

Figure 6-7. *Product inventory changes at the destination warehouse*

When the distribution truck arrives at the regional store, the driver will use the Dynamics 365 Field Service Mobile app to offload the items to the destination. For this, the driver will create a new Inventory Transfer record and replenish the store. Notice that the Transfer Type field is set to Replenish Regional Store (Figure 6-8).

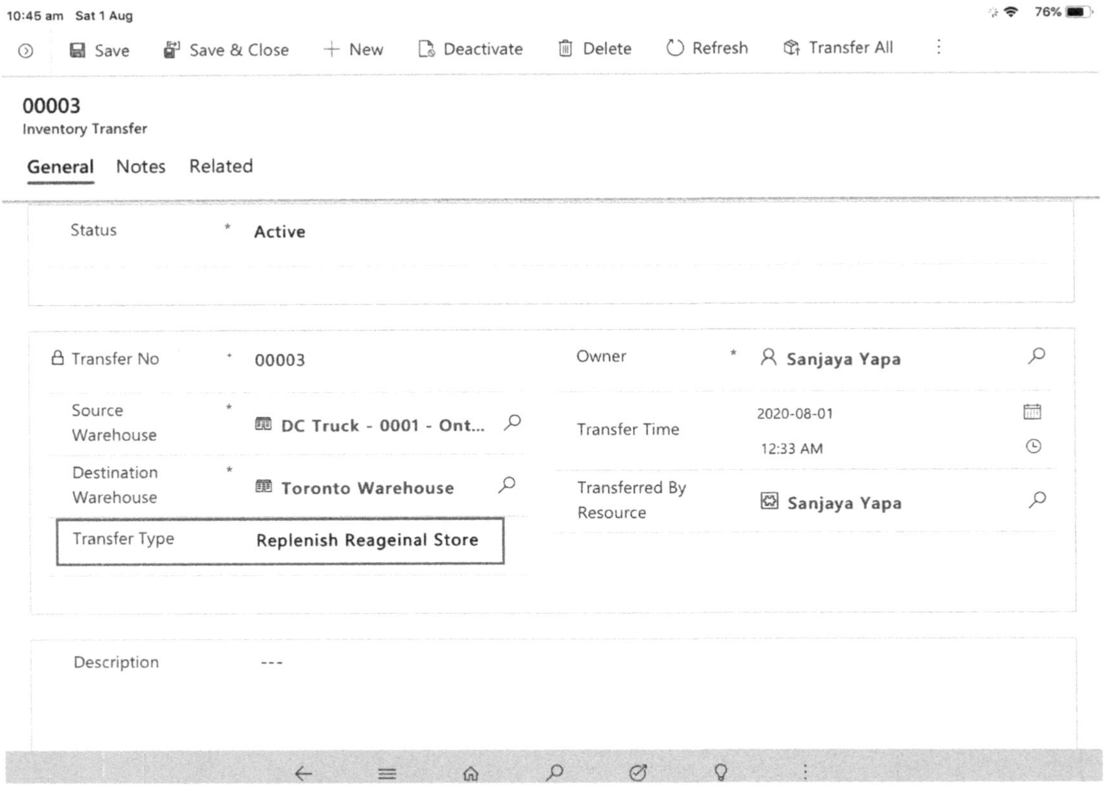

Figure 6-8. *Inventory Transfer record created on Field Service Mobile*

Adding products to the Inventory Transfer record is the same as before. As shown in Figure 6-9, the Inventory Adjustment Product drop-down list will automatically list the inventory available in the source warehouse. After saving the Inventory Transfer record, the driver will add the required products, which will increase the products at the destination warehouse and decrease the inventory at the source warehouse.

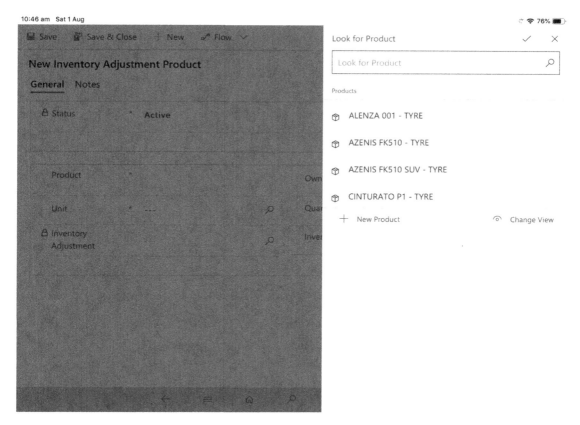

Figure 6-9. *Adding inventory adjustment products to the transfer*

As with the previous inventory transfer, the items are added to the Inventory Transfer record based on the requirements of the destination warehouse (Figure 6-10).

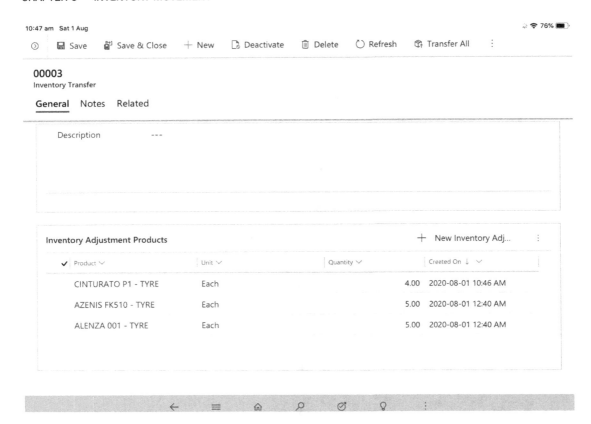

Figure 6-10. *Products added to the inventory transfer in Field Service Mobile*

The driver can verify the stock counts by looking at the Warehouse record in Field Service Mobile (Figure 6-11). This is a good example of inventory moving out from the main distribution center.

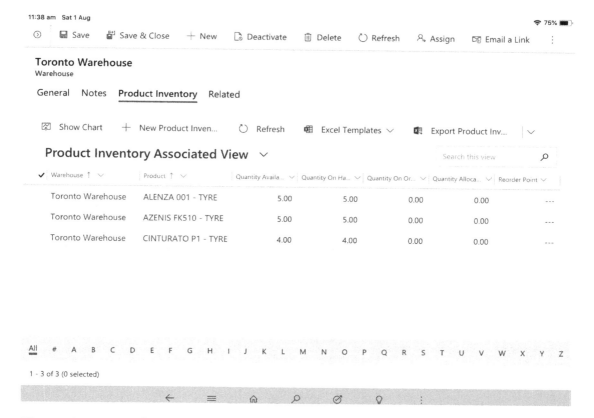

Figure 6-11. Verifying inventory in the destination warehouse

TyreWorx field operatives need to replenish their vehicles daily to provide support to the customers. Before they start work, the field operatives visit the company's closest tire store and replenish their vehicles using inventory transfers.

The first step is to create an Inventory Transfer record, where the source warehouse is the store and the destination warehouse is the service vehicle. Notice the Transfer Type field is set to Restock Service Vehicle and the Transfer Status field is set to New (Figure 6-12).

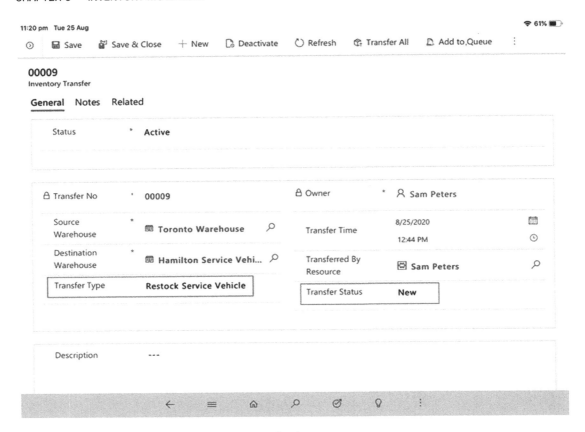

Figure 6-12. *Restocking the service vehicle*

All the other steps are the same as the previous scenarios. When the transfer completes, the inventory will get updated at both ends. Now the technician can use these items when processing work orders.

Note   To transfer all the inventory from the source warehouse to the destination warehouse, click the **Transfer All** button from the toolbar of the **Inventory Transfer** record (Figure 6-12).

Exception Scenarios

When several thousands of inventories move back and forth from warehouses, there will be exceptions. Let's examine a few specific scenarios.

SCENARIO 1: In this scenario, a warehouse has no inventory of a specific tire (Figure 6-13).

Toronto Warehouse
Warehouse

General   Notes   **Product Inventory**   Related

⊡ Show Chart   ✎ Edit   ⎀ Activate   ⎀ Deactivate   🗑 Delete Product Invent...   ⊠ Email a Link   ▣ Run Report ∨   ⬚ Word Templates ∨

Product Inventory Associated View ∨   Search this view   ⌕

✓	Warehouse ↑ ∨	Product ↑ ∨	Quantity Available ∨	Quantity On Hand ∨	Quantity On Order ∨	Quantity Allocated ∨	Reorder Point ∨	
	Toronto Warehouse...	ALENZA 001 - TYRE...	5.00	5.00	0.00	0.00	---	
	Toronto Warehouse...	AZENIS FK510 - TYRE...	5.00	5.00	0.00	0.00	---	
	Toronto Warehouse...	CINTURATO P1 - TYRE...	4.00	4.00	0.00	0.00	---	
✓	Toronto Warehouse...	SINCERA SN831 - TYRE...	0.00	0.00	0.00	0.00	---	

Figure 6-13. *Warehouse with no inventory of a specific product*

When the technician selects this warehouse as the source warehouse for the inventory transfer, the product list does not show the product with no inventory items (Figure 6-14).

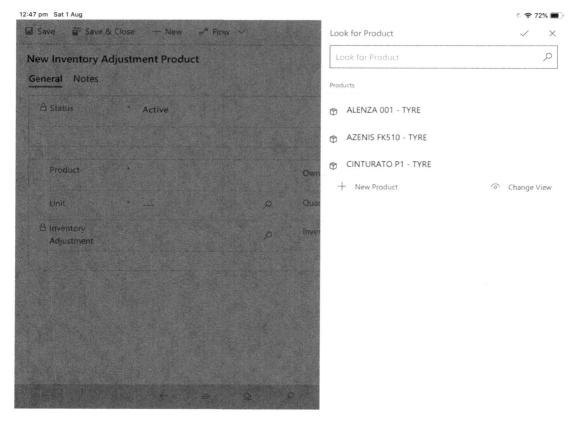

Figure 6-14. *Filtering the products with no inventory items*

Now let's use an inventory adjustment to increase the inventory by two (Figure 6-15.) Please refer to Chapter 5 for more details about inventory adjustments.

Toronto Warehouse
Warehouse

General   Notes   **Product Inventory**   Related

🔲 Show Chart   ✏ Edit   ⬜ Activate   ⬜ Deactivate   🗑 Delete Product Invent...   📧 Email a Link   📄 Run Report ∨   📧 Word Templates ∨

Product Inventory Associated View ∨   Search this view   🔍

✓	Warehouse ↑ ∨	Product ↑ ∨	Quantity Available ∨	Quantity On Hand ∨	Quantity On Order ∨	Quantity Allocated ∨	Reorder Point ∨
	Toronto Warehouse	ALENZA 001 - TYRE	5.00	5.00	0.00	0.00	---
	Toronto Warehouse	AZENIS FK510 - TYRE	5.00	5.00	0.00	0.00	---
	Toronto Warehouse	CINTURATO P1 - TYRE	4.00	4.00	0.00	0.00	---
✓	Toronto Warehouse	SINCERA SN831 - TYRE	2.00	2.00	0.00	0.00	---

Figure 6-15. *Increasing the inventory from 0 to 2*

Now the item is visible to the technician to add to his vehicle (Figure 6-16). This scenario demonstrates Field Service's built-in validations to prevent negative inventories.

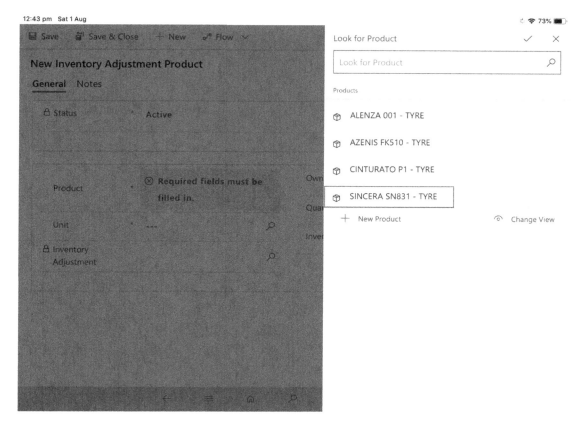

Figure 6-16. *Listing items with an inventory count greater than 0*

SCENARIO 2: Consider a scenario where the technician enters a quantity more than the items in the source warehouse. See the current stock levels in the source warehouse in Figure 6-15. In the Inventory Adjustment Product record, select one of the products from the list and enter a Quantity greater than the stock level. The selected product has an inventory count of 5 in the source warehouse and the transfer quantity is specified as 6 (Figure 6-17).

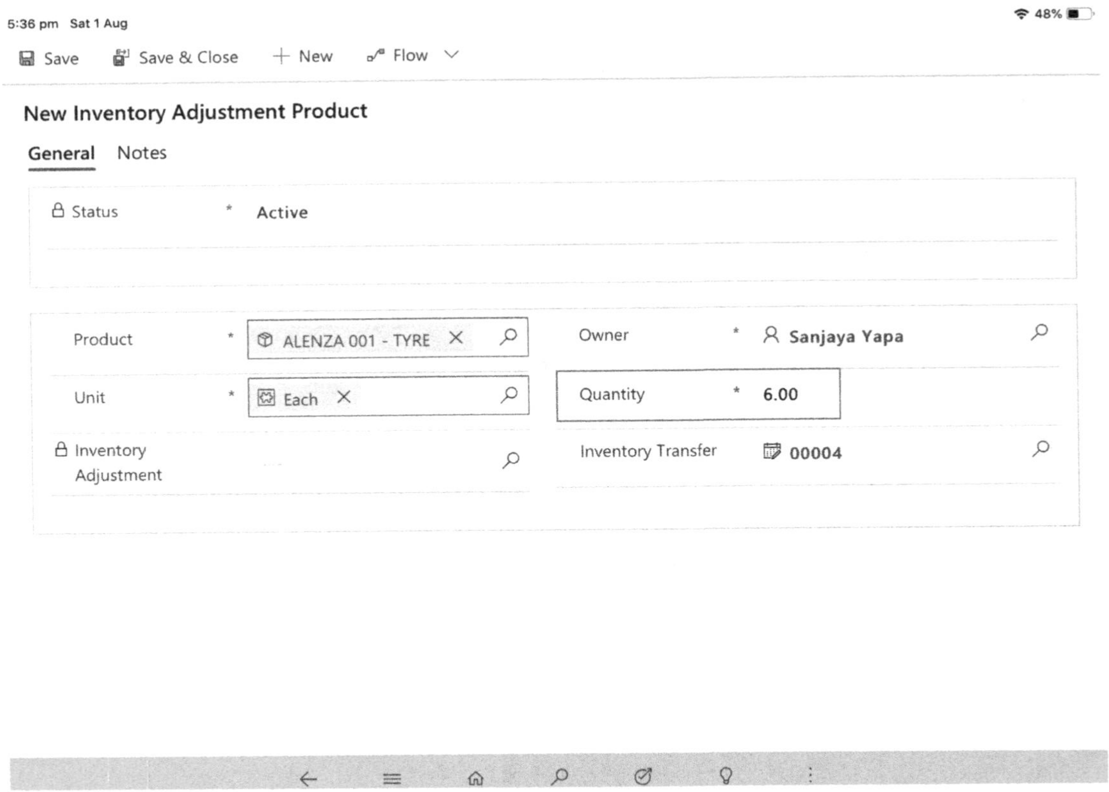

Figure 6-17. *Transfer quantity is greater than the source warehouse inventory.*

When the user clicks Save, the system throws the error message shown in Figure 6-18.

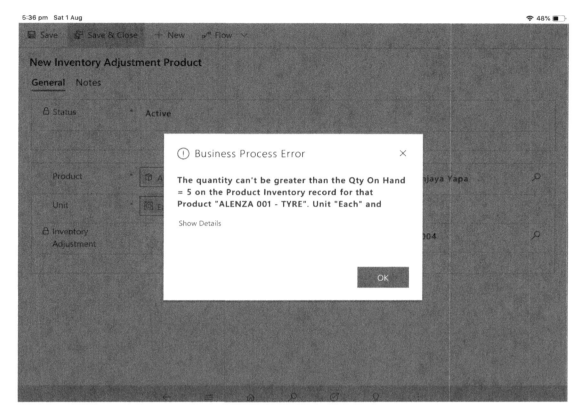

Figure 6-18. *The error message for an incorrect inventory quantity in the inventory transfer*

This validation will prevent negative inventory in the source warehouse and mismatches between the physical inventory and the system inventory.

SCENARIO 3: Sometimes the field staff makes mistakes during replenishing runs. In such scenarios, they might want to reverse the transfer. As previously mentioned, as soon as the inventory adjustment product is added to the inventory transfer, the products are transferred from the source warehouse to the destination warehouse. The transaction can be rolled back only via another inventory transfer by swapping the source and destination warehouses.

Further customization is required to automate this process. For instance, if the requirement is to roll back the entire transfer if the user makes a mistake, then a Power Automate flow can be configured. In this solution, the user selects the Transfer Type as Rollback Transfer (Figure 6-19) and saves it.

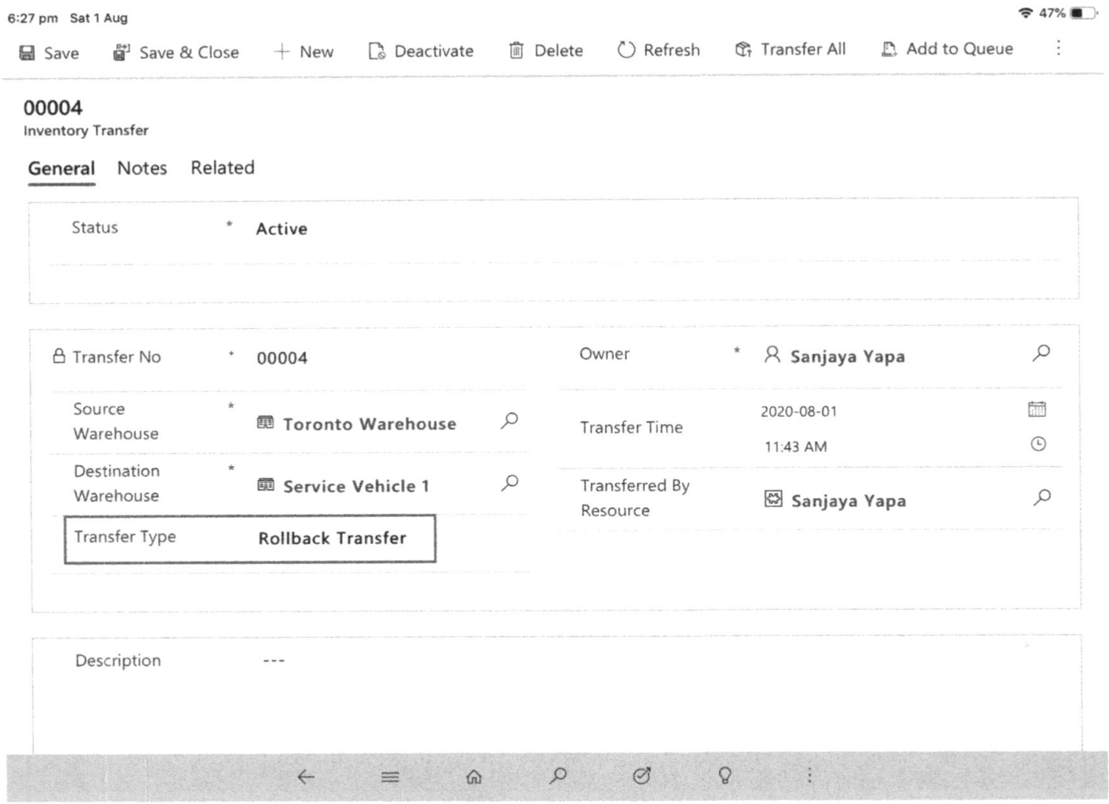

Figure 6-19. *Rolling back the inventory transfer*

Then, the Power Automate flow will trigger the update event of the inventory transfer. Following is a high-level view of the automated flow:

1. The flow triggers when the Transfer Status is changed. It triggers only if the Transfer Type is set to Cancelled.

2. The flow retrieves the list of inventory adjustment products associated with the inventory transfer.

3. The flow creates a new inventory transfer by swapping the source and destination warehouses.

4. The flow iterates through the list of inventory adjustment products retrieved and creates new inventory adjustment products for the new inventory transfer.

To design the flow, we will be using the new DataFlex connectors—previously known as Common Data Service (current environment) connectors. These connectors are versatile to include in the solution because of the ease with which they can be deployed from one environment to another.

The first step of the flow is to create the triggering action (Figure 6-20). As you can see, the flow Trigger Condition is set to Update. Most importantly, notice the Filtering Attributes and the Filter Expression fields. The Filtering Attributes field will ensure the flow will trigger only when change occurs on the transfer type of the inventory transfer. Here, the transfer type act as the record update trigger and the transfer status is the filters the update to specified transfer status value. That is, the Filter Expression field will narrow the execution further and ensure that the flow is executed only when the Transfer Type is set to Rollback.

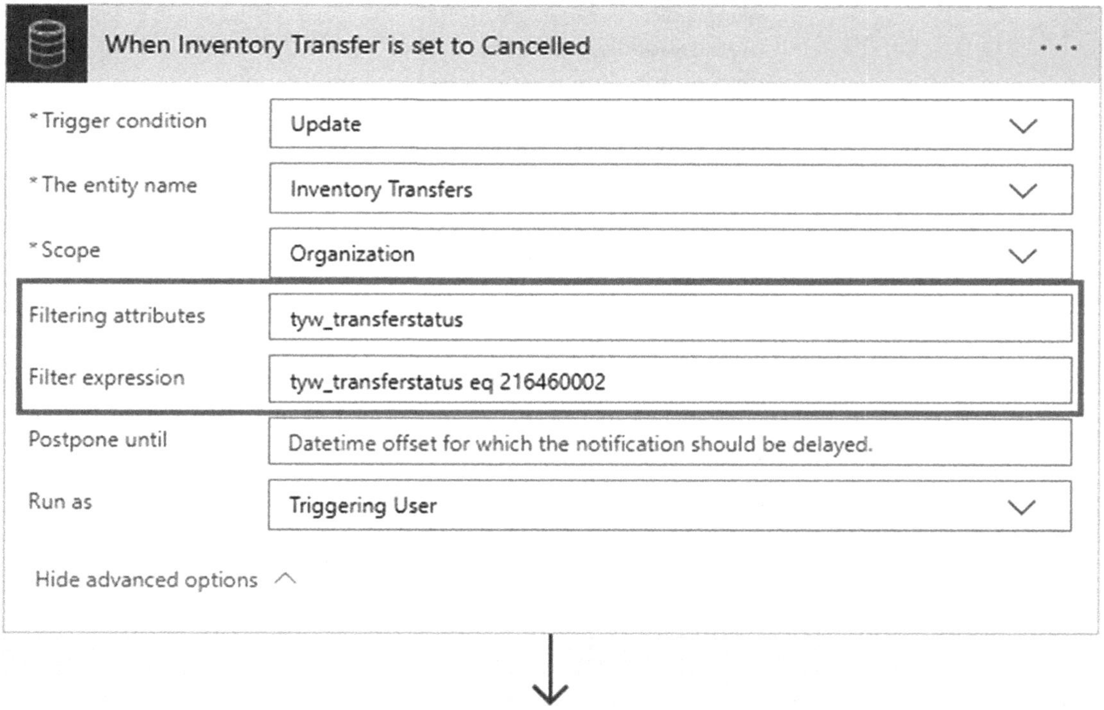

Figure 6-20. *Power Automate flow to reverse the inventory transfer*

The second step of the flow is to get the list of inventory adjustment products associated with the inventory transfer (Figure 6-21). A Fetch XML query is used to extract the list of inventory adjustment products.

Figure 6-21. *Reading the list of inventory adjustment products via Fetch XML*

The next step of the flow is to create the inventory transfer for rolling back the original transfer (Figure 6-22). Notice that the values in the Destination Warehouse and Source Warehouse fields are swapped. As previously explained, this action will revert the inventory transfer. Also, the Transfer Type field is set to Transfer Cancellation and the Transfer Status field is set to Completed.

⬛ Create a new Inventory Transfer for Rollback	
* Entity name	Inventory Transfers
* Destination Warehouse	msdyn_warehouses/ ⬛ Source Wareho... ×
* Source Warehouse (Warehouses)	msdyn_warehouses/ ⬛ Destination Wa... ×
Auto-Numbering	Internal field used to generate the next name upon entity creation. It is optiona
Description	Rollback Inventory Transfer- ⬛ Transfer No ×
Import Sequence Number	Shows the sequence number of the import that created this record.
Inventory Transfer	Shows the entity instances.
Owner (Owners)	Owner Id
Record Created On	Shows the date and time that the record was migrated.
Status Reason	Reason for the status of the Inventory Transfer
Time Zone Rule Version Number	For internal use only.
Transfer No	Enter the name of the custom entity.
Transfer Status	Completed
Transfer Time	
Transfer Type	Transfer Cancellation
Transferred By Resource (Bookable Resources)	Unique identifier for Resource associated with Inventory Transfer.
UTC Conversion Time Zone Code	Shows the time zone code that was in use when the record was created.
Hide advanced options ⌃	

Figure 6-22. *Creating the new inventory transfer for rolling back the original transfer*

The final step of the flow is to iterate through the inventory adjustment product list retrieved in Step 2 and create the same set of inventory adjustment products for the new inventory transfer (Figure 6-23).

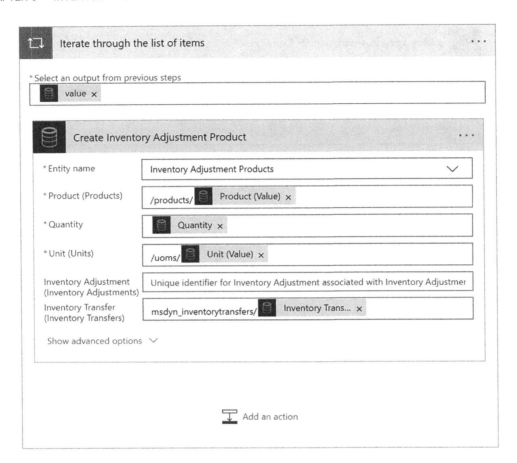

Figure 6-23. *Creating inventory adjustment products for the new transfer based on the products transferred originally*

Let's see this process in action.

1. Compare the inventories at the source warehouse (Figure 6-24) and the destination warehouse (Figure 6-25).

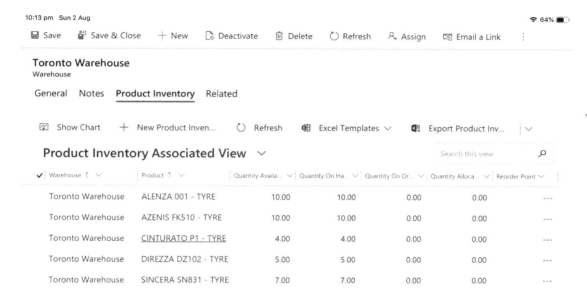

Figure 6-24. *The current stock level of the source warehouse*

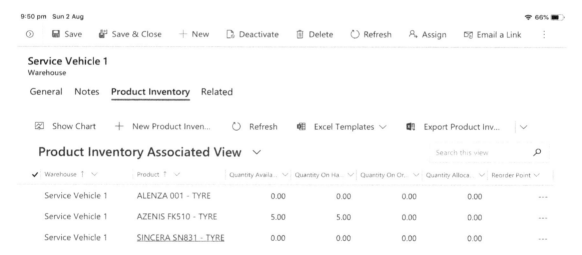

Figure 6-25. *The current stock level of the destination warehouse*

2. Create the inventory transfer and check that the source warehouse inventory has dropped down (Figure 6-26). The changes to the inventory are visible when compared with Figure 6-21.

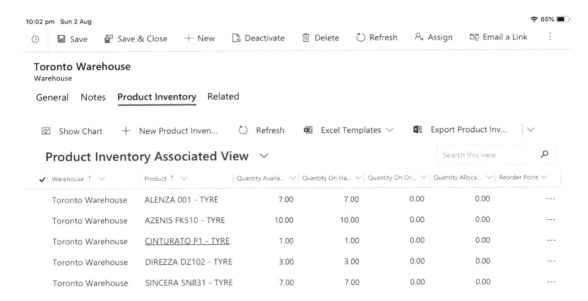

Figure 6-26. *Inventory depleted at the source warehouse after the inventory transfer*

3. Note that the inventory at the destination warehouse is increased (Figure 6-27). Refer the Figure 6-22 for comparison. Also notice that new items are added to the inventory.

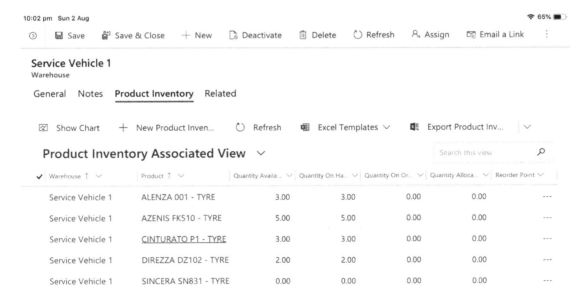

Figure 6-27. *Inventory increased at the source warehouse*

4. Roll back the inventory transfer by changing the **Inventory Transfer Status** field to **Cancelled**, and then click **Save** (Figure 6-28).

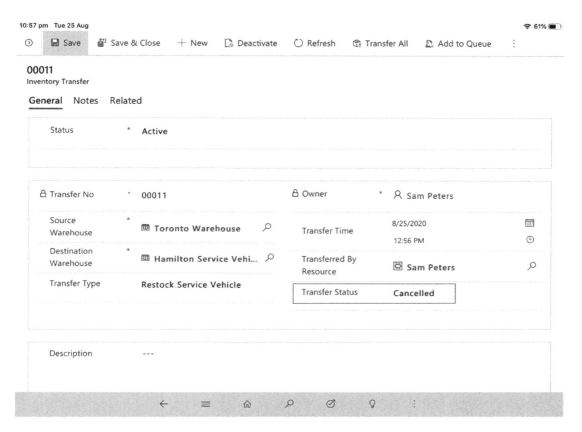

Figure 6-28. *Changing the transfer status*

5. At this point, the flow triggers and will create a new inventory transfer by swapping the source warehouse and the destination warehouse. As shown in image 6-29, the Description field has details about the transfer it relates to. We used this approach to make it simpler; ideally, however, this should be linked with the original inventory transfer.

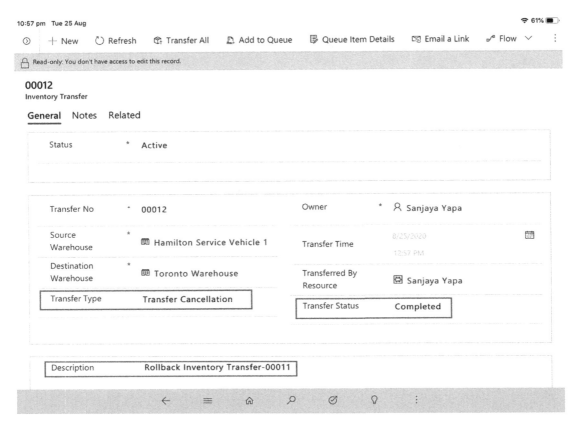

Figure 6-29. *New inventory transfer created to roll back the previous one*

6. This flow will also create the products in the original transfer with the same quantities, ensuring that the same quantities will be transferred back (Figure 6-30).

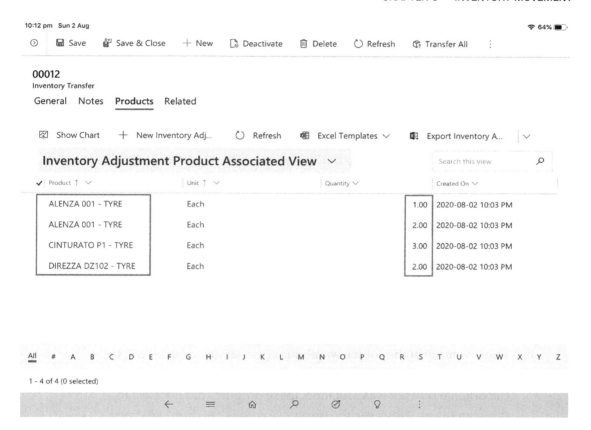

Figure 6-30. *Inventory adjustment products associated with the new transfer record for rollback*

7. Once all the inventory adjustment products are added, the inventory at the destination warehouse will be increased by the same amounts (Figure 6-31). It will be moved back to the original state (refer to Figure 6-24).

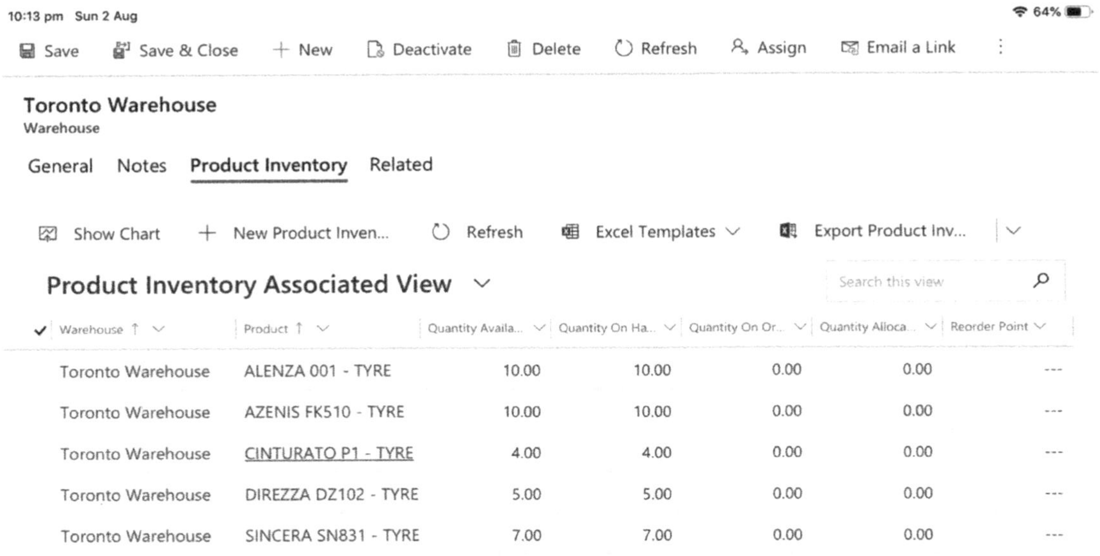

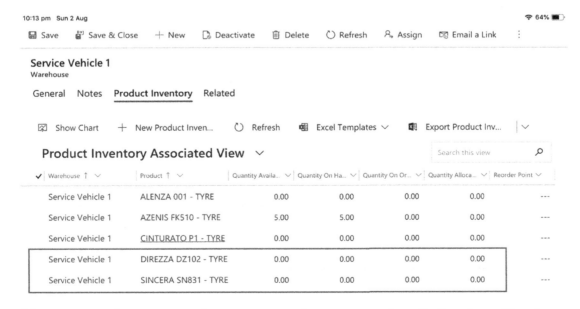

Figure 6-31. *Inventory increased at the destination warehouse after the rollback*

8.   The inventory at the source warehouse (the service vehicle) will be depleted (Figure 6-32). Notice the additional product entries. When the original transfer was executed, these products did not exist in this warehouse. However, the inventory counts are dropped down.

Figure 6-32. *Inventory at the source warehouse gets reduced after the rollback*

This section looked at some of the out-of-the-box validations to support some exceptions common to any field operation business conducting inventory management. We also looked at the possibility of extending the functionality with customizations using Power Automate. This is not where the validation configuration stops. The capabilities can be further extended using plug-ins.

Processing Purchase Orders

For the TyreWorx solution, processing purchase orders is essential in the following two scenarios:

1. When ordering tires from the vendors for the distribution centers

2. When the technician does not have the tires to complete the work order, in which case they can raise the purchase order to buy tires from a third-party vendor

For both these scenarios, TyreWorx deals with specific vendors, which are set up as accounts in the system. The first scenario is done by the warehouse manager. The second scenario occurs in the field. The following sections discuss these scenarios in detail.

Processing Purchases for the Company

TyreWorx warehouse managers keep track of the warehouse's inventory. Each distribution center has a scheduled cycle of purchasing tires from their overseas vendors. Every three months, the main distribution centers receives a shipment. The warehouse manager determines the number and types of tires required, and creates the purchase order. This functionality is available under the Inventory section of Field Service. Click the **+New** button to create a new purchase order (Figure 6-33). You can also create purchase orders through the business process flow.

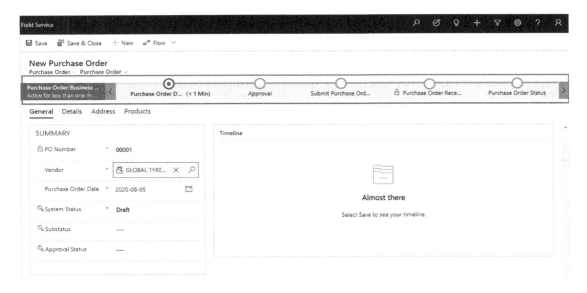

Figure 6-33. *New Purchase Order form*

In the Summary section under the General tab, the user must select the vendor. Notice that the System Status field is set to Draft. The warehouse manager will set the destination warehouse from the Details tab (Figure 6-31). This will indicate where the items in the purchase order will be shipped to.

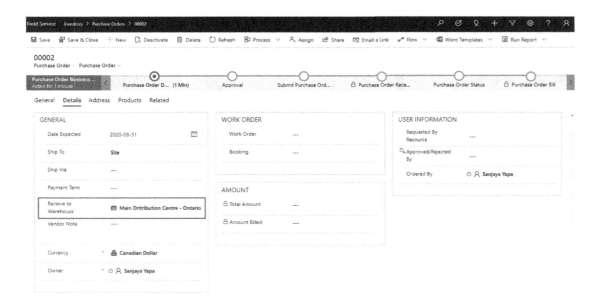

Figure 6-34. *The Details tab of the Purchase Order form*

Some of the fields on the Details tab are not required for purchase orders raised to replenish the main distribution center. The address of the warehouse will appear under the Address tab. The warehouse manager will enter the products for the next shipment under the Products tab. When adding the new purchase order product, the manage selects the product and specifies the required quantity (Figure 6-35). When the manager specifies the unit price, the total cost is calculated automatically and, by default, the Item Status field is set to Pending.

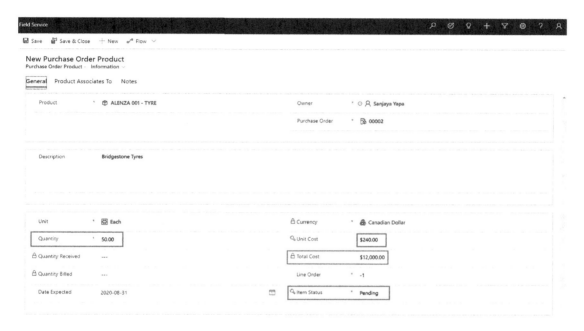

Figure 6-35. *Adding new purchase order products to the purchase order*

As shown in Figure 6-36, the purchase order now includes a few products.

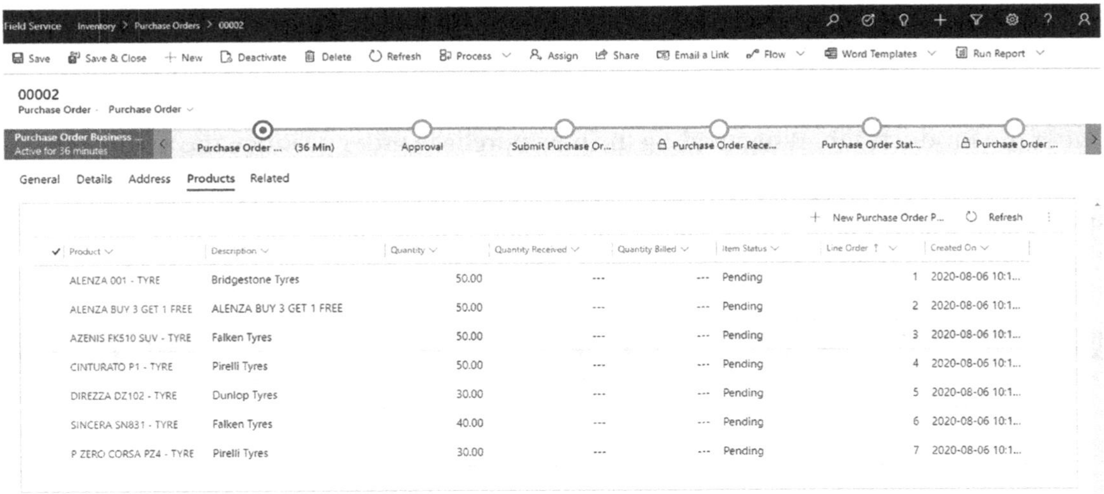

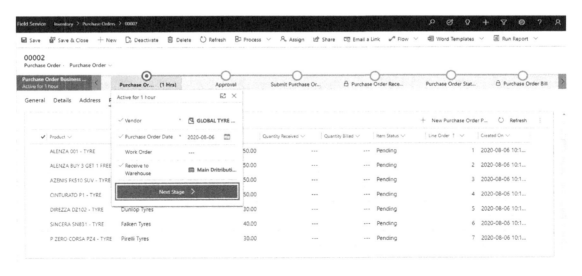

Figure 6-36. *List of purchase order products added to the purchase order*

After adding the products, the manager clicks Next Stage from the business process flow to navigate to the next step (Figure 6-37).

Figure 6-37. *Moving to the next stage after adding products*

The second stage is where the purchase order gets approved or rejected (Figure 6-38). Once the purchase order has been approved, the flow will move to the next stage.

Figure 6-38. *The purchase order approval stage*

The next step is to submit the purchase order, which indicates the purchase order is ready for the vendor (Figure 6-39). At this point, the vendor can be notified regarding the purchase order. In most situations, an email is sent to the vendor with the details of the purchase order. Sometimes this process needs to be integrated with external systems, such as external organizations that handle shipments.

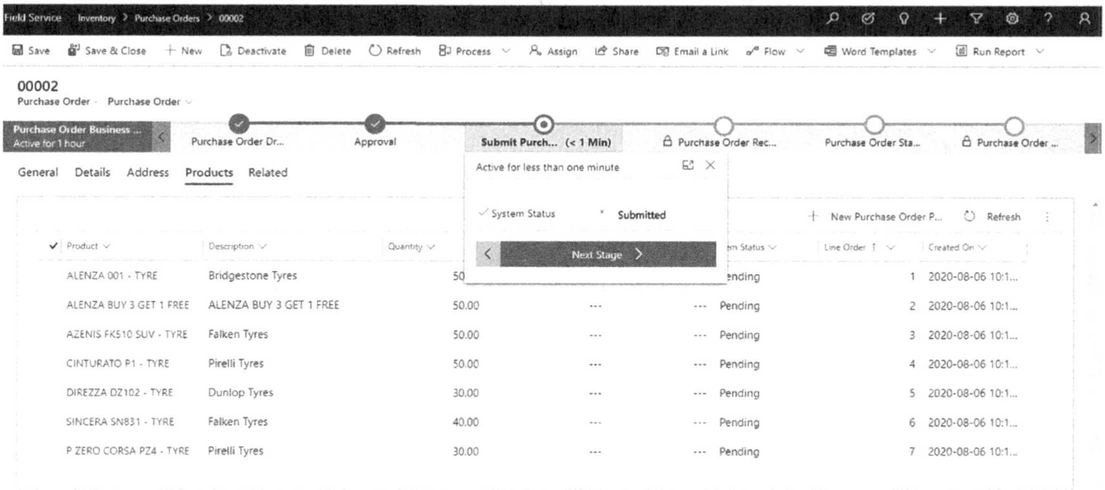

Figure 6-39. *Purchase order submitted for processing*

As part of receiving the products, a purchase order receipt must be created for the purchase order (Figure 6-40). This is used to accept the products defined in the purchase order at the warehouse.

Figure 6-40. *Purchase order receipt creation stage*

At the base of the pop-up, a Create New option is available to create the purchase Order Receipt form (Figure 6-41). The key information required on this form is the person responsible for accepting the shipment at the warehouse.

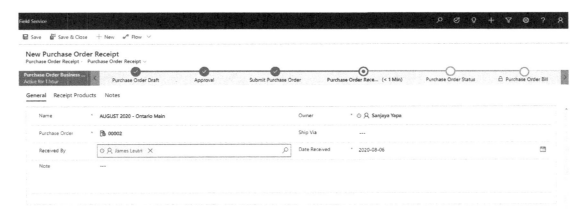

Figure 6-41. *New Purchase Order Receipt form*

When the products arrive at the warehouse, they should be entered under the Receipt Products tab. As shown in Figure 6-42, add new receipt products to the receipt by checking the physical items received. The Purchase Order Product lookup field will list the products associated with the purchase order. When the product is selected, the rest of the information will be auto-populated.

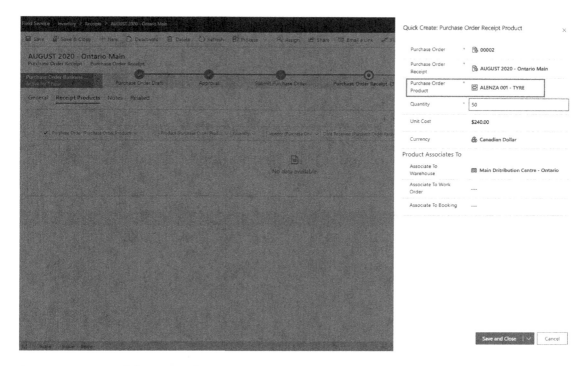

Figure 6-42. *Adding purchase order receipt products to the receipt*

All the products should be added to the receipt in order for the status of the purchase order to be changed to received. As shown in Figure 6-43, the Bill Date column is still blank. This will be filled when the bill is created. (Please refer to Chapter 2 for more details about purchase order bills.)

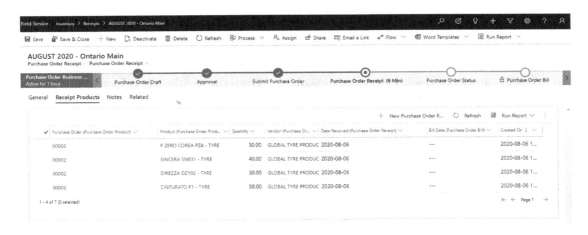

Figure 6-43. *Listing receipt products associated with the receipt*

On the next stage of the process flow, click **Next Stage** to accept the Received By and Date Received entries (Figure 6-44).

Figure 6-44. *Updated purchase order product's Received By and Date Received entries*

As shown in Figure 6-45, the products have been received at the warehouse and accepted.

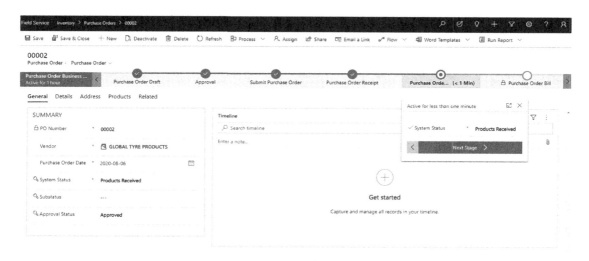

Figure 6-45. *The System Status field updated to Product Received*

The next step is to create the purchase order bill (Figure 6-46). Click the **+Create** button to open the new form.

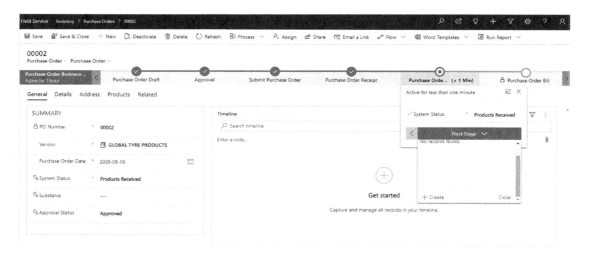

Figure 6-46. *Creating the purchase order bill after receiving the products*

Preparing the bill is the last step of this process. As shown in Figure 6-47, all prices will be auto-calculated based on the prices entered in the Purchase Order Product.

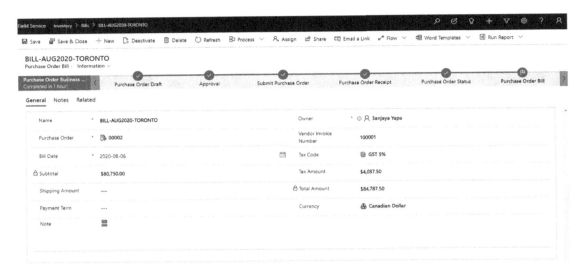

Figure 6-47. *Purchase order bill*

Notice that the System Status field of the Purchase Order record is changed to Billed (Figure 6-48).

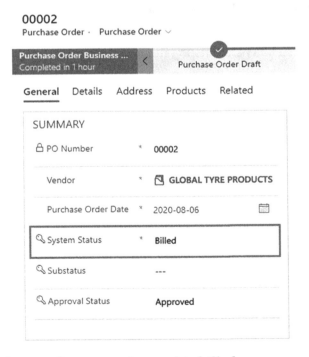

Figure 6-48. *Purchase order status changed to billed*

Processing Purchases in the Field

TyreWorx field technicians can require purchase orders because in some scenarios when they attend to a job, the required tire is not available in the service vehicle stock. So, the technician creates a purchase order. This will trigger an email notification to the manager, who either approves or rejects the purchase order. If the purchase order is approved, the technician can visit the vendor and buy the items required for completing the job. Let's see this process in action.

Out of the box, the purchase order process is not available in the Field Service Mobile. You must ensure that all the required entities are available for the Field Service Mobile. The following entities are required to process purchases in the field: purchase order, purchase order product, purchase order receipt, and purchase order receipt product. Also, the user should be assigned with Field Service - Inventory Purchase security role.

1. The user creates the purchase order from the Field Service Mobile. Notice that the System Status at this point is Draft (Figure 6-49).

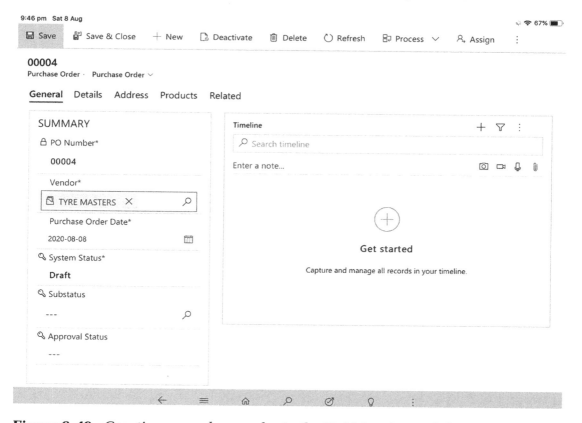

Figure 6-49. *Creating a purchase order in the Field Service Mobile*

2. On the Details tab of the Purchase Order record, the user selects the service vehicle as the warehouse, and notices that the Work Order and Booking fields are selected, as required to complete a work order (Figure 6-50).

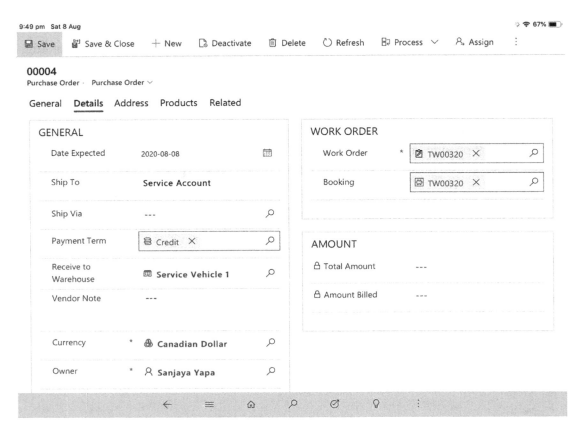

Figure 6-50. *Purchase Order Details tab in the Field Service Mobile*

3. Under the Products tab, the user can enter the required product (Figure 6-51).

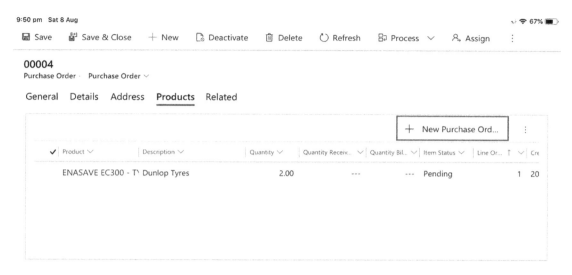

Figure 6-51. *Adding the required products to the purchase order in the Field Service Mobile*

4. After adding the product, the user changes the System Status field of the purchase order to Submitted (Figure 6-52). As per the TyreWorx requirements, the system should generate the notification email to the warehouse manager.

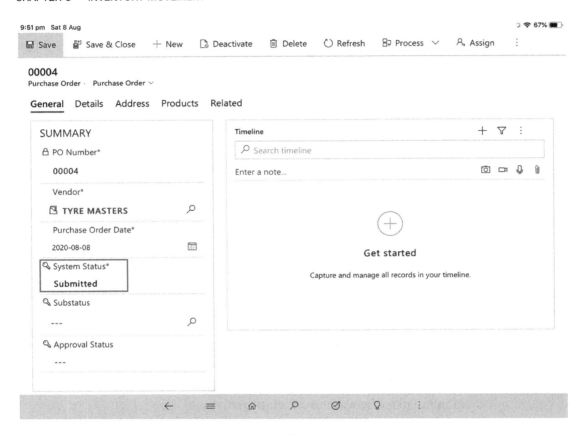

Figure 6-52. *Purchase order submitted for approval*

5. Now the warehouse manager can see the purchase order appearing on the web application at his desktop. The manager opens the record and moves down the stages of the business process flow. The required information is already populated (Figure 6-53).

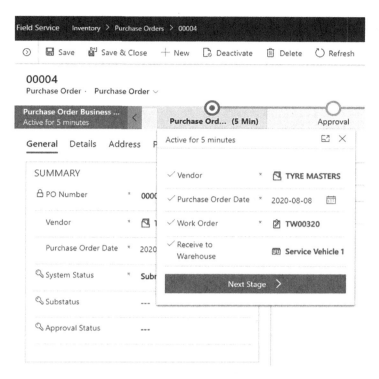

Figure 6-53. *Purchase order ready for approval*

6. The warehouse manager approves the purchase order request
    (Figure 6-54).

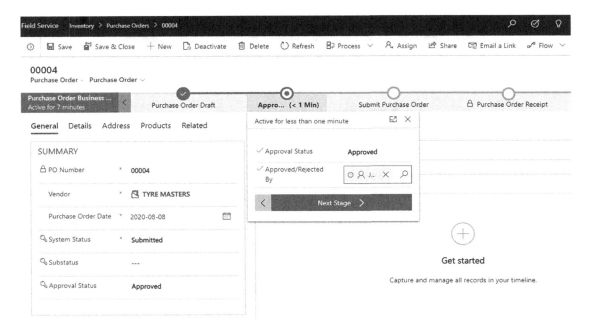

Figure 6-54. *Purchase order approved*

7. The warehouse manager creates the receipt manually. Or, it can
be automated via a Power Automate flow when the purchase
order is approved. Now the field technician can see that the
purchase order has been approved and can go to the vendor to
collect the tires to complete the job (Figure 6-55).

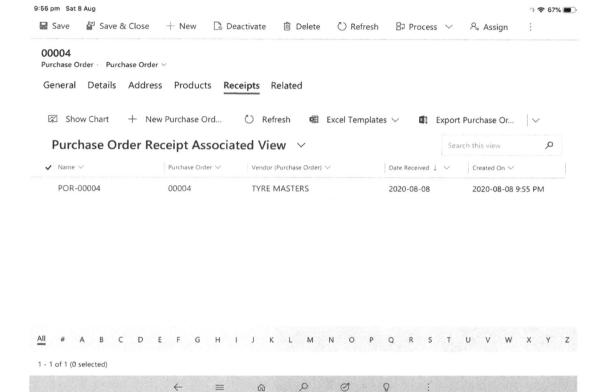

Figure 6-55. *Purchase order receipt in the Field Service Mobile*

8. The field technician opens the receipt. Under the Purchase Order Receipt Products, the field technician can add the product after accepting it at the vendor site. Notice that the product lookup will filter the item(s) based on the product requirement in the purchase order (Figure 6-56).

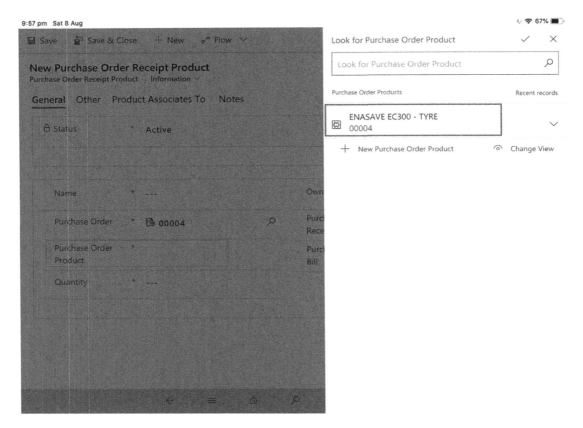

Figure 6-56. *Accepting products at the vendor*

9. Now the product is added to the receipt by the field technician. The receipt product will contain the quantity requested (Figure 6-57).

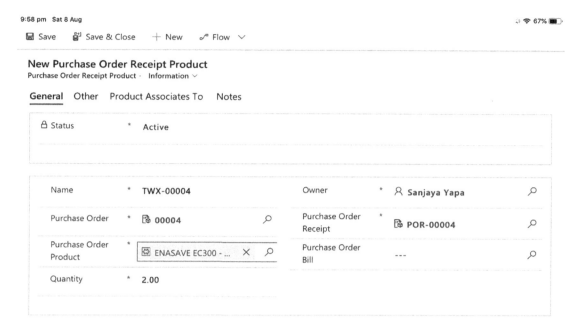

Figure 6-57. *New purchase order receipt product in the Field Service Mobile*

> 10.   The pricing details appear under the Other tab (Figure 6-58).

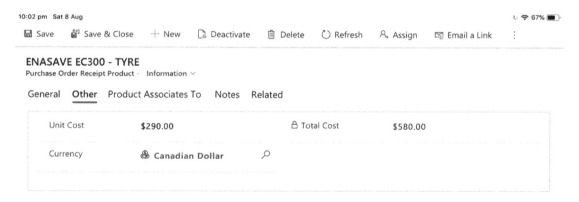

Figure 6-58. *Pricing details of purchase order receipt product*

> 11.   All the details of the work order and the booking are located under
>   the Product Associates To tab (Figure 6-59). This association will
>   ensure that the product is purchased to complete the work order.

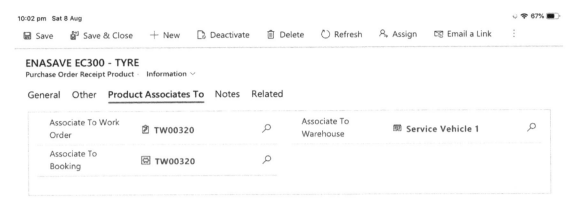

Figure 6-59. *Work order and booking details in the Purchase Order Receipt Product form*

> 12. Once the product is received, the System Status field will change to Product Received (Figure 6-60).

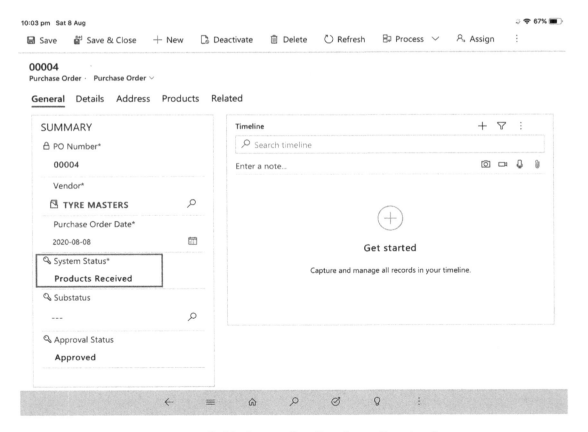

Figure 6-60. *System Status field changed to Products Received*

As explained in the previous section, the final stage of the purchase order is to prepare the bill for the vendor. In this transaction, the warehouse manager will generate the bill when the vendor emails the invoice to TyreWorx. The takeaway from this section is that both the desktop app and the Field Service Mobile can be used to process purchase orders. Field Service has the flexibility to support various business scenarios and can be extended.

The Return Merchandise Authorization Process

As explained in Chapter 2, the RMA feature is used for managing the items returned. TyreWorx uses this feature for their wholesale business. Sometimes the items sold by TyreWorx have damages; other times, some tires are not sold at all. When the sales rep visits the wholesale customer, an RMA process is initiated to handle returns. The RMA process should be enabled for the Field Service Mobile, as it is not enabled in the out-of-the-box application.

1. After inspecting the items to be returned, the sales rep will create an RMA record. Almost all the fields on this record are self-explanatory. The Requested By Contact field will be the contact person of the wholesale customer, as specified in the Service Account field (Figure 6-61).

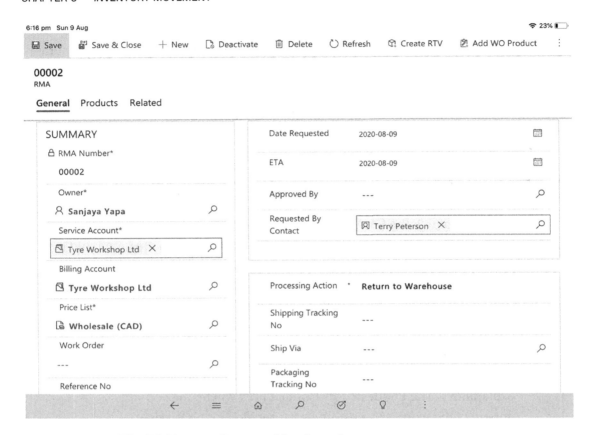

Figure 6-61. *The RMA record created by the sales rep*

2.   The sales rep creates the returning products under the Products
     tab. The processing action will define where the items will be
     returned. For this example, it will be the main warehouse of the
     province (Figure 6-62).

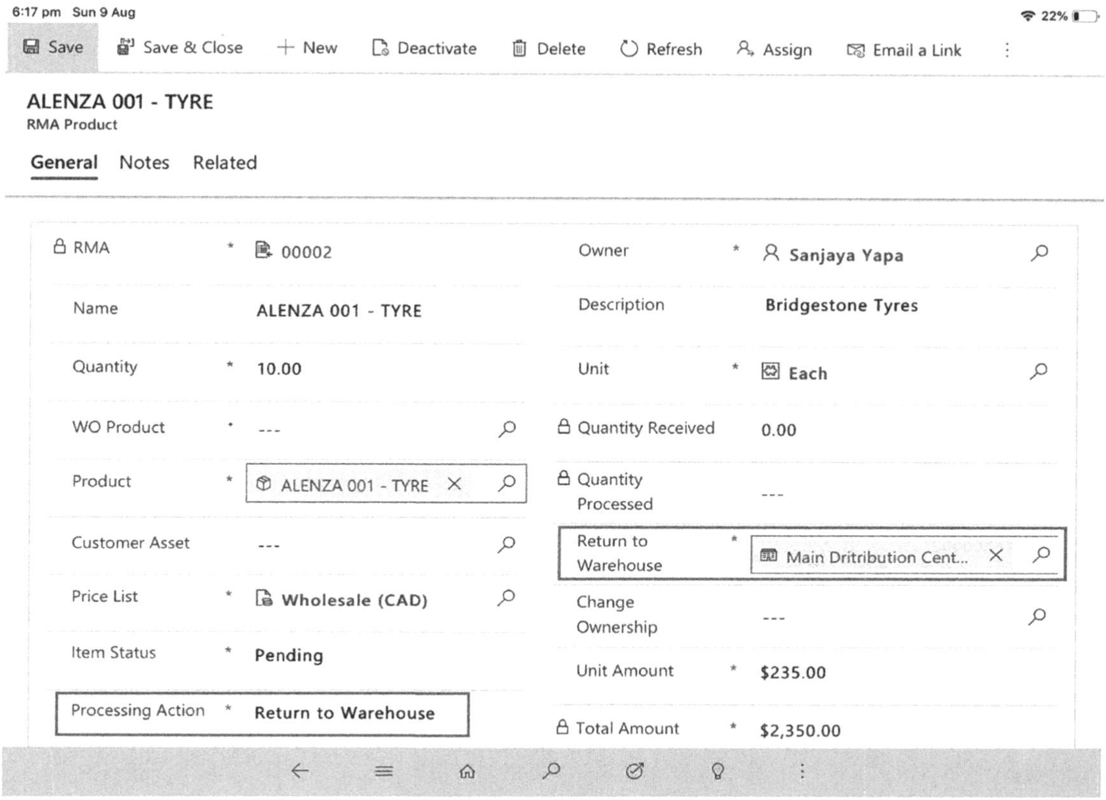

Figure 6-62. *RMA Product record to track the items returned*

3. As shown in Figure 6-63, the items are added to the RMA record. As per the business process of TyreWorx, at this point, the sales rep will collect the goods from the customer.

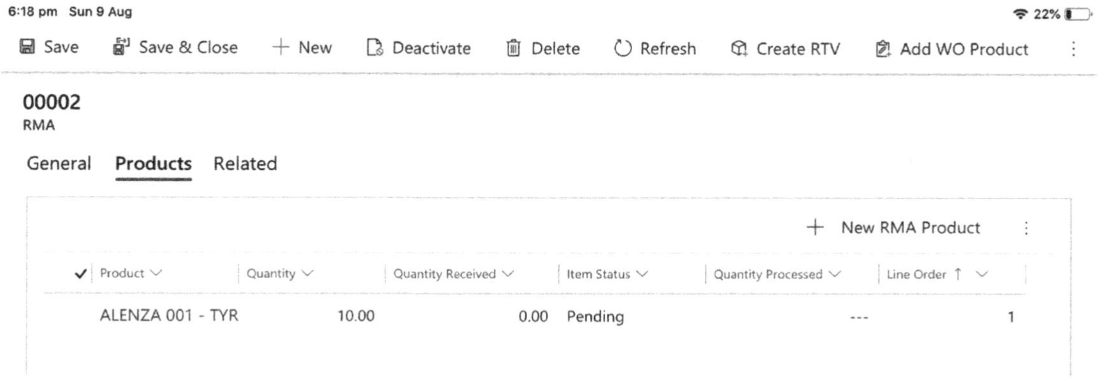

Figure 6-63. *RMA Products sub-grid*

4. The next step is to create the RMA Receipt record by the sales rep,
    which the warehouse manager will use to accept the returning
    products at the warehouse (Figure 6-64).

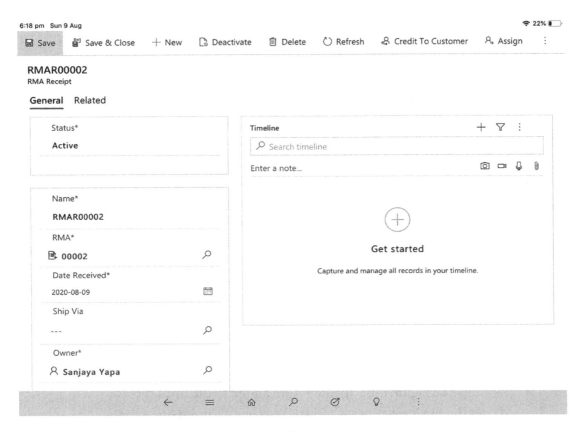

Figure 6-64. *RMA Receipt record created*

5. When the sales rep comes back to the warehouse, the
    warehouse manager will accept the RMA via the RMA Receipt
    record. The warehouse manager can see the receipt in the
    system (Figure 6-65).

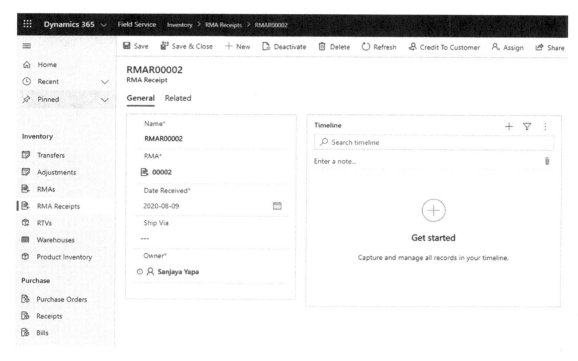

Figure 6-65. *RMA Receipt record in the web application*

6. The warehouse manager can inspect the items returned and add the RMA Receipt Product record to the RMA receipt (Figure 6-66). When the manager selects the RMA Product lookup field, it will filter the products attached to the RMA record. This task indicates the product is received.

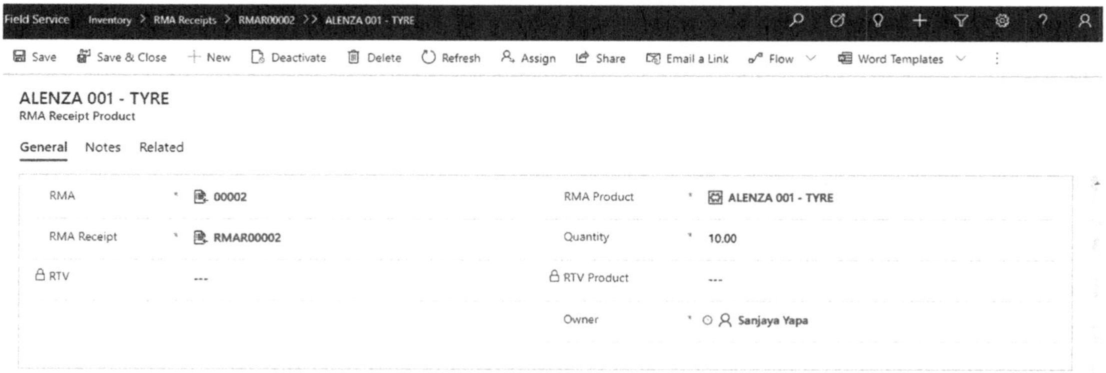

Figure 6-66. *RMA Receipt Product record created for the RMA receipt*

7. Once the RMA Receipt Product is added, you can see the System Status of the RMA record is changed to Products Received (Figure 6-67).

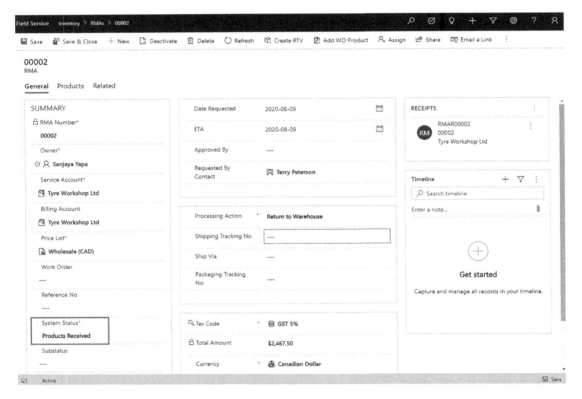

Figure 6-67. *System Status changed to Product Received*

The next step is to create the RTV. The items received at the warehouse should be returned to the vendor so that they can recycle the tires.

The Return to Vendor Process

As explained in Chapter 2, RTV is the process to return the items to the vendor. The TyreWorx warehouse manager performs this process. TyreWorx main warehouses occasionally receive RVMs. Once a bulk of return items is available, the warehouse manager will create an RTV record to ship the items back to the vendor.

Note   The RTV can be initiated from the RMA as well. For this example, however, TyreWorx collects a bulk of return items and sends them back quarterly as one shipment.

1. The warehouse manager creates the RTV record and by default the System Status field is set to Draft (Figure 6-68). The Originating RMA field can be linked if this RTV is created via an RMA.

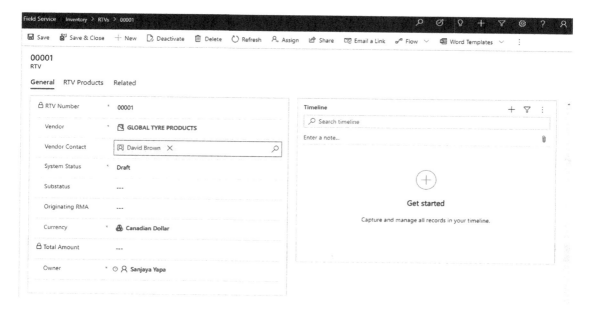

Figure 6-68. *RTV Record created by the warehouse manager*

2. The products to be returned to the vender will be added under the RTV Products tab (Figure 6-69). As you can see, all these fields are self-explanatory. The Work Order field and the Work Order Products field will be filled if the item is related to a specific work order. In this example, it is a bulk return.

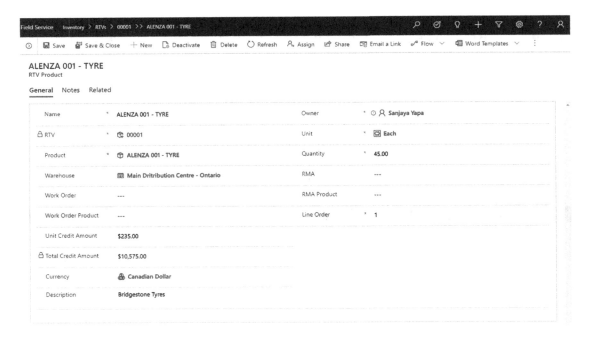

Figure 6-69. *RTV Product record*

3. The list of RTV products appears under RTV Products tab of the RTV record (Figure 6-70).

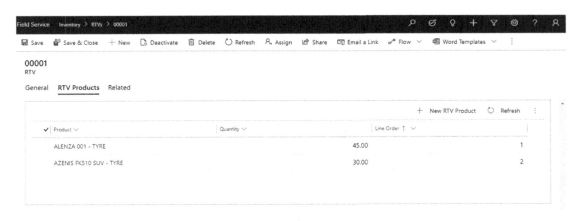

Figure 6-70. *List of RTV products*

4. Finally, the RTV products are shipped back to the vendor, so the
    System Status field can be changed to Shipped (Figure 6-71). Note
    that the requirements might require additional customizations.

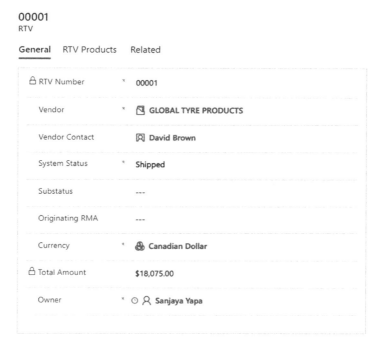

00001
RTV

General   RTV Products   Related

🔒 RTV Number	ˣ	00001
Vendor	ˣ	🔲 GLOBAL TYRE PRODUCTS
Vendor Contact		🔲 David Brown
System Status	ˣ	Shipped
Substatus		---
Originating RMA		---
Currency	ˣ	🪙 Canadian Dollar
🔒 Total Amount		$18,075.00
Owner	ˣ	⊙ 👤 Sanjaya Yapa

***Figure 6-71.** System Status field changed to Shipped*

Summary

This chapter explored inventory movements by discussing inventory transfers, purchase
order processing, and the RMA (return merchandise authorization) and RTV (return to
vendor) processes. The scenarios described used both the web application and the Field
Service Mobile. We also explored the flexibility of these processes for further extensions
with customizations. The next chapter looks at how to complete a work order in both
retail and wholesale scenarios.

CHAPTER 7

Processing Work Orders

The first six chapters of this book discussed creating and preparing the required components for performing business-as-usual (BAU) functions. This final chapter looks at the execution part of these components for completing BAU functions. A work order is created and assigned to the field staff, who then process and complete it. This chapter covers the steps involved in processing a work order. To demonstrate this in action, a work order for both retail and wholesale will be executed, because there are slight differences worth noticing.

Processing Retail Work Orders

Chapter 3 examined creating a work order, including the prerequisites and the scheduling aspects. Figure 7-1 shows several work orders assigned to resources.

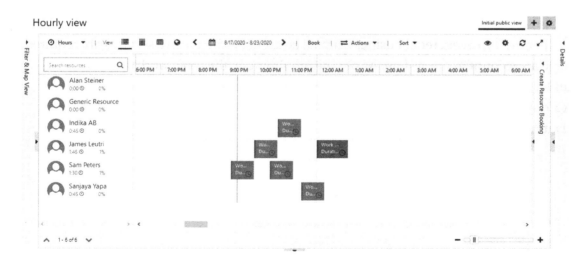

Figure 7-1. *Schedule board with work orders assigned to resources*

S. Yapa and I. Abayarathne, *Dynamics 365 Field Service*, https://doi.org/10.1007/978-1-4842-6408-9_7

When the field technician logs in on the Field Service Mobile, they can see the work assigned to them (Figure 7-2).

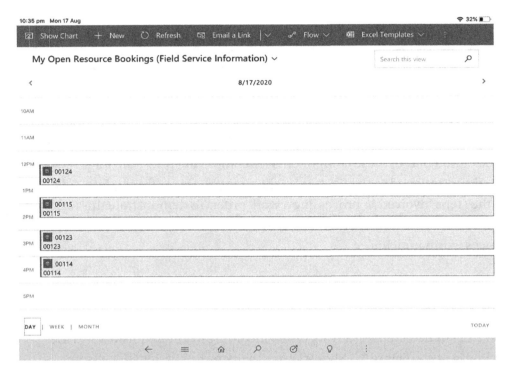

Figure 7-2. *Work orders assigned to the field technician*

For the TyreWorx retail business, not all customers who receive services are required to be an account in the system. As per the requirement, the retail work will be done under TyreWorx retail account. Therefore, both the Service Account and the Billing Account fields of the Bookable Resource Booking record will be set as TyreWorx Retail (Figure 7-3).

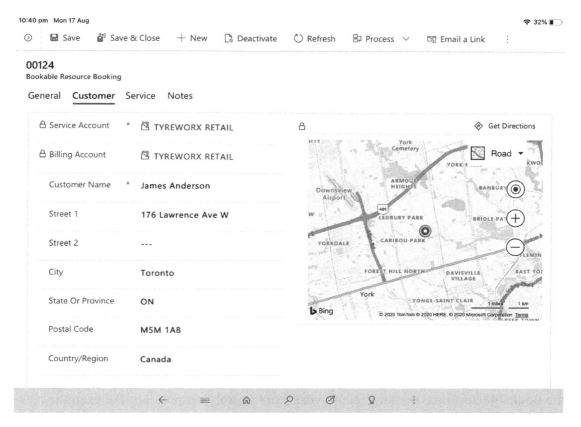

Figure 7-3. *Bookable Resource Booking record showing customer details and service billing accounts*

As shown in Figure 7-3, the customer details are stored under the Customer tab of the Work Order.

Some customers are actual businesses, such as taxi services, currier services, car dealerships, etc. For the work orders created for these customers, the Service Account and Billing Account fields of the Bookable Resource Booking record are set to the specific account. The Customer Type field of the Work Order record helps to segregate these transactions (Figure 7-4).

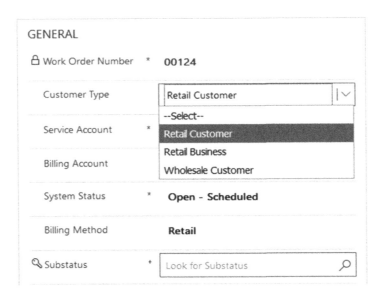

Figure 7-4. *Customer Type field on the Work Order record*

Even though the job is created as a work order, on the Field Service Mobile, the field technician will be using the Bookable Resource Booking record to process the work order. Multiple records are created for work orders, some of which are exposed on the Bookable Resource Booking record via Form Control Components. For example, the Services tab has a reference to the work order (Figure 7-5). A quick view form can also be used, although it has limitations and is not ideal—for example, the form is not editable. For more information, please refer to https://docs.microsoft.com/en-us/ dynamics365/customerengagement/on-premises/customize/quick-view-control- properties-legacy.

Note   If you are using the current Power Apps form designer, then you have to switch to the classic form editor to edit this component, until the Power Apps Form Designer supports the editing of Power Apps custom components.

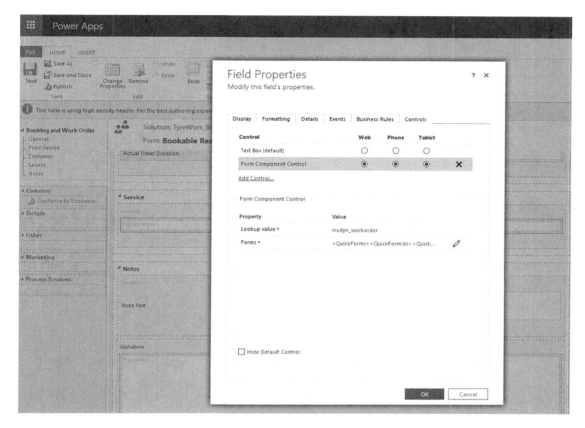

Figure 7-5. *The Form Component Control in the classic form editor*

As you can see the from Figure 7-6 the details of the Work Order is exposed on the Bookable Resource Booking record.

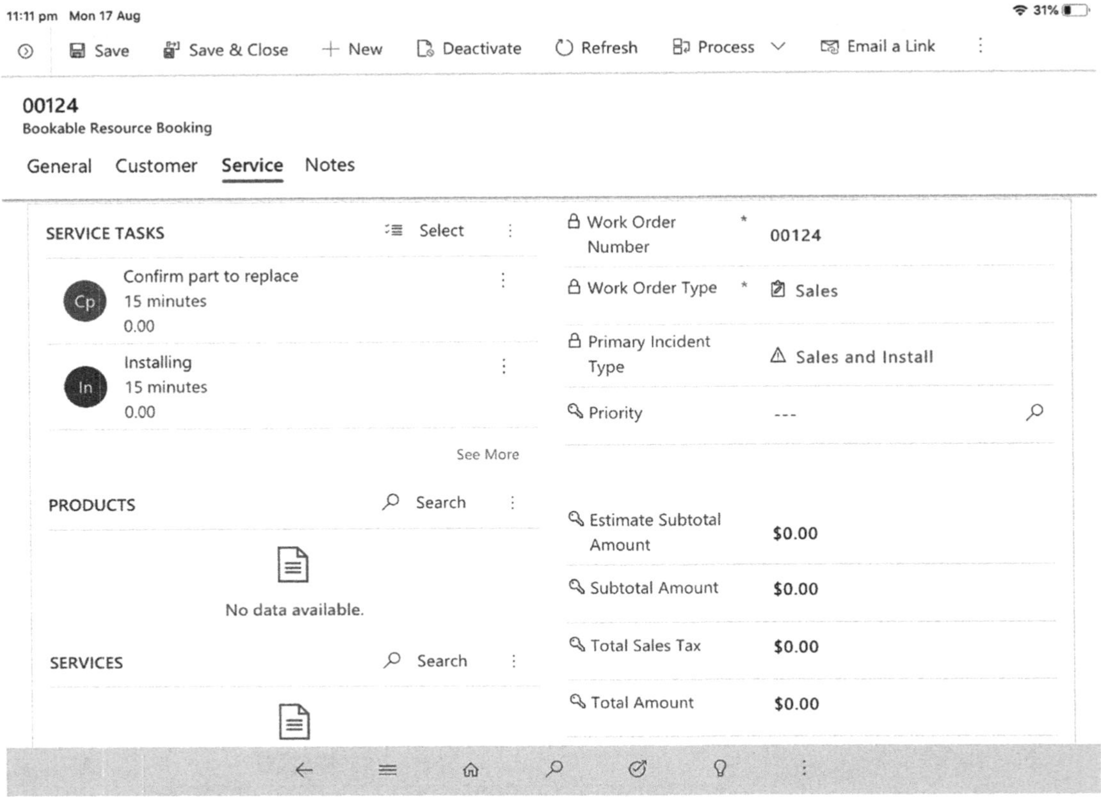

11:11 pm Mon 17 Aug

⊙ 🖫 Save   🖫 Save & Close   ＋ New   🗋 Deactivate   ⟳ Refresh   🗐 Process ∨   🖾 Email a Link   ⋮

00124
Bookable Resource Booking

General   Customer   **Service**   Notes

| SERVICE TASKS | ≔ Select | ⋮ | 🔒 Work Order Number | * | 00124 |

Cp Confirm part to replace
15 minutes
0.00   ⋮

🔒 Work Order Type   *   🗐 Sales

In Installing
15 minutes
0.00   ⋮

🔒 Primary Incident Type   ⚠ Sales and Install

See More

🔗 Priority   ---   🔍

PRODUCTS   🔍 Search   ⋮

📄

No data available.

🔗 Estimate Subtotal Amount $0.00

🔗 Subtotal Amount $0.00

🔗 Total Sales Tax $0.00

SERVICES   🔍 Search   ⋮

🔗 Total Amount $0.00

📄

←   ≡   ⌂   🔍   ⊘   ♀   ⋮

Figure 7-6. *Service tab of the Bookable Resource Booking record showing work order details*

Now the work order is ready and assigned to the field staff member. If the field staff member doesn't know how to get to the location, they can click the Get Directions button above the Map view, which will open the device's native Maps app and provide the directions (Figure 7-7).

00124
Bookable Resource Booking

General   **Customer**   Service   Notes

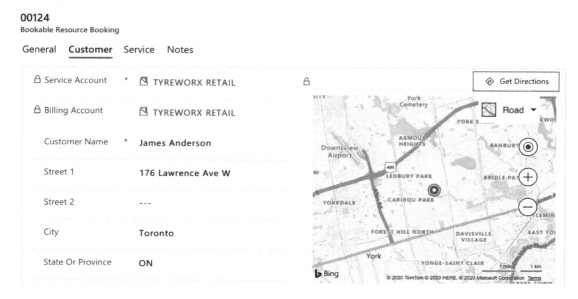

🔒 Service Account	* 🔳 TYREWORX RETAIL
🔒 Billing Account	🔳 TYREWORX RETAIL
Customer Name	* James Anderson
Street 1	176 Lawrence Ave W
Street 2	---
City	Toronto
State Or Province	ON

Figure 7-7.   Map view of the location of the incident

Adding Work Order Products

The next step is to add the work order products to the work order. To do this, the technician should navigate to the Services tab and click the New Work Order Product option from the Products sub-grid (Figure 7-8).

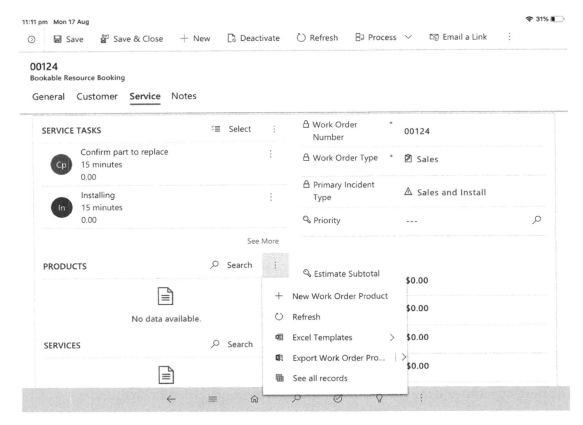

Figure 7-8. *Adding a new work order product to the work order*

The technician then clicks the Products lookup and searches for the product. Once the product is selected, all the required fields get populated automatically (Figure 7-9). You can add multiple products to the work order, but for this TyreWorx scenario, we will add one product line item. If you want to add multiple items from the same product, you can define them in the Quantity field.

As shown in Figure 7-9, the warehouse is selected automatically. This is the warehouse assigned to the bookable resource working on this work order.

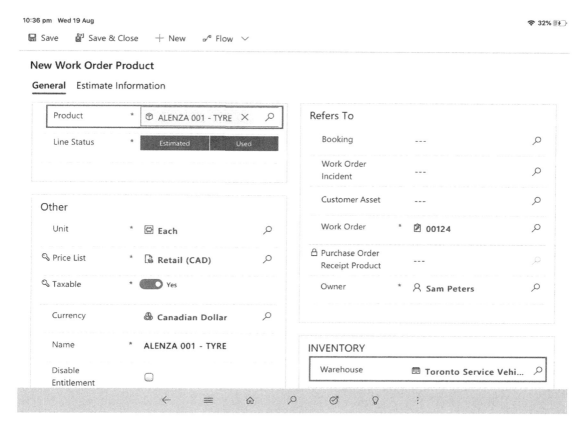

Figure 7-9. *Work order product selected with all the required information*

Note   If your business requires scanning, this is where you can enable it. Out of the box, scanning is enabled for the device camera. Although barcode scanning works on regular phones and tablets, consider an infrared barcode scanner. For example, Zebra offers a wide range of devices built specifically for Field Service applications.

On the Estimate Information tab, the user should enter the estimated quantity (Figure 7-10). When the quantity is entered, the system will calculate the estimated subtotal and the estimated total amount. You can add a discount, if required, which also will be auto-calculated.

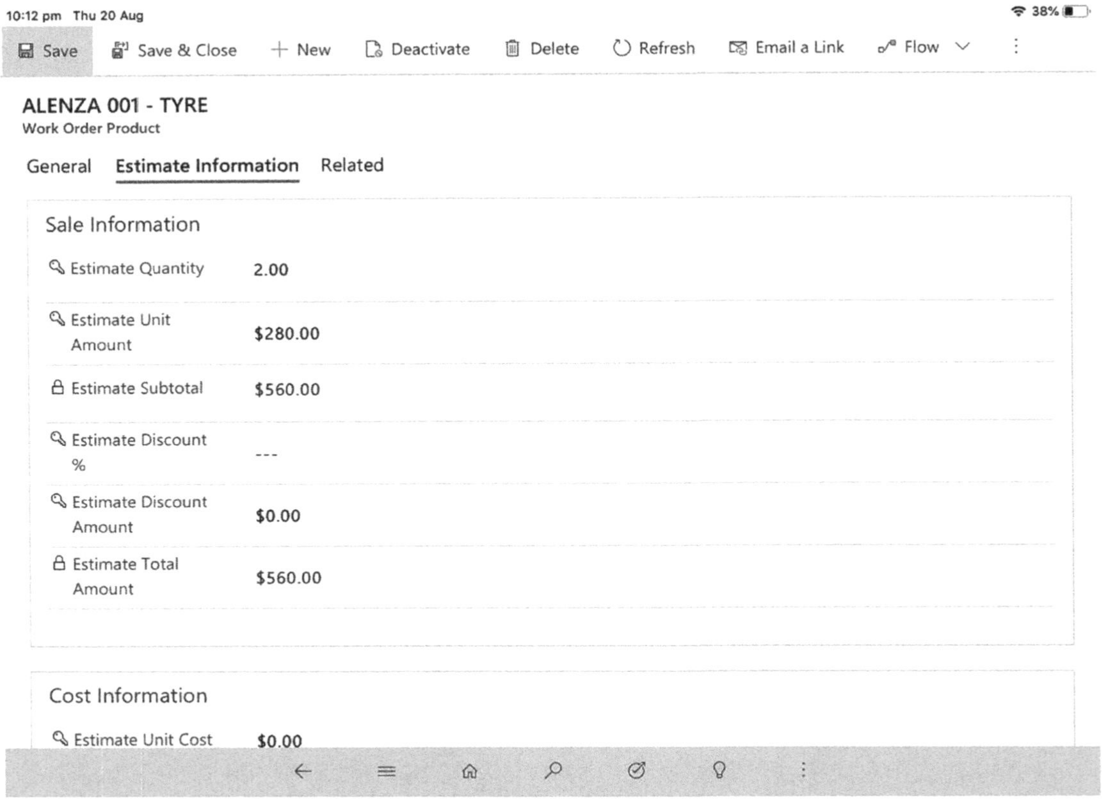

10:12 pm   Thu 20 Aug   38%

🖫 Save   📑 Save & Close   + New   ⟲ Deactivate   🗑 Delete   ⟳ Refresh   ✉ Email a Link   ⚡ Flow ⌄   ⋮

ALENZA 001 - TYRE
Work Order Product

General   **Estimate Information**   Related

Sale Information

🔍 Estimate Quantity   2.00

🔍 Estimate Unit
   Amount $280.00

🔒 Estimate Subtotal $560.00

🔍 Estimate Discount
   %   - - -

🔍 Estimate Discount
   Amount $0.00

🔒 Estimate Total
   Amount $560.00

Cost Information

🔍 Estimate Unit Cost $0.00

←   ≡   ⌂   🔍   ⊘   💡   ⋮

Figure 7-10.   Estimate Information tab

After adding the product to the work order, the user must set Line Status field to Used (Figure 7-11). The Estimated setting means at this point it is just an estimation. Once the field is set to Used, the price will be calculated and the quantity will be deducted from the warehouse.

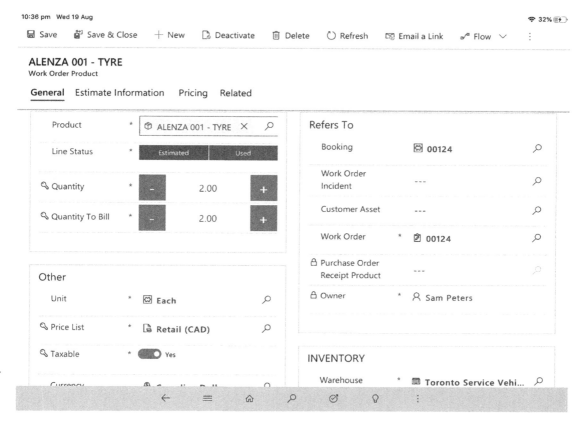

Figure 7-11. *Line Item status set to Used*

As shown in Figure 7-12, the pricing will also be calculated, based on the unit price derived from the price list and the quantity. This information is available under the Pricing tab.

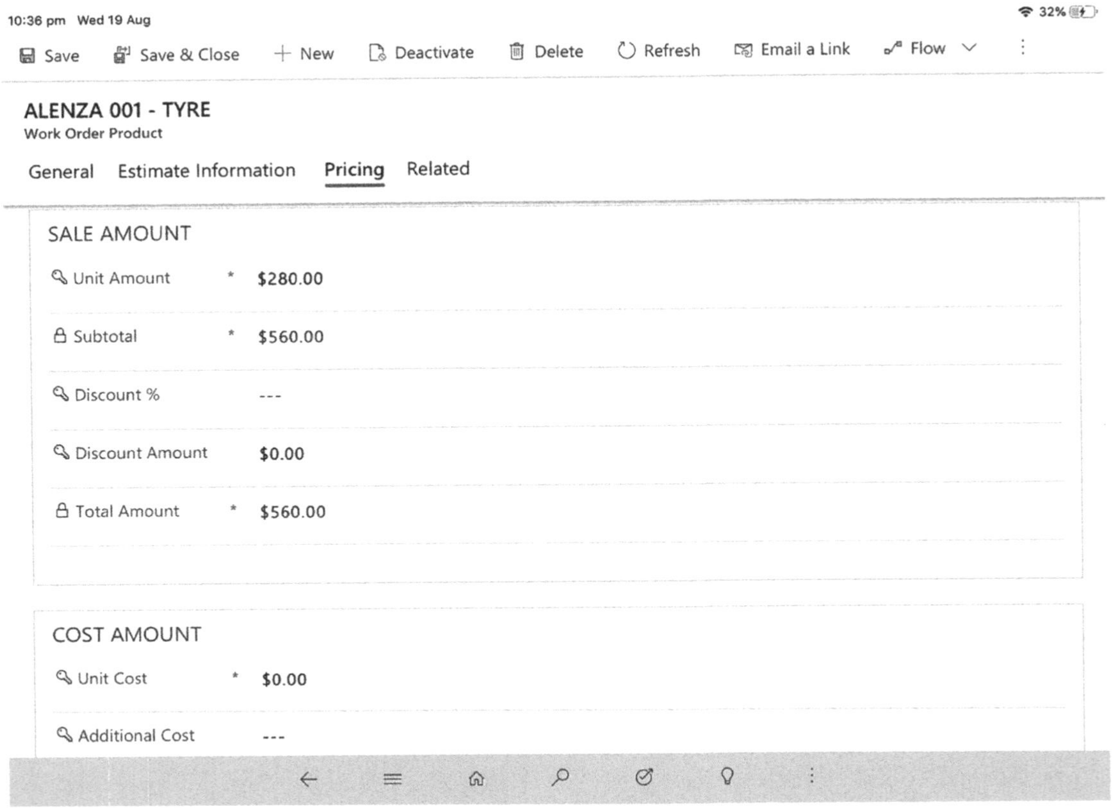

💾 Save   💷 Save & Close   + New   🗋 Deactivate   🗑 Delete   ⟳ Refresh   🖾 Email a Link   ⤭ Flow ∨   ⋮

ALENZA 001 - TYRE
Work Order Product

General   Estimate Information   **Pricing**   Related

SALE AMOUNT

🔍 Unit Amount   * $280.00

🔒 Subtotal   * $560.00

🔍 Discount %   ---

🔍 Discount Amount $0.00

🔒 Total Amount   * $560.00

COST AMOUNT

🔍 Unit Cost   * $0.00

🔍 Additional Cost   ---

←   ≡   ⌂   ◌   ⊙   ♡   ⋮

Figure 7-12. Pricing tab of Work Order Product record after the Line Status field is changed to Used

Adding Work Order Services

Let's assume that the technician is going to provide some services. Under the **Services** sub-grid, click the **New Work Order Service** option (7-13).

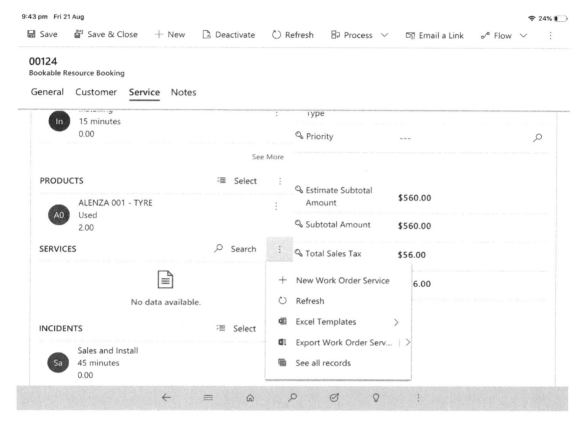

Figure 7-13. *Adding work order services*

Similar to adding a work order product, search for the particular work order service and add it to the work order. Figure 7-14 shows a time-based service added to the work order with a duration of one hour.

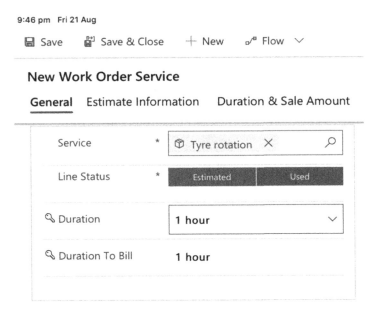

Figure 7-14. *Adding a time-based work order service to the work order*

Under the Estimate Information tab, you can see that the pricing is calculated based on the time spent on the service work (Figure 7-15).

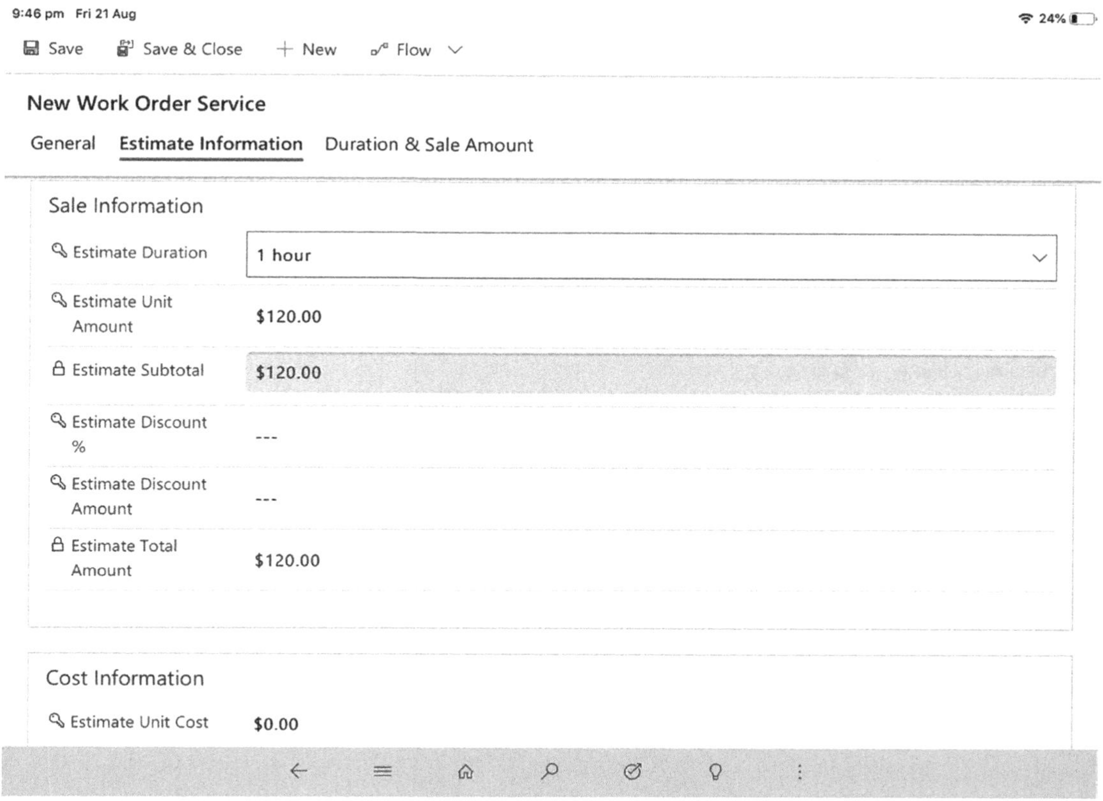

9:46 pm   Fri 21 Aug   24%

💾 Save   📑 Save & Close   + New   ₀╱ᵃ Flow ⌄

New Work Order Service

General   **Estimate Information**   Duration & Sale Amount

Sale Information

🔍 Estimate Duration	1 hour	⌄
🔍 Estimate Unit Amount	$120.00	
🔒 Estimate Subtotal	$120.00	
🔍 Estimate Discount %	---	
🔍 Estimate Discount Amount	---	
🔒 Estimate Total Amount	$120.00	

Cost Information

| 🔍 Estimate Unit Cost | $0.00 |

← ≡ ⌂ 🔍 ⊘ 💡 ⋮

Figure 7-15. *Estimated pricing information for the services provided*

If the number of hours increases, the pricing will be calculated automatically
(Figure 7-16).

271

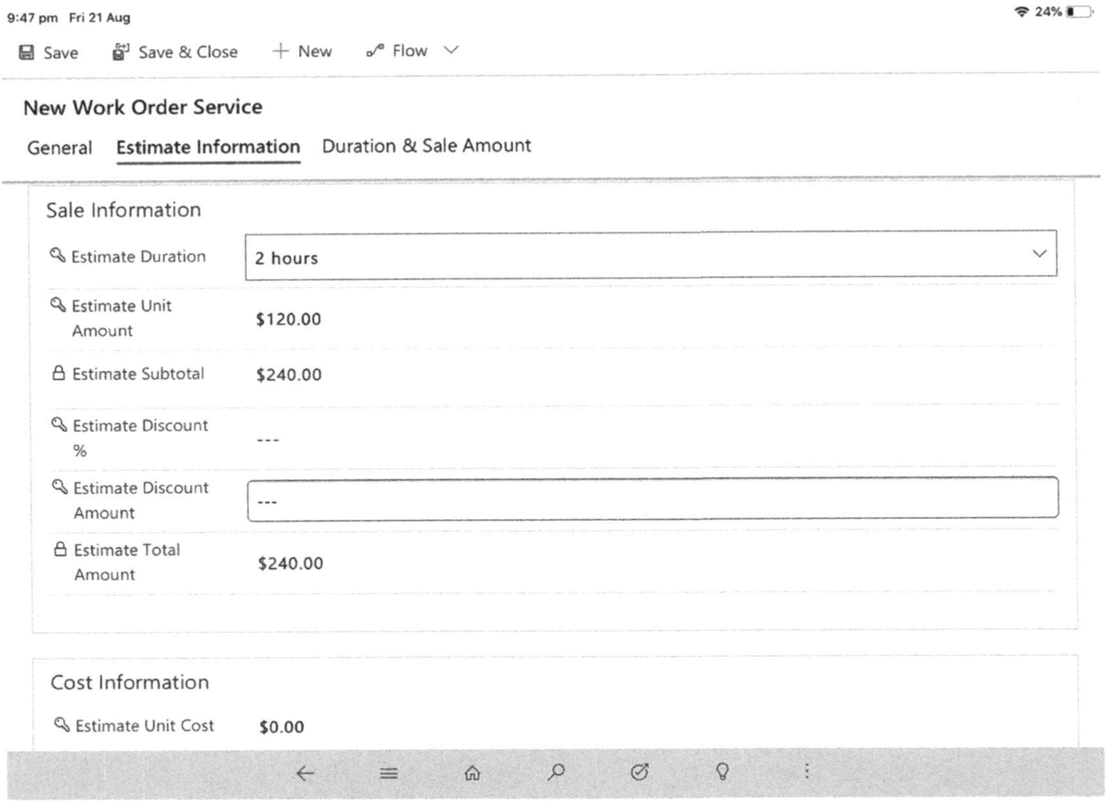

9:47 pm Fri 21 Aug   24%

💾 Save   📑 Save & Close   + New   ⚙ Flow ⌄

New Work Order Service

General   **Estimate Information**   Duration & Sale Amount

Sale Information

🔑 Estimate Duration   2 hours   ⌄

🔑 Estimate Unit $120.00
   Amount

🔒 Estimate Subtotal $240.00

🔑 Estimate Discount
   %   ---

🔑 Estimate Discount
   Amount   ---

🔒 Estimate Total
   Amount $240.00

Cost Information

🔑 Estimate Unit Cost $0.00

← ≡ ⌂ 🔍 ⊘ 💡 ⋮

Figure 7-16. *Automatic price calculation for the estimated duration*

Next, set the **Line Status** field to **Used** (Figure 7-17). This indicates that the service work is completed and finalized. The total amount for the work order service is located under the **Duration & Sale Amount** tab. You can also add multiple work order services for the same work order.

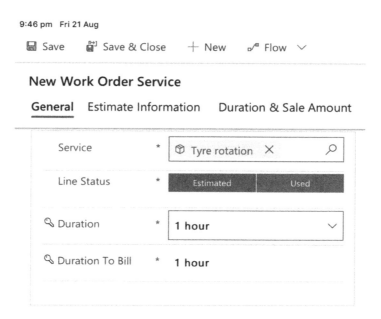

Figure 7-17. *Setting the work order service status to Used*

On the Bookable Resource Booking record, both the product and the service are added to the work order. Also, the full total amount is calculated, including sales tax (Figure 7-18).

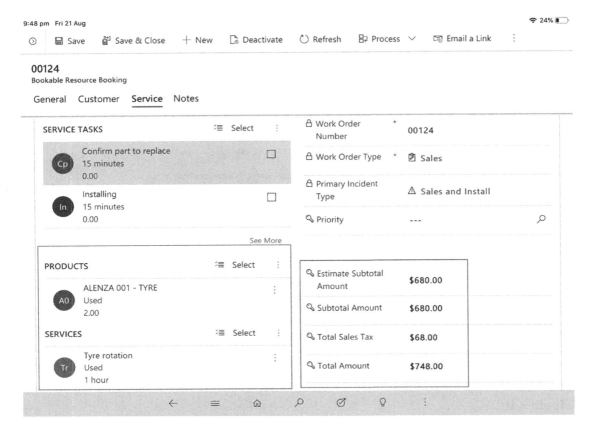

Figure 7-18. *The final total amount after adding the work order product and work order service*

Completing the Service Tasks

Now that the product(s) and service(s) are added, the next step is to complete the service tasks. Service tasks are the checklist items that every field technician should complete. As shown in Figure 7-19, multiple service tasks can be selected.

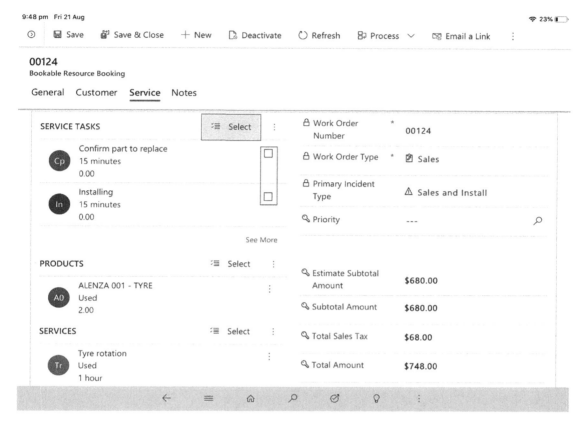

Figure 7-19. *The list of service tasks for the work order*

The field technician can see the entire list of service tasks associated with the work order by clicking the dots next to the Select option. Notice the % Complete column, which indicates the current status (Figure 7-20).

Figure 7-20. *All service tasks associated with the work order, ready for completion*

The user can select them all and click Mark Complete. The user will be prompted with the message shown in Figure 7-21.

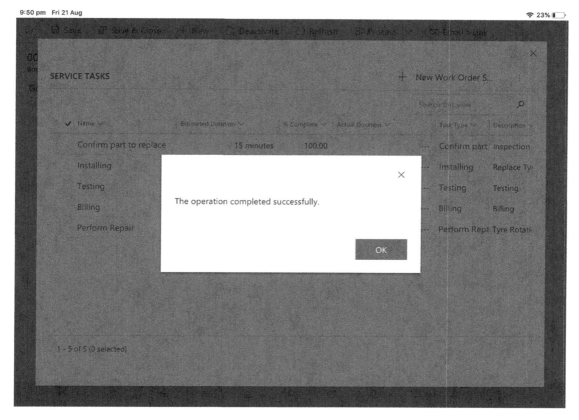

Figure 7-21. *All service tasks completed successfully*

On the individual service task, the Progress is set to 100% (Figure 7-22). The user can open each task and update them one by one.

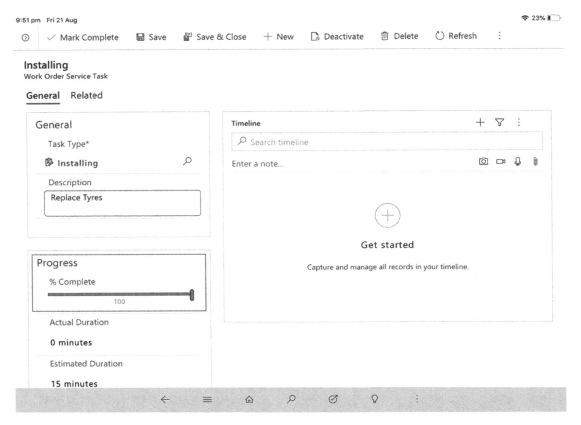

Figure 7-22. Service task progress

The field technician can add comments about the task in the Timeline field.

Completing the Work Order

The last step for the field technician is to complete the Bookable Resource Booking record. The final input required from the customer is their signature, which can be captured under the Notes tab (Figure 7-23).

Note   Different businesses require unique validations to complete work orders. These validations can be implemented using business rules, JavaScript, or plug-ins.

Figure 7-23. *Capturing the customer's signature*

Open the **General** tab to complete the work order. Click the **Booking Status** field and select the **Completed** option, as shown in Figure 7-24.

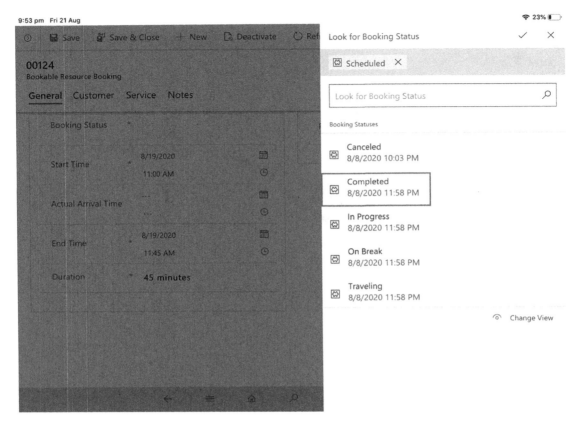

Figure 7-24. Completing the Bookable Resource Booking record to complete the work order

TyreWorx has a business rule to show the booking substatus, which is a reporting requirement for the business. That is, management wants to know the number of tire sales for a given period. So, the technician will set the appropriate Booking Sub Status field in the Bookable Resource Booking record (Figure 7-25).

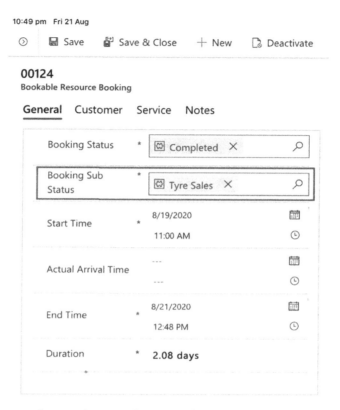

Figure 7-25. *Setting the Booking Sub Status field to complete the work order*

Because the business rule (Figure 7-26) set the field as a mandatory field, if it is not filled, the booking cannot be completed. As per the rule, the field will be visible only when the Booking Status is set Completed. You can find more details about business rules at `https://docs.microsoft.com/en-us/dynamics365/customerengagement/on-premises/customize/create-business-rules-recommendations-apply-logic-form`.

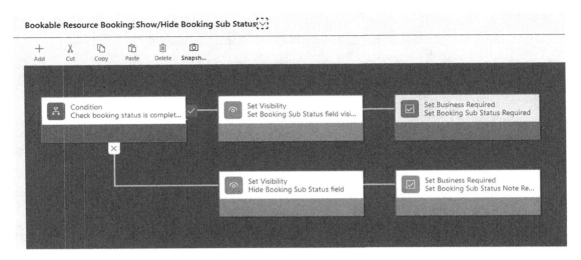

Figure 7-26. *The business rule to validate the booking sub status*

Generating the Invoice

From the field technician's perspective, the work is now completed. The out-of-the-box behavior of Field Service is to set the System Status field of the Work Order record to Open-Completed (Figure 7-27), and then a supervisor would inspect the work and complete the work order from the back end.

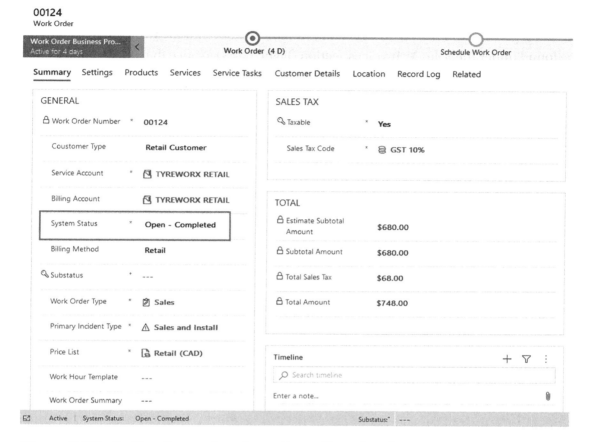

Figure 7-27. *Setting the work order to Open-Completed*

On the business process flow, the user must set the status to Closed-Posted and, finally, to Finish (Figure 7-28).

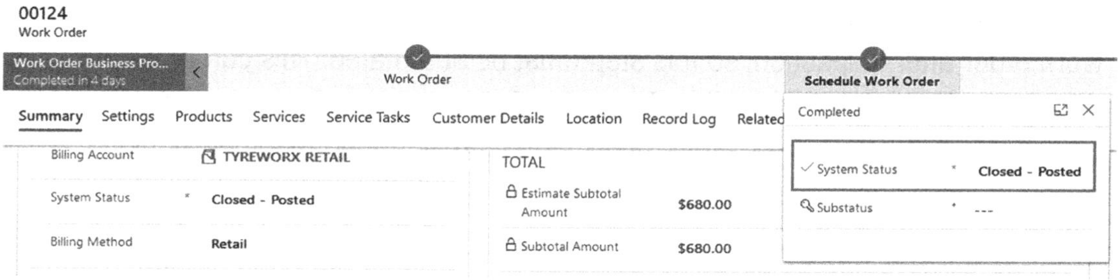

Figure 7-28. *Setting the work order to Closed-Posted*

Once the Work Order record's System Status field is set to Closed-Posted, the Invoice record is generated. There is no direct link with the invoice and the work order. It can be found under the Sales ➤ Invoices section (Figure 7-29). Notice that all the details entered in the field are available here.

***Figure 7-29.** The Invoice record generated for the work order*

Note   For businesses like TyreWorx, the invoice should be generated on the spot and emailed to the customer. No other user will change the system status of the work order after inspection, so this step must be automated. This can be easily done with a Power Automate flow. When the field technician completes the work order, the system sets the status Open-Completed, and then the flow should trigger. It checks the value and sets it to Closed-Posted.

It is highly recommended to use the Common Data Service (current environment) connector. For more information about the connectors, visit `https://docs.microsoft.com/en-us/power-automate/connection-cds-native`.

1. The first step of the flow is to trigger only when the system status of the work order is Open-Completed (Figure 7-30).

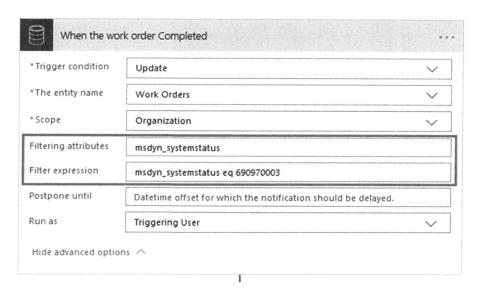

Figure 7-30. *The trigger step*

2. Update the **System Status** of the work order to **Closed-Posted** (Figure 7-31).

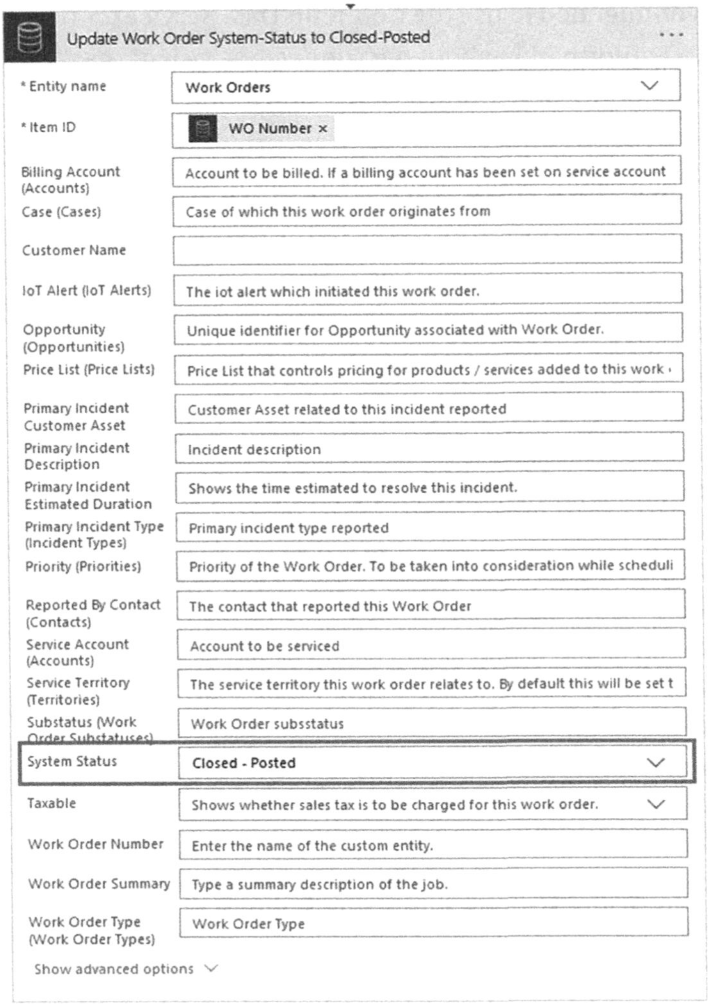

Figure 7-31. *The update step*

After creating the flow, you can include it in a solution, which can be deployed to multiple environments (Figure 7-32).

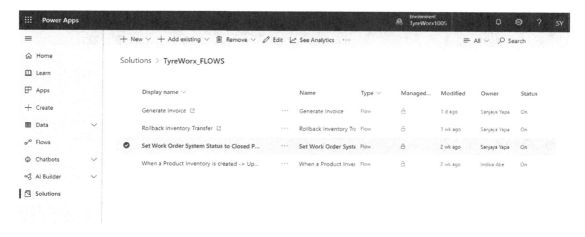

Figure 7-32. *Solution containing the Power Automate flows*

Processing Wholesale Work Orders

The TyreWorx wholesale business differs from the retail business. The wholesale business sells products in bulk. The work orders are pre-created using agreements, as explained in Chapter 4. This section looks at how to process wholesale work orders.

As explained in the previous section, the sales rep will see the list of bookings on the Calendar view on the mobile device (7-33).

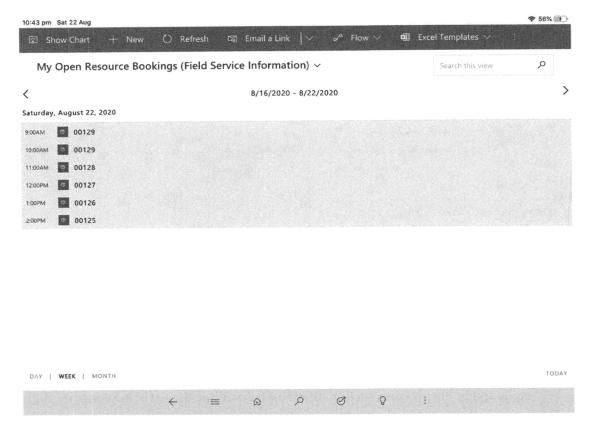

Figure 7-33. *Bookable resource bookings for wholesale work orders*

Adding Products to the Work Order

The previous section explained how to add the work order products to the work order. The difference here is that the work order products are already added to the work order (Figure 7-34). This is because when selling bulk in the wholesale business, the sales reps cannot spend time on adding multiple products to the work order one by one. So, a specific incident type was used to add the products to the work order when it was generated. Please refer to Chapter 4 for more details.

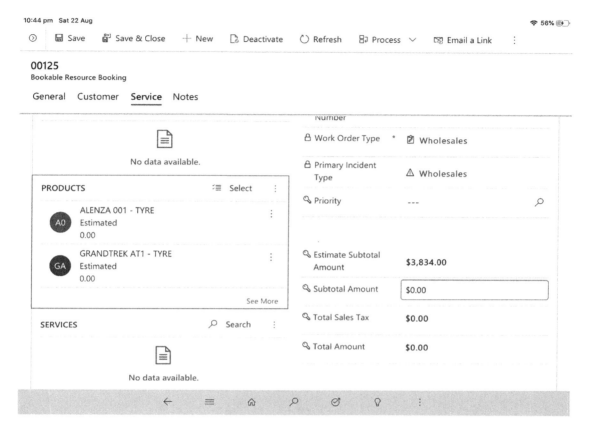

Figure 7-34. *Work order products already added to the work order*

At this point, based on the estimated quantity and unit prices of each item in the list, an estimated subtotal amount is also calculated.

When the Work Order Product record is opened, the Line Status field is set to Estimated (Figure 7-35). This allows the sales rep to adjust the record before committing it.

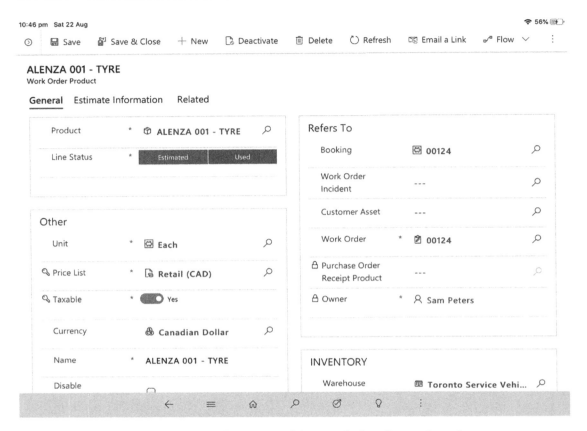

Figure 7-35. *Work Order Product record for a wholesale work order*

For example, suppose the customer wants additional products. The sales rep simply opens the Work Order Product record and changes the estimated quantity, and the estimated subtotal will be calculated automatically (Figure 7-36).

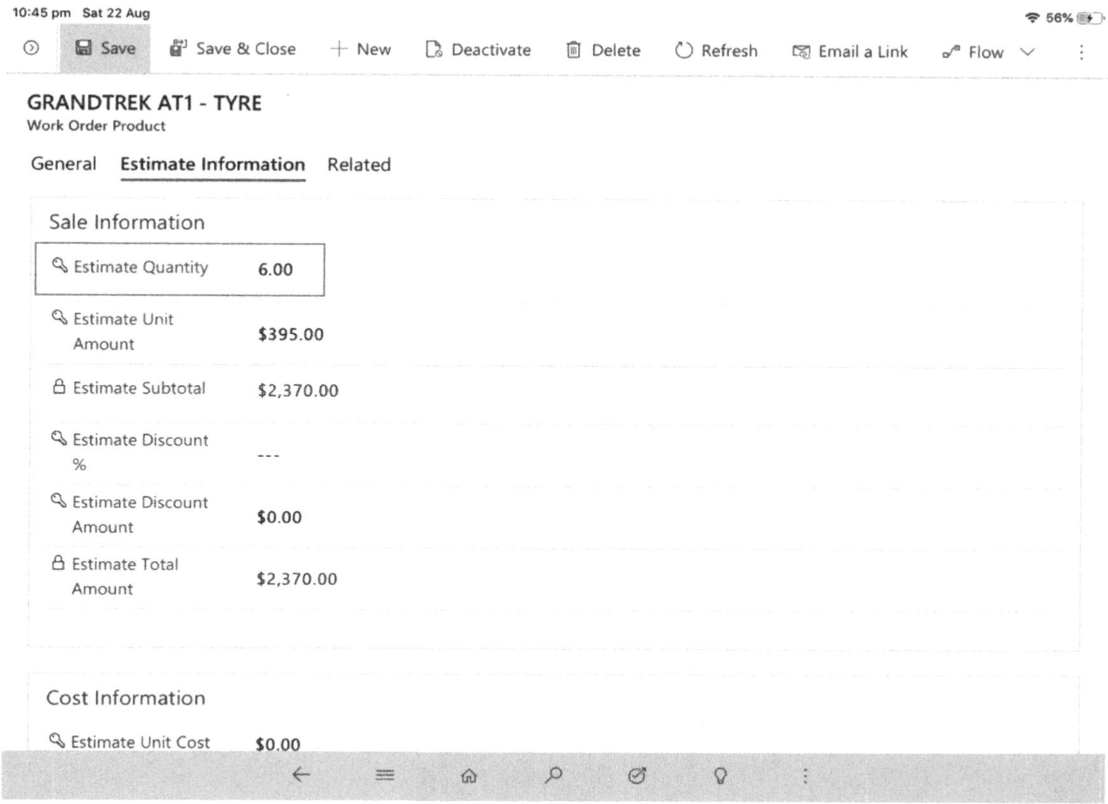

10:45 pm   Sat 22 Aug   📶 56% 🔋

⊙   💾 Save   💾 Save & Close   ＋ New   📄 Deactivate   🗑 Delete   ↺ Refresh   📧 Email a Link   ⚡ Flow ∨   ⋮

GRANDTREK AT1 - TYRE
Work Order Product

General   **Estimate Information**   Related

Sale Information

🔍 Estimate Quantity   6.00

🔍 Estimate Unit
   Amount $395.00

🔒 Estimate Subtotal $2,370.00

🔍 Estimate Discount
   %   ---

🔍 Estimate Discount
   Amount $0.00

🔒 Estimate Total
   Amount $2,370.00

Cost Information

🔍 Estimate Unit Cost $0.00

←   ≡   ⌂   🔍   ⚙   ♀   ⋮

Figure 7-36. *Changing the estimated quantity for the work order product*

To view the full list of work order products associated with the work order, click the **See More** option on the **Products** list under the **Service** tab of the **Bookable Resource Booking** record (refer to Figure 7-34). The list of products will be filtered for the work order associated with the booking (Figure 7-37).

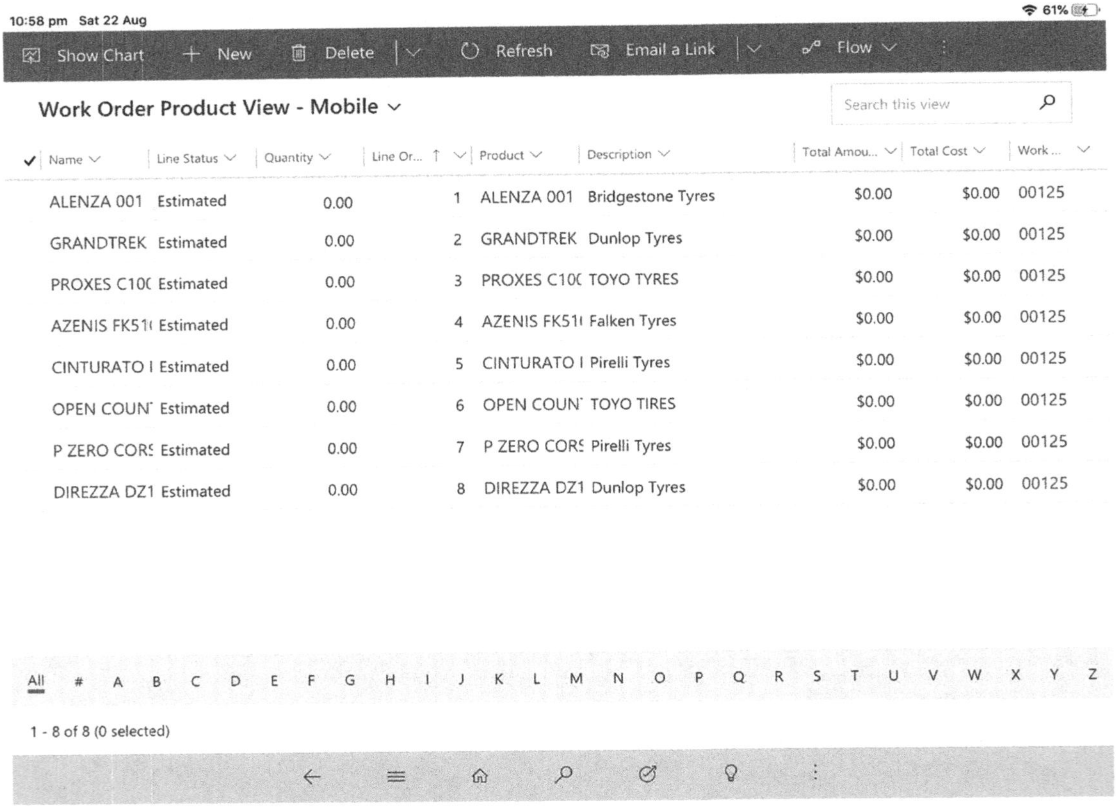

Figure 7-37. *The full list of work order products associated with the wholesale work order*

Now the sales rep can open each record and set the Line Status field to Used (Figure 7-38). Notice that the Quantity field gets auto-populated based on the estimated quantity. To edit the quantity, click the + or – button.

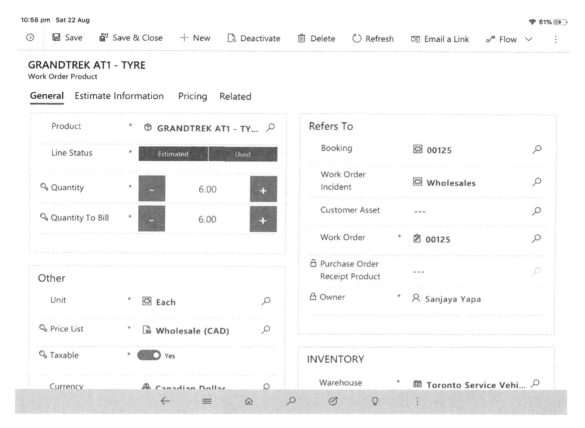

Figure 7-38. *Work Order Product record's Line Status field set to Used*

Because the sales rep is doing this retrospectively, they can open each record, verify the quantities offloaded to the customer site, and set the Line Status field of the records one by one. As shown in Figure 7-39, now the full list of products is set to Used, and the totals for the consumed products are displayed.

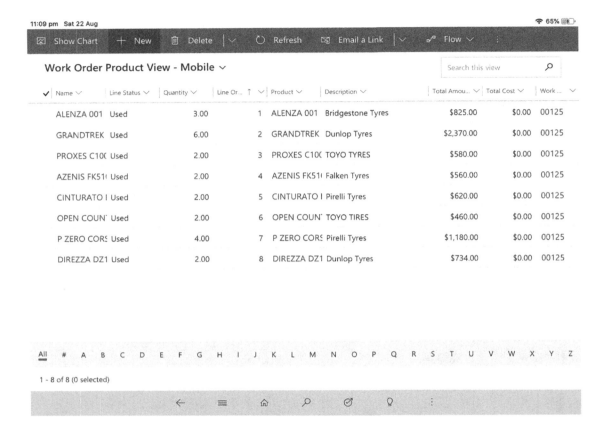

Figure 7-39. *Line Status and Quantities fields updated for the full list of work order products*

Completing the Work Order and Generating the Invoice

Now the work order is ready to be completed. The TyreWorx wholesale business has no requirement for adding services. As shown in Figure 7-40, the final total has been calculated, including the sales tax.

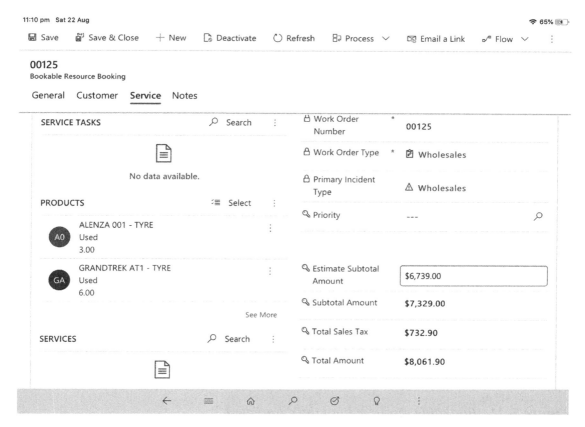

Figure 7-40. *Work order finalized and ready for completion*

As explained in the previous section, the signature of the customer can be captured in the Signature section under the Notes tab. Now the sales rep can open the General tab and set the Booking Status field to Completed and the Booking Sub Status field to Tyre Sales (Figure 7-41).

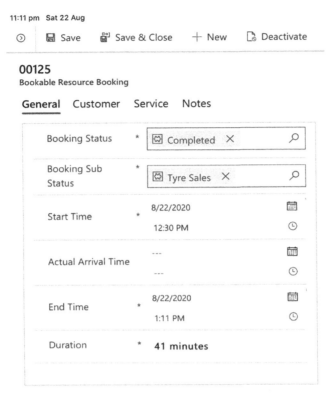

Figure 7-41. *Bookable resource booking completed*

At this point, the Power Automate flow that we created in the previous section kicks in and changes the system status of the work order to Closed-Posted (Figure 7-42).

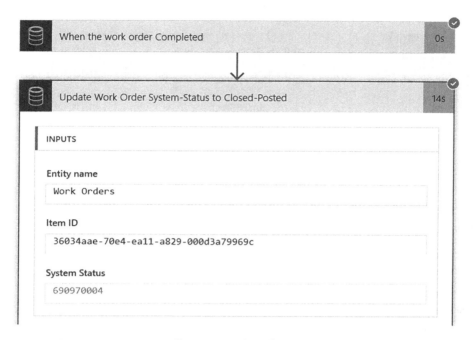

Figure 7-42. *Power Automate flow completed*

As shown in Figure 7-43, the Work Order System Status is set to Closed-Posted. Because of the simple automation technique, no manual intervention is required here.

00125
Work Order

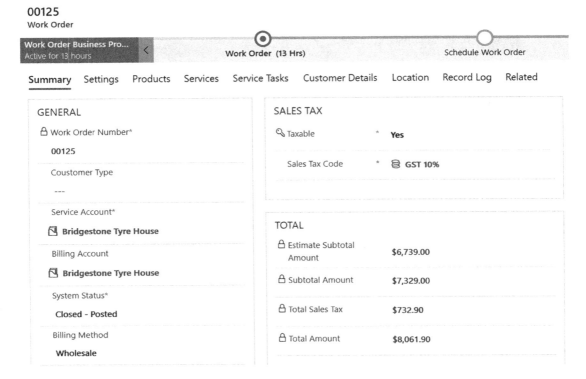

Figure 7-43. *Work order completed*

When the Invoice record is opened, it displays all the details of the completed work order (Figure 7-44).

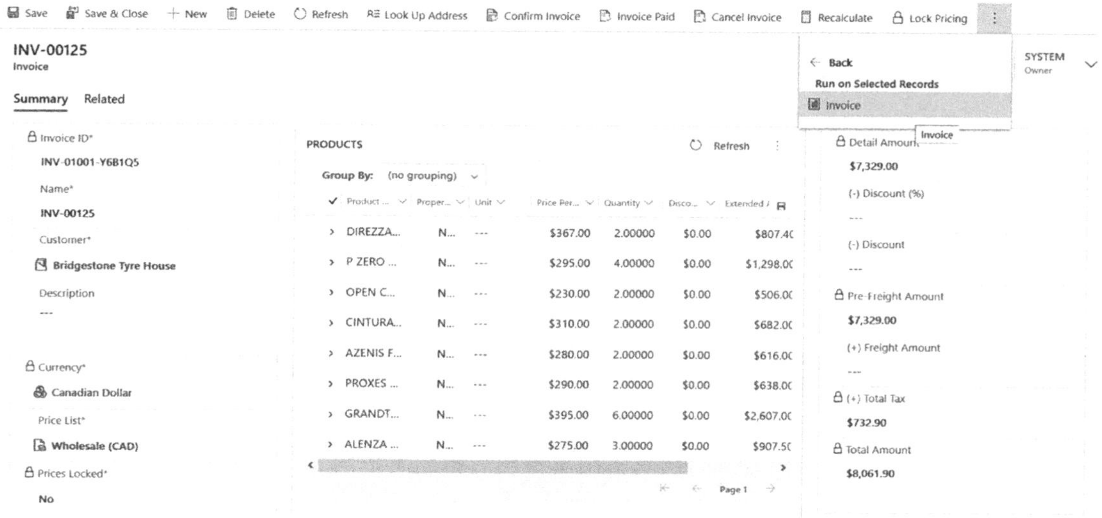

Figure 7-44. *Invoice record for the work order completed*

Notice the Invoice option under the three dots on far right corner of the command menu. This enables you to generate a printable version of the invoice (Figure 7-45) and save it as a PDF. To automate the process, you could easily create a Power Automate flow to generate the PDF version of the invoice and mail it to the customer.

Edit Filter

Select information that needs to be displayed in the Item Details area: | Product ID,Quantity,Price per unit | ∨

|◁   <   1   of 1   >   ▷| ↻   ⊝   100% ∨   🖫 ∨   🖶   [   ] Find | Next

Invoice: tyreworx1005

To: **From:**

Bridgestone Tyre House   SYSTEM

Summary

Total Amount:	$8,061.90		Invoice ID:	INV-01001-Y6B1Q5
Shipping Method:			Date:	8/23/2020
Payment Terms:				

Shipping Information

Ship To: **Bill To:**

                                           Bridgestone Tyre House

Details

Product ID	Product	Quantity	Price	Sub Total
	AZENIS FK510 - TYRE	2.00	$280.00	$616.00
	DIREZZA DZ102 - TYRE	2.00	$367.00	$807.40
	PROXES C100 PLUS SUV - TYRE	2.00	$290.00	$638.00
	ALENZA 001 - TYRE	3.00	$275.00	$907.50
	P ZERO CORSA PZ4 - TYRE	4.00	$295.00	$1,298.00
	GRANDTREK AT1 - TYRE	6.00	$395.00	$2,607.00
	CINTURATO P1 - TYRE	2.00	$310.00	$682.00
	OPEN COUNTRY H/T - TYRE	2.00	$230.00	$506.00
			Total Tax	$732.90
			Total	$8,061.90

8/22/2020 11:33 PM	Prepared by : Sanjaya Yapa	Page 1 of 1

Figure 7-45. *Invoice generated from back end*

Generating the Invoice from Power Automate

Following is a step-by-step process to generate the invoice using a Power Automate flow. We will use the following components:

- Common Data Service (current environment) connector

- Append to Array

- Populate a Microsoft Word template

- Convert Word Document to PDF

To begin, you should prepare the invoice template. The invoice is generated using a document template. For this template, you must add the placeholders for the Dynamics Field Service content. First, you must enable the Developer tab in Word (Figure 7-46). On Microsoft Word, the Developer menu is not enabled by default. To enable the Developer menu, follow the steps below.

1. On the File tab, go to Options ➤ Customize Ribbon.

2. Under Customize the Ribbon and under Main Tabs, select the Developer check box.

Figure 7-46. *Developer tools of Microsoft Word*

The template should look something like Figure 7-47.

TYREWORX PTY LTD – TAX INVOICE

TORONTO CANADA

Invoice No:

Invoice Date:

Customer Name:

Products	Unit Cost	Quantity	Unit Total

Detail Amount ($)	
Total Tax ($)	
Total Amount ($)	

Figure 7-47. *Invoice template before adding the placeholders*

You can create the template based on the end user's requirements. Now let's start adding the placeholders. Use the Plain Text Content control to add the placeholders (Figure 7-48). At the time of writing, the Rich Text control does not work when generating an invoice via Power Automate.

Figure 7-48. *Using the Plain Text Content control to add placeholders*

To add the placeholder for the Invoice No: on the template, place the cursor next to the word and click the control from the ribbon. This will add the placeholder with dummy text. Replace the dummy text with one space (Figure 7-49).

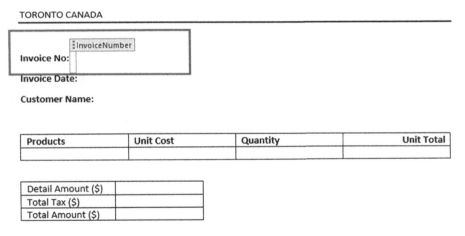

Figure 7-49. *Inserting a placeholder*

Next, select the placeholder and select **Properties** from the ribbon (Figure 7-50).

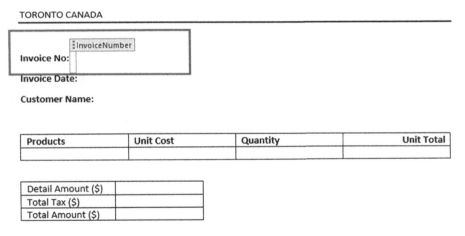

Figure 7-50. *Selecting the Properties option from the ribbon*

In the **Content Control Properties** dialog box, enter the appropriate names in the Title and Tag fields (Figure 7-51).

TYREWORX P

TORONTO CANADA

Invoice No:

Invoice Date:

Customer Name:

Products	Uni		Unit Total

Detail Amount ($)	
Total Tax ($)	
Total Amount ($)	

Content Control Properties   ?   ✕

General

Title: InvoiceDate

Tag: InvoiceDate

Show as: Bounding Box ⌄

Color: 🎨 ▾

☐ Use a style to format text typed into the empty control

Style: Default Paragraph Font ⌄

A₊ New Style...

☐ Remove content control when contents are edited

Locking

☐ Content control cannot be deleted

☐ Contents cannot be edited

Plain Text Properties

☐ Allow carriage returns (multiple paragraphs)

OK   Cancel

Figure 7-51. Setting properties for placeholders

Follow the same steps to add placeholders for other fields, except for the product list, because there will be multiple line items in an invoice. For this, select the row where the data is going to be added, which is the second row of the product table, and add the **Repeating Section Content** control from the ribbon (Figure 7-52).

Figure 7-52. Inserting the Repeating Section Content control as the placeholder

This will ensure that when there are multiple line items in the invoice, they will be shown on the generated invoice. Since there are four columns in the table, after adding the repeating section, insert placeholders for all the columns, like you did before. Be sure to set the Properties and the Title and Tag fields. Once the template is created, save it in a folder within OneDrive for Business. Now the Invoice Template is created and the next step is to create the Power Automate Flow. Let's jump into creating the Power Automate flow.

As usual, the first step of the flow will be the trigger. In this case, the trigger is when the Invoice record is generated (Figure 7-53). As we discussed in the previous section, when the work order is set to Close-Completed the system generates the Invoice record.

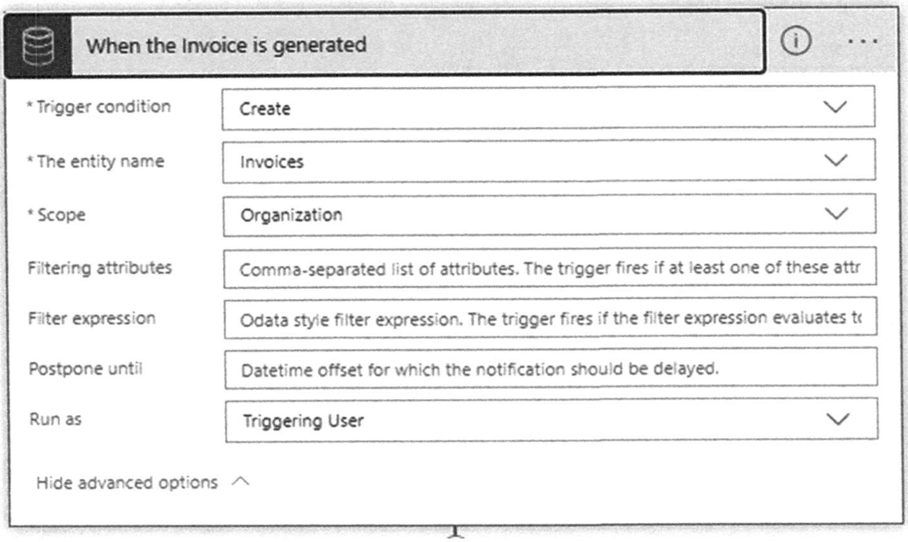

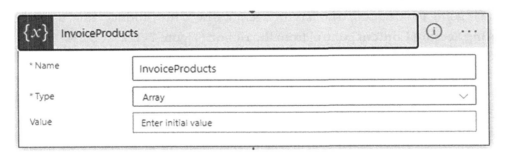

Figure 7-53. *Power Automate flow triggers when the invoice is generated*

The next step is to declare an array to hold the list of invoice line items (Figure 7-54).

Figure 7-54. *Declaring an array to hold the invoice line items*

After declaring the array, use a **List Record** component to retrieve the invoice products (Figure 7-55).

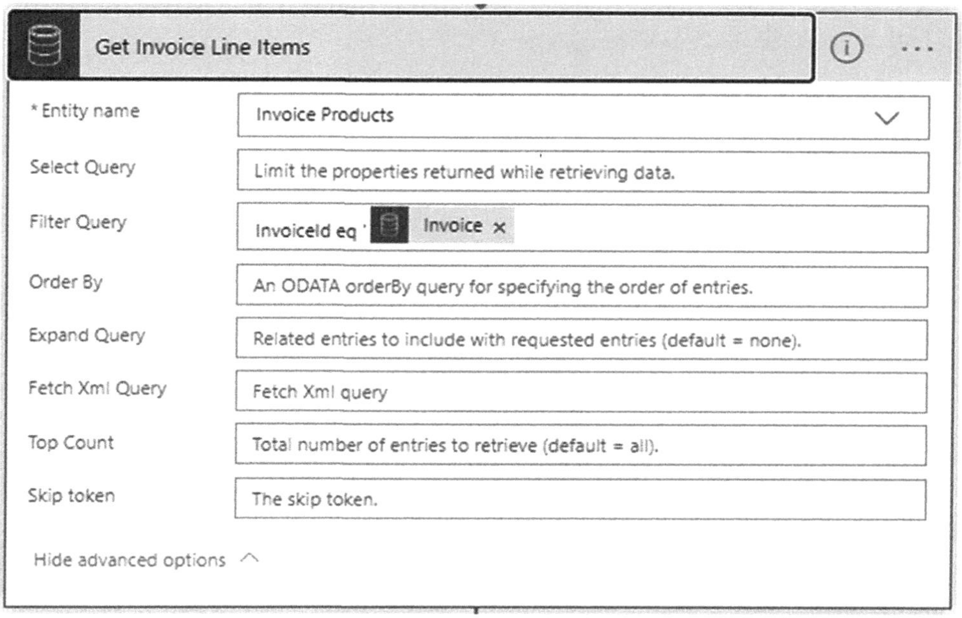

Figure 7-55. *Retrieving the list of invoice line items*

Use the **Apply to Each** component and populate the array with the items retrieved from the previous step. For this, use the **Append to Array variable** component (Figure 7-56). As you can see, the array item is a JSON object within the Append to Array variable component and each item name is the tag name given to the placeholder of each column in the product table of the template.

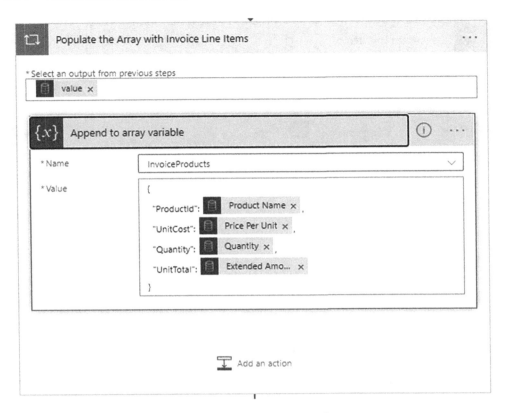

Figure 7-56. *Populating the array with the invoice line items*

Now we need to add the step to populate the template. For this, you need to add the **Populate a Microsoft Word Template** component (Figure 7-57). Keep in mind that this works only with OneDrive for Business and SharePoint locations within the tenancy. Select the location, document library, and file. Click the folder icon to show the folder structure. As you can see, the component picks up the placeholders.

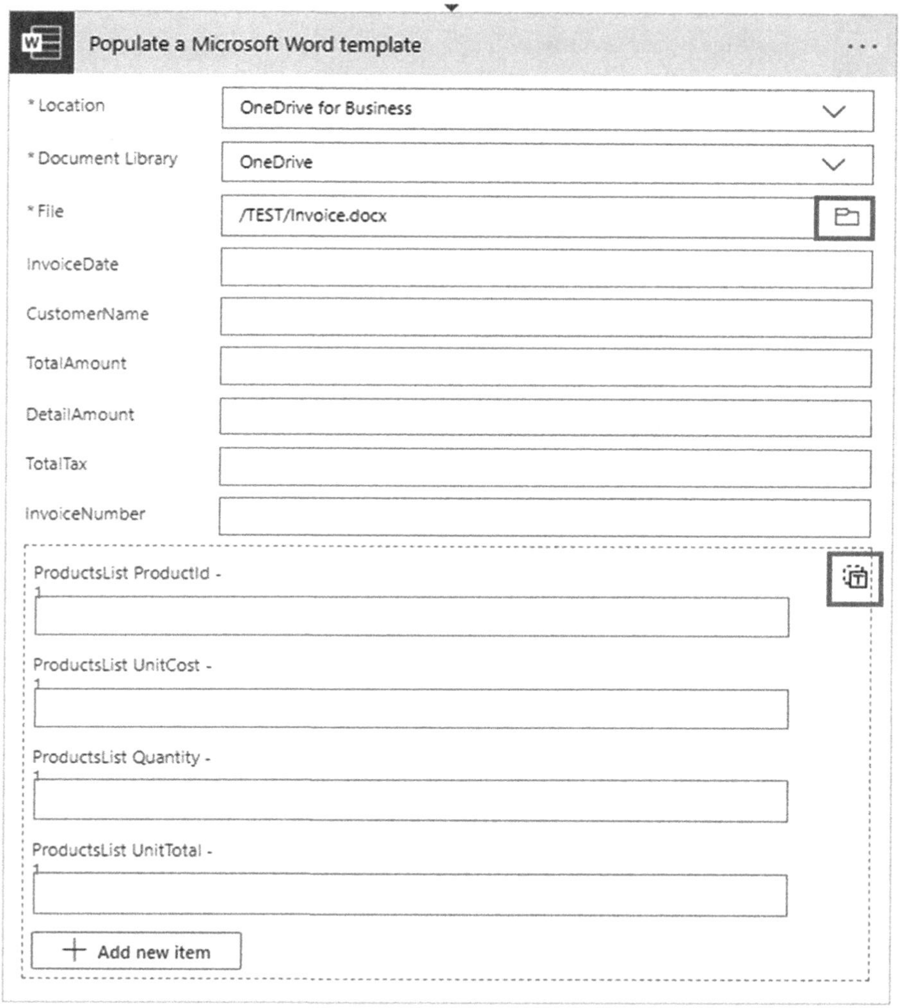

Figure 7-57. *Populating a Microsoft Word Template component*

As you can see, the product list is shown as a static list, which fine if you know the list of items. In this scenario, however, the number of invoice products will be different from one invoice to another. That is the primary reason for creating and populating the array. The component where you add the array items includes a small icon with a "T" in upper-right corner (highlighted). When you click the icon, the view changes to add the full array (Figure 7-57). Once all the placeholders are mapped, the component will look like something Figure 7-58.

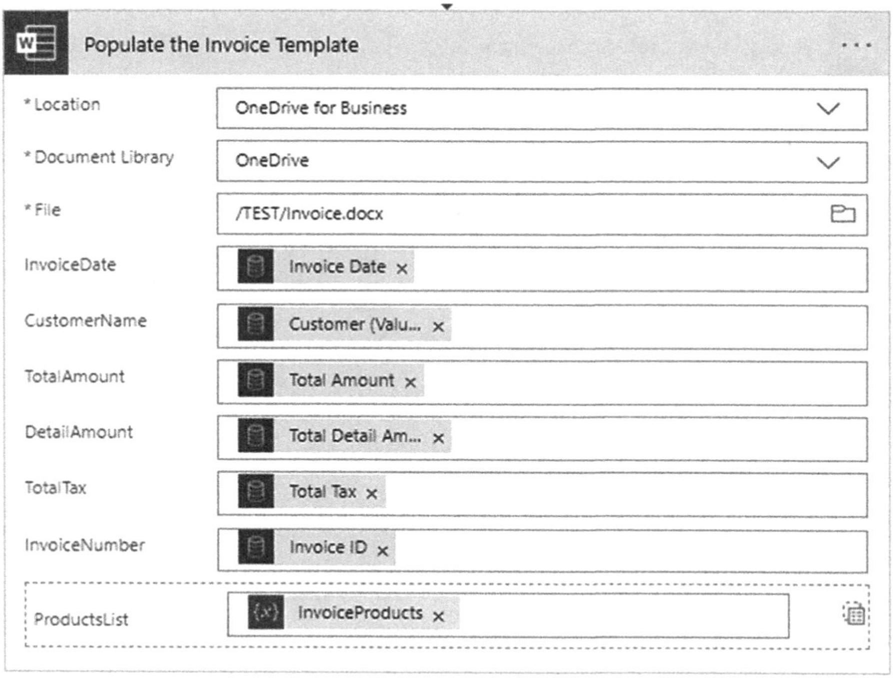

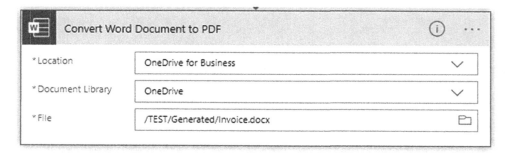

Figure 7-58. *Updated Word Template component*

The final step of the flow is to convert the document to a PDF (Figure 7-59). To do that, add a **Convert Word Document to PDF** component. Set the **Location** to **OneDrive for Business**, the **Document Library** to **OneDrive,** and the **File** to the target document.

Figure 7-59. *Converting the Word document to PDF*

As soon as the invoice is created, you should attach the document to the Invoice record using the Notes entity (Figure 7-60). You also need to set the Regarding Object ID to the invoice ID for this component.

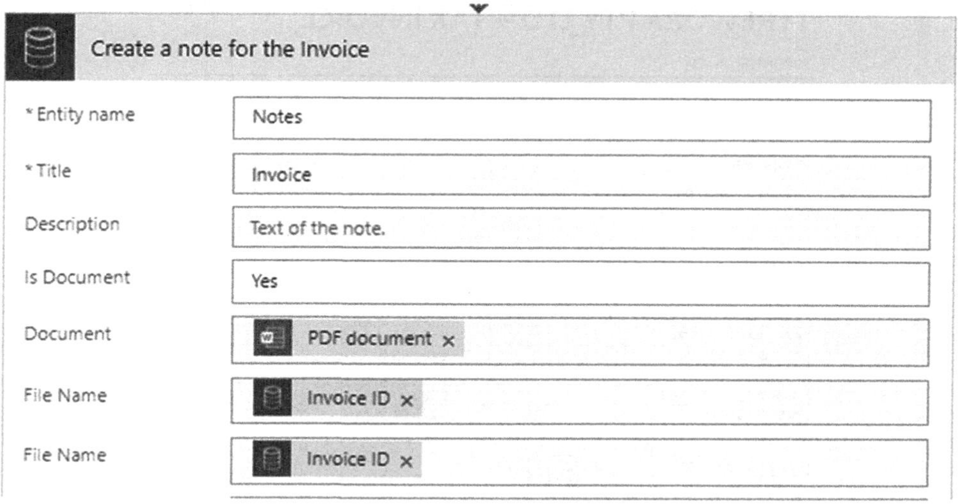

Figure 7-60. *Creating a note by attaching the invoice generated*

When the invoice is generated, it will look something like Figure 7-61.

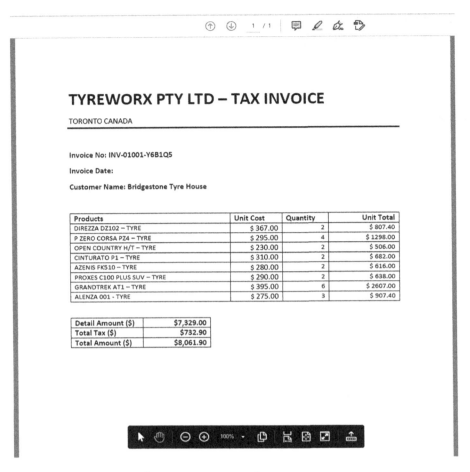

Figure 7-61. *The generated invoice in PDF format*

Summary

The focus of this last chapter was to complete a work order in two different business domains: retail and wholesale. We also looked at utilizing Microsoft Power Automate to automate the business process.

To conclude, we hope this book will be a stepping stone for your start with Dynamics 365 Field Service.

Index

© Sanjaya Yapa and Indika Abayarathne 2021
S. Yapa and I. Abayarathne, *Dynamics 365 Field Service*, https://doi.org/10.1007/978-1-4842-6408-9

Printed in the United States
By Bookmasters